SCREWBALL

Screwball

Hollywood's Madcap Romantic Comedies

ED SIKOV

Foreword by Molly Haskell

Crown Publishers, Inc., New York

For Bill Paul and Carole Lombard

Published by Crown Publishers, Inc., 201 East 50th Street,
New York, New York 10022

CROWN is a trademark of Crown Publishers, Inc.

Manufactured in Japan

Library of Congress Cataloging-in-Publication Data
Sikov, Ed.
Screwball: Hollywood's madcap romantic comedies / by Ed Sikov
Includes index
1. Comedy films—United States—History and criticism.
2. Comedy films—United States—Pictorial works.   I. Title.
PN1995.9.C55S5   1989
791.43'09'0917—dc19   89-1154
ISBN 0-517-57302-4

Design by Draper Shreeve

1   3   5   7   9   10   8   6   4   2

FIRST EDITION

LUCY: You're all confused, aren't you?
JERRY: Uh-huh. Aren't you?
LUCY: No.
JERRY: Well, you should be, because you're
wrong about things being different
because they're not the same. Things
are different, except in a different
way. You're still the same, only I've
been a fool. Well, I'm not now. So, as
long as I'm different, don't you think
things could be the same again? Only
a little different?

Irene Dunne and Cary Grant
in *The Awful Truth*

TABLE OF CONTENTS

FOREWORD

*T*HE SCREWBALL COMEDIES WERE A SORT OF EXISTENTIAL American version of the French *l'amour fou:* a challenge, in the name of love, to the very precepts on which a sane and civilized society is based. In turning the world upside down, in releasing their behavioral inhibitions, in scraping against each other, in discovering their affinities for another person through this mutual mayhem, the men and women of these often anarchic and exhilarating movies were in effect "finding themselves." The mating games played within their frames were testimonials to the fact that the choice of a partner—the most important choice most people ever make—is nothing less than earthshaking, an assertion of one's deepest instincts and destiny through love, a leap of faith into the void.

The screwball comedies that flourished in the decade between the onset of the Depression and the end of World War II have left a mark on our memories far greater than could have been expected from their impact at the time. By no means as popular as more dominant genres such as Sentimental Drama or Edifying Adventure, these fables of love masquerading as hostility were largely an elitist variant of the eternal battle of the sexes. The specific personalities we think of as representative of the genre—Carole Lombard, Cary Grant, Irene Dunne, Melvyn Douglas, Katharine Hepburn, Robert Montgomery, Claudette Colbert, Fred MacMurray, Ginger Rogers, James Stewart, Jean Arthur, Henry Fonda, Margaret Sullavan, Barbara Stanwyck, and even such superhero types as Clark Gable and Gary Cooper—whirl in the orbit of a New York smart set (many of the scripts were by writers with more than a nodding acquaintance with *The New Yorker*) who have the time and leisure to be crazy. Carole Lombard rescuing William Powell from a dump and "rehabilitating" him as a butler in *My Man Godfrey;* Jean Arthur and James Stewart turning a nightclub upside down in the name of non-conformity in *You Can't Take It With You;* Katharine Hepburn and Cary Grant clumping around Connecticut after a leopard in *Bringing Up Baby:* even as metaphors, these hardly evoke the struggles of ordinary people in a workaday world.

One of the great attractions of the screwball genre is its binary system: in its

OPPOSITE: Brainy Cary Grant reaches the end of his rope with a blithely distracted, superbly willful Katharine Hepburn in *Bringing Up Baby.*

universe, women are on an equal footing with men. Often, it's money and class that place them there: among the wives (not "housewives" but penthouse and on-the-town wives) there are no children to be seen; and among the single women, there are no domestic chores to enslave the free spirit. Enhanced by independent wealth, they can talk to men and give as good as they get. Even when the plot stipulates working girls—like Jean Arthur in *Easy Living* and Carole Lombard in *Nothing Sacred*—fate thrusts upon them all the trappings of luxury and celebrity. And even when the plot provides children, as in the sequels to *The Thin Man,* the little boy produced by Myrna Loy and William Powell is hustled off to military school so he won't get underfoot, and marriage is rescued from daily routine by drinking and detecting.

In terms of film history, what is fascinating is that the genre achieved its merriment at a time when censorship was more rigid than ever before. Since sex could not even be implied, it was sublimated into the furor of one-on-one combat, in which the double standard itself was overturned in a noisy contest of verbal assault and insult battery, with women the aggressors as often as men.

The cinema itself provided the arena for actors and actresses to get off the couches of the Coward-Maugham-Barry-Behrman theatrical drawing rooms and engage in pratfalls and somersaults. Slapstick, which had been the province of sexless clowns, became the activity of courting lovers, and allowed an acrobat—Cary Grant—to become one of the greatest of them all. In the relaxation of inhibitions through violence, passion was translated into physical antagonism, a peculiarly American form of expressing love in a country where civilized courtship is often construed as deceptive and insincere. From the frontier days to the present, men and women have never been as comfortable with each other as they have been in older countries and more sybaritic, less Puritanical civilizations. Men are uneasy with their feminine side; women inexperienced in their masculine side. Classy ladies of spirit and spunk, liberated from the imperatives of ladylike behavior, allowed themselves to look temporarily awkward, ill at ease; and found their way psychologically in the overturning of the normal rules and roles of courtship. For these comedies were in essence voyages of self-discovery, fed by the Protestant work ethic: to make romance palatable, men and women had to earn it, and each other.

Ed Sikov's comprehensive account has captured this fascinating period both in terms of its sensuous surface and its provocative subtexts. Instead of succumbing to the usual rationale that mere escapism from the Depression propelled the best of these films into sublimity, he shows many of the immediate social influences that hovered around the edges, the general and specific ways in which literature, the theater, and politics came into play. More centrally, however, Sikov identifies a uniquely American art form based on Puritanism, optimism, and prodigious energy.

The great value of this book is that it makes us smile with fond reminiscences even as it makes us ponder more seriously its implications about an era that still remains timely for us today. Marx and Freud make strange bedfellows in Sikov's ruminations; but, as we have long known, Hollywood movies in general, and screwball comedies in particular, can sustain the most paradoxical analyses without ever ceasing to be great fun. We may wonder whether the supposed sexual liberation of recent decades has made movies (and women) too "easy" for real romance. Do we now treasure the beautifully passionate Puritans of the screwball era precisely because they respected and even revered the fearsome chasm between yes and no in sexual consent? Do we unconsciously yearn for repression, for a return to old rules and standards of behavior? Or is it simply that we ruefully mourn a pre-Holocaust world of genuine lightness and grace? Sikov does not provide any facile answers to these and other perplexing questions. He has written a provocative and intelligent book, and has succeeded in bringing a scintillating period in our cultural history back to glittering life.

MOLLY HASKELL

INTRODUCTION

Pitching Screwballs

WHAT IS THE SINGLE MOST ROMANTIC MOMENT IN THE CINEMA? Most of us are drawn to the thirties, to the sleek and elegant era of backlit stars and streamlined sets, the imaginary world of Hollywood's golden age where, legend has it, romance reigned. Starry-eyed dreamers could point to Fred Astaire and Ginger Rogers dancing "Cheek to Cheek" in *Top Hat* (1935). Those with a morbid streak might choose the sequence in *Young Mr. Lincoln* (1939) when the unassuming future president, played by Henry Fonda, kneels stoically at the grave of Ann Rutledge, the love of his life. And though film buffs would probably roll their eyes in contempt, a huge number of people would say without hesitation that the most romantic moment, maybe even the single most memorable image in the history of film, occurs when Clark Gable drapes Vivien Leigh over his arm on the advertising poster for *Gone With the Wind* (1939). But *some* people would instantly flash on the final scene of *The Lady Eve* (1941), where a befuddled and demoralized Henry Fonda is forced to admit that he is helplessly in love with Barbara Stanwyck, who has spent most of the film conning, torturing, and ruining him. This book is for that kind of romantic.

In the world of screwball comedy, there is one primary axiom: Hatred is no reason to give up on a relationship. Just because two people seem to despise each other doesn't mean

OPPOSITE: Hopsie Pike (Henry Fonda) and Jean Harrington (Barbara Stanwyck) getting acquainted in *The Lady Eve*.

they're not in love. It could, on the contrary, provide the final proof of a couple's delight in one another, their passion, devotion, and joy. Classically, American movies have thrived on visions of ideal love. But in the 1930s, a whole genre developed around the perverse idea that love could only be enhanced by aggravation. In screwball comedies, the thornier the relationship, the better. If a man and woman seem to like each other in the first reel, they are inevitably doomed. If, on the other hand, they respond to each other with a quick and overpowering sense of disgust, chances are that they will eventually find themselves caught up in the ceaseless bliss of an ongoing war without which they would never live happily ever after.

Think of Cary Grant in *Bringing Up Baby* (1938). Who could look at the scene in which Grant traipses nervously around Katharine Hepburn's lovely Connecticut farmhouse dressed in a white boa-collared dressing gown and not see an image of potential happiness? His life as a paleontologist has been so drab until then, and the flighty, abrasive, independent Hepburn provides just the kind of nonstop torment he needs. Cary's metamorphosis might be painful in the short run, but he's clearly on the road to some sort of recovery. Only by going through a terrible ordeal can genuine progress be made in a screwball comedy. It's a kind of cathartic therapy, both for the characters who are trapped in its logic and for audiences who willingly enter into it.

Because screwball comedies first exploded in the mid-thirties, and because everyone knows that movies have something to do with the world in which they are made, most accounts of the genre begin with the idea that screwball comedy grew out of the Depression. Life was bleak in the thirties, the story goes, so when people went to the movies they wanted to laugh. In this vision, the thirties were a time when millions of oppressed souls went scurrying into theaters to escape from their poverty into the happy world of luxury, the mythic land of lavish musicals and sprightly romantic comedies.

It's certainly true that comedies can take your mind off trouble, but there is really no evidence that Depression audiences liked comedies and musicals more than melodramas, historical dramas, or horror films. All kinds of movies were popular during the thirties. If audiences were simply paying for a means of escape, they were escaping frequently into a world in which mobsters gunned each other down (*Scarface,* 1932), gigantic apes terrorized midtown Manhattan (*King Kong,* 1933), and neurotic women ruined their lives (*Stella Dallas,* 1937; *Jezebel,* 1938). *Snow White and the Seven Dwarfs* (1937) was a big hit, but so was *Angels with Dirty Faces* (1938). *Wee Willie Winkie* (1937) was a smash, but so was *The Hunchback of Notre Dame* (1939).

Despite the Depression, Hollywood did very well in terms of output. The studios saw the value of their stocks plummet, and the stagnating economy pushed some of them into the red, but both film production and attendance remained substantial considering the extent of the financial devastation. Even in 1932, the worst year of the Depression, somewhere between 65 and 90 million tickets were sold each week. While this represented a sizable drop from 1928 when, at the height of the twenties boom, Americans made over 125 million trips to the movies weekly, the average ticket price continued to hover around $.23 throughout the Depression, keeping movies affordable for many people. Movies were also entertaining, for reasons that have little to do with the population's putative need for froth.

In too many accounts of screwball comedy, the brute fact of the Depression is paramount, even though the myths might be strictly MGM. Economic hardship becomes the only reality to consider, and it must be insistently reflected in every single screwball comedy no matter what it's about. This theory of screwball's evolution makes it possible to have a good idea of what hundreds of movies are like without ever having taken the trouble of

seeing them, but it's not very plausible. Despite the fact that most screwball heroes and heroines either have, acquire, or simply witness the effects of a lot of cash at some point in the film, screwball comedies usually have as much to do with sex (or its absence) as with money.

Screwball comedy, like any film genre, expresses a whole range of meanings—the news of the day, cultural obsessions, psychological dynamics, and aesthetic conventions. An individual film or the films of a given director might reach tentative conclusions about the state of the world, but an entire genre is necessarily much less specific. Screwball comedy—not just a series of classic moments, but *a genre*—is more like a loosely structured artistic

forum. It's a way of organizing and reflecting certain issues with endless repetitions and variations— adding some here, ignoring others there, but never clumping all together into a unified ideology or point of view. Screwball comedies range from the liberal (*Easy Living,* 1937) to the reactionary (*Public Deb No. 1,* 1940); from the sexually liberating (*My Favorite Wife,* 1940) to the sexually repressive (*Turnabout,* 1940); from the overtly class-conscious (*It Happened One Night,* 1934) to the relatively class-disregarding (*Twentieth Century,* 1934). As a genre, screwball comedy presents a much wider, more contradictory picture of the world out of which it arose than the individual films we remember best.

Theories of genre and society aside, there's

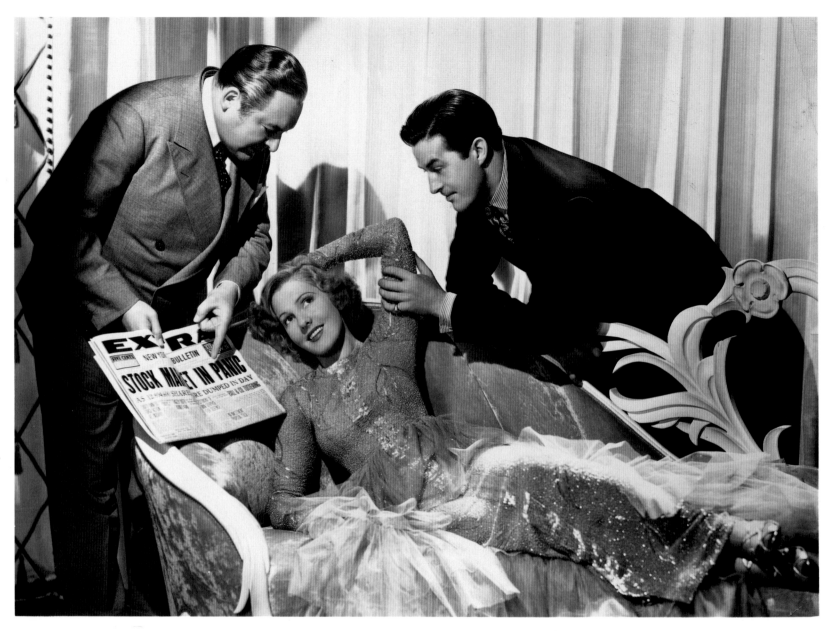

High-living Edward Arnold, Jean Arthur, and Ray Milland ponder the sorry state of current events in Paramount's *Easy Living* (1937).

another danger in seeing the world as a series of Big Events that determine the course of human experience: everyday life gets lost. The fact is, the many gray Fridays that followed Black Thursday were days on which people loved and hated each other for reasons that had little to do with the financial news they read in the morning paper or the rumors they heard on the unemployment line. Movies—not just screwball comedies, but gangster films and horror films, melodramas and historical epics as well—look and sound and feel the way they do be-

cause of a whole range of real-life events. When screwball films get the chance to speak for themselves on the screens of repertory houses, museums, and televisions, they tell a different story from the one we're accustomed to hearing. Looking at the screen, at the wealth of detail, gesture, physical beauty, and style in films like *The Awful Truth* (1937), *Easy Living,* and *Nothing Sacred* (1937), and hearing the smart dialogue of *His Girl Friday* (1940), *The Thin Man* (1934), and *My Man Godfrey* (1936), another picture of the thirties may emerge. Even if it doesn't, a close and fresh-eyed look at screwball comedy will reveal at least one subplot in the intricate tale that movies tell about themselves.

"The entire story has, in our specific judgment, a definitely unacceptable flavor that is certain to be highly offensive to motion picture audiences everywhere."—Letter from Joseph I. Breen, head of the Production Code Administration, to RKO Radio Pictures, rejecting the script of *My Favorite Wife*

Discussions of screwball comedy typically begin with a list of screwball favorites, like *It Happened One Night, Twentieth Century, My Man Godfrey, The Awful Truth, Nothing Sacred, Easy Living, Bringing Up Baby, Midnight* (1939), *His Girl Friday, My Favorite Wife, The Lady Eve, The Palm Beach Story* (1942) . . . Most critics know which films count as the classics. But when it comes time to define what makes screwball screwball, their commentary becomes much less accurate. Some critics, for instance, tell us that screwball comedies satirize the rich. Others say that they're not satiric enough, that screwball comedies are too complacent. Finally, while they're appreciated for being a lot of fun, screwball comedies are usually seen as charming fluff, an observation that can only be true if we find the essential and demoralizing failure of two individuals to live together in peace to be simply one of life's little inconveniences.

To see what screwball comedy is and how it came to be, it might be best to look not at other critics' generalizations, but at the world of sports, where the word *screwball* was coined. In baseball, a screwball is an erratic pitch that is produced in an exact and deliberate way. The pitcher throws the ball at great speed, letting it come off his middle finger while turning his wrist to the side. Whatever the variations in style between right-handers and lefties, the point of the pitch is that the batter is supposed to be confused.

When the pitch was first developed by the great Christy Mathewson of the New York Giants in the early 1900s, it was called the fadeaway. But it was another New York Giant, Carl Hubbell, the best screwball pitcher in baseball history, who perfected the pitch and (according to one etymologist) coined the term *screwball* somewhere around 1930. For most pitchers then and now, the screwball is a variety pitch; Hubbell, however, used the screwball so often that his wrist became permanently twisted. Hubbell's most famous use of the screwball occurred in the All-Star Game of 1934, when Hubbell struck out five future Hall-of-Famers in a row—Babe Ruth, Lou Gehrig, Jimmie Foxx, Al Simmons, and Joe Cronin—all with screwballs. It was also in 1934 that the screwball comedy was born.

The word *screwball* entered the language in the 1930s not only to describe a baseball pitch, but also as an adjective meaning insane or eccentric and as a nominal term for lunatic. In the early 1800s the British used the word *screwy* to describe a drunk. This evolved into "having a screw loose" in the latter part of the century and finally back to "screwy" in the 1920s, both as expressions of eccentricity or craziness. As a result, by the early 1930s "screwball" successfully brought together a number of connotations in a single slang and streetwise term: lunacy, speed, unpredictability, unconventionality, giddiness, drunkenness, flight, and adversarial sport.

Moving away from the pitcher's mound and back to the screen, one of the qualities that distinguishes screwball comedy is a sense of confusion about romance and human relations usually expressed by verbal and sometimes physical sparring. In these films, it's generally the fighting that helps convince two people they are (or should be) deeply in love. The Marx Brothers' films are not screwball comedies, nor are the films of Laurel and Hardy, Abbott and Costello, or, careening rapidly down the scale, the Ritz Brothers or Wheeler and Woolsey. While some of these movies offer a love story in the midst of the craziness, it usually occurs between secondary characters, men and women whose sanity stands in dull contrast with the liberating anarchy of the all-male stars. A similar split between love and lunacy occurs in the romantic comedies that preceded the birth of screwball, only there it happens in reverse. Those films feature a love relationship between the principals but leave physical comedy to the secondaries.

In the early to middle thirties, something changed in the way comedies represented romance. Why did so many fast-paced, contentious, romantic comedies begin to hit the world's theaters in 1934, continue at a furious pace through the early forties, subside through the war, and then fade away almost completely? If we can't see the genre as filling the gap between the height of the Depression and the beginning of World War II, how else can we see it? What could screwball comedies be if not blithely evasive responses to economic catastrophe?

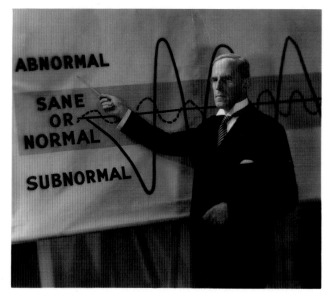

A no-nonsense psychiatrist pronounces his diagnosis of Longfellow Deeds in Frank Capra's *Mr. Deeds Goes to Town*. The expert's distinction between "abnormal" and "subnormal" is particularly illuminating.

If screwball comedy has to be traced to a single real-world event—and much of this book will try to show why it shouldn't be—that event would be the establishment in 1934 of the now infamous Production Code. The code was the result of more than a decade of outrage and protest on the part of religious leaders who saw movies and moviemakers leading America's flocks to perdition. Dirty Hollywood was corrupting America, the

moralists cried, and since somebody had to put a stop to it, it might as well be they.

Catholic clergymen all across America were ready to take up the sword against the Hollywood smut machine, and in the spring of 1934, cheered on by representatives of other denominations, they formed the National Legion of Decency as an agency of the Catholic Bishops of the United States. Justifiably concerned that pressure from the Legion might result in some form of governmental censorship, and absolutely terrified that the Legion's threatened boycott would put a crimp in their business, Hollywood's producers responded by requiring all scripts to be submitted to a central censoring agency, the Production Code Administration, for approval.

The code's proponents evidently believed that if Hollywood gave the public virtue, then the public would learn to be virtuous. Whether or not Americans lived better, cleaner lives during the Production Code years is debatable, though hotel rooms, bars, pool halls, and confessionals probably continued to reverberate with the sounds of sin even after movie theaters no longer could.

There's little doubt that the vast bulk of Hollywood's output didn't improve in quality because of the code, but there may have been a hidden dividend or two. Crusader Daniel A. Lord, S.J., may have inadvertently predicted the rise of the screwball comedy when he wrote that the code "seemed to open possibilities for simply magnificent pictures that would never be done as long as the industry lazed about in gutters and dirt and crime." Talented directors, writers, and stars were certainly not about to get rid of sexuality, so they simply found ways to slip it in on the sly. As Andrew Sarris puts it in one of the two best essays on the genre, screwball comedies are sex comedies without the sex; as William K. Everson puts it in the other, screwball comedies "hit back at the conventions and sexual restraints of the polite new comedies" that toed the censors' line.

Fred MacMurray and Carole Lombard obviously adore each other in Paramount's *True Confession*. As film critic Molly Haskell has written, "The battle of the sexes is a battle of equals, and the language of sexual antagonism tells as passionate a love story as Jerome Kern's music and Rogers's and Astaire's dancing in *Swing Time*."

Irene Dunne and Cary Grant capture the spirit of true romance in a publicity shot for *The Awful Truth*.

Since they could no longer base romantic comedies on suggestions of sexual combat, crafty writers and directors discovered that if they removed the sex, they could still have the combat. In this light, it's not surprising that 1934 is not only the year the Production Code went into full swing, but also the year often credited as witnessing the birth of the classic, wranglingly romantic screwball comedies, Frank Capra's *It Happened One Night* and Howard Hawks's *Twentieth Century*.

Watching and hearing any screwball comedy, then, there's a distinctive sound, barely audible, behind the smart dialogue and the bang of fist meeting jaw. It's not the crashing of stocks and stockbrokers onto the Wall Street pavement but rather the fitful hiss of a censor's pen across the pages of the script. In the films of the strongest

directors, we can also make out bits and pieces of conversation in certain silences on the soundtrack—religious figures telling the censors what to do, censors telling filmmakers what not to do, and directors and screenwriters laughing over what they were getting away with. Beginning in 1934, directors and screenwriters who wanted to make romantic comedies were forced to remove every overt suggestion of physical love from a genre that depended on suggestions and sublimations of physical love. Little wonder, then, that they created comic characters who found themselves doing verbal and physical cartwheels as a way of dealing with frustrated passions.

Was sexual repression itself an outgrowth of the Depression, a way of imposing institutional authority on the individual during a period of economic stress? After all, the favorable depiction of crime was forbidden with equal vigor, and it doesn't stretch the imagination to see the Production Code Administration's efforts as a means of governing America's libidos during an era of potential (and sometimes expressly threatened) anarchy. The major studios—MGM, Twentieth Century-Fox, RKO, Paramount, Warner Brothers, Columbia, and Universal—were large corporations that obviously had an economic interest in suppressing the more rebellious aspects of a populace that, in some quarters, at any rate, was seen to be edging toward revolt.

It isn't necessary to impute conscious political motives to the studios. Their effective institutional power spoke loudly enough. The three-way relationship among the Great Depression, the Production Code, and the rise of screwball comedies is obvious, though it might be easier to see if the dates matched up more snugly. There were two years between the worst year of the Depression on the one hand and the imposition of film censorship and the birth of screwball comedy on the other. During the declining years of 1929–1932, when the economy was collapsing, Hollywood was in the thick of

Lolita à la Production Code: Director Billy Wilder reduced Ginger Rogers to a nubile preteen in his 1942 *The Major and the Minor*, in which Ray Milland falls in love with the infantilized little Ginger. Wilder explained Rogers's transformation bluntly: "We had Ginger's marvelous tits strapped down." Thus the code's demand for cleaner pictures enabled the production of a lighthearted comedy about pedophilia.

its raciest, most innuendo-ridden period. By 1934, when adherence to the code was mandated, the first New Deal was in full swing, the economy was recovering after the 1932 bottom-out, and the phantasmic threat of socialist revolution was fading. But the dream factory has always been energized by resources other than current events. It is, and was, a magnificent process of production and influences, elaborate causes and mixed-up effects, which is why it's best not to judge the meaning of the screwball comedies until they've had a chance to be seen and heard.

"The sorrows of life are the joys of art."
John Barrymore in *Twentieth Century*

Even if there hadn't been a Production Code or a Depression, comedies of the thirties would bear another historical imprint—that of Broadway. The development of synchronized-sound film and the rapid conversion of projection equipment throughout the country opened the way for Broadway plays to be adapted for the screen and presented to a much wider audience than any theatrical producer could have dreamed. One of the most striking features of screwball comedies is that so many of them are set in New York, the city that not only epitomized the sophistication of urban America, but had also served as the stomping ground of many screwball scriptwriters. Most of the best comedies are filled with people who talk New York, act New York, and even threaten suicide in what might be called a New York way—the slick, theatrical effect of the suicide threat far outweighing the likelihood of the act ever taking place.

American comic theater in the late twenties and early thirties has survived in our memory as a vital if lightweight period in which witty writers dashed off plays for a literate, cosmopolitan audience. After sound film produced the need for dialogue, playwrights such as George S. Kaufman, Ben Hecht, Charles MacArthur, and others were quickly lured not only by the money Hollywood

Looking for Trouble

Censorship advocates of the early thirties were obsessed by the very details they sought to eliminate. One anti-Hollywood crusader, Father Daniel A. Lord, S.J., cataloged offenses with a preservationist's zeal. "In 133 screen plays released from January 15 to May 15, 1934," Father Lord crisply noted in the *New York Times,* "there were 107 major violations of sex morality." Father Lord found: 26 plots or episodes of illicit love; 13 plots or main episodes of seduction accomplished; 12 plots or episodes with seductions as attempted or planned; 2 episodes of rape; 1 attempted incest; 18 (mostly leading) adulterous characters; 7 characters planning or attempting adultery; 3 prostitutes as leading characters (whereas prostitutes as incidental characters were frequent); 25 scenes, situations, dances, or dialogues of indecent or obscene or antimoral character.

The antiseptic vision of life as put forth by the Production Code of Ethics seems as ridiculous as Father Lord's list of "offenses." Here are some excerpts:

GENERAL PRINCIPLES
1. No picture shall be produced which will lower the standards of those who see it. Hence, the sympathy of the audience should never be thrown to the side of crime, wrongdoing, evil, or sin.
2. Correct standards of life, subject only to the requirements of drama and entertainment, shall be presented.
3. Law, natural or human, shall not be ridiculed, nor shall sympathy be created for its violation.

PARTICULAR APPLICATIONS—SEX
The sanctity of the institution of marriage and the home shall be upheld. Pictures shall not infer that low forms of sex relationship are the accepted or common thing.
1. Adultery, sometimes necessary plot material, must not be explicitly treated, or justified, or presented attractively. . . .
2. Scenes of passion: a. They should not be introduced when not essential to the plot; b. Excessive and lustful kissing, lustful embracing, suggestive postures and gestures, are not to be shown; c. In general, passion should be so treated that these scenes do not stimulate the baser element.

uncredited rewriting that studio bosses forced upon scripts, the hack work that is inevitably cited as evidence of the great writers' lack of independence. At the very least, Hollywood forced a relaxation of the archly conventional theatrical language of the Broadway elite, a means of expression that has dated far more drastically than the quicker, more idiomatic speech the hacks substituted in its place. Rather than being destroyers of the playwrights' creations, the anonymous journeymen-writers whose job it was to meddle with famous authors' work were at least partly responsible for bringing comedy alive for people whose speech hadn't congealed into the aesthetic and linguistic conventions of upper-middle-class New Yorkers. On screen, New York was still the center of wit and style, but Hollywood broadened it into a place where *anyone* could live and laugh.

The best Broadway playwrights brought cleverness and technical dexterity. The best unsung hacks brought patter. The best Hollywood actors brought an unaffected, nearly invisible style. And even the worst studio bosses brought an unnervingly savvy sense of popular entertainment, not to mention a knack for corralling and merchandizing human talent on an unparalleled scale. But the period itself seems to have had something to offer—a set of cultural assumptions about romance and comedy. Reviewer Pauline Kael correctly describes as distinctively American the kind of humor that Hecht, Kaufman, and others infused into the movies. But if one had to name a single playwright who most significantly tapped into the emerging spirit of farcical romance that would, later in the decade, find expression in the screwball comedy, that writer would be Noël Coward.

Hecht and MacArthur turned a pair of squabbling egomaniacs into romantic leads in *Twentieth Century,* which opened on Broadway in 1932. Coward had done it two years earlier in *Private Lives.* In both *Private Lives* and *Design for Living,* Coward presented battling, strong-willed

New York, New York: William Powell dances on the edge in MGM's vastly underrated Love Crazy.

offered them, but also by the extraordinary worldwide exposure the cinema could give to their work. Standard discussions of this era described Hollywood's employment of these talented men and women in degrading terms; the words *prostitution, corruption,* and *vulgarization* are used so mechanically that one cannot help but be suspicious of their accuracy. But after reading the plays and comparing them with the films adapted from them, it's difficult to see why anyone would ever complain about the couples whose wrangling was the essence of their love. Coward's comedy gulls the constricting, blandly pleasant normality that is supposed to reign over most people's lives, and if the results are abrasive, at least there's relief from the usual boredom. *Private Lives,* with its deep appreciation of the amorous value of anger, and *Design for Living,* with its love of scandal, look ahead to screwball comedy's sense of release, though neither counts as screwball comedy. Not only is the genre particular to the cinema, but the language of British aristocracy is too haute, too institutionally stagy, to be truly screwball. Moreover, without the restrictions of the Production Code, Coward was free to be as lurid as he wanted (though it's worth noting that *Design for Living,* which played a successful run on Broadway, didn't open in London until 1939—six years after it opened in New York—because of concerns about the play's indecency).

Paramount's film version of *Design for Living* (1933), written by Ben Hecht and directed by Ernst Lubitsch, bears only a passing resemblance to Coward's play. Americanized in language and casting (Gary Cooper, Miriam Hopkins, and Fredric March appearing in place of Alfred Lunt, Lynn Fontanne, and Coward himself), the cinema's *Design for Living* is sometimes categorized as a screwball comedy, but—as later chapters will show—it's really on the periphery of a genre that focused more on bourgeois domestic disharmony than on bohemian scandal.

In the end, screwball comedy didn't grow out of the theater as much as it bounced off of it. The dramatic conventions the cinema borrowed from Broadway were molded into something new, and the character types it stole ended up looking very different in close-up from the way they appeared from the second balcony. These weren't simple formal developments; they were massive transformations that gained artistic force from being blown up to the twenty-five-foot silver screen and energetically distributed throughout the world.

Paramount's *Design for Living* (1933): *(left to right)* Gary Cooper, Fredric March, Edward Everett Horton, and Miriam Hopkins.

Central to their glory is how these film comedies looked and felt to audiences who had never seen anything close to a real penthouse, a long white mink coat, or a real knockdown brawl between two breathtakingly beautiful, supremely articulate human beings.

Screwball comedy hit its stride in the middle thirties, the very peak of Art Deco and post-Deco Hollywood set design. The Deco look invaded

George Curtis (Gary Cooper, *left*) and Tom Chambers (Fredric March, *right*) compare notes on Gilda Farrell (Miriam Hopkins) in *Design for Living.* George loves Gilda, Tom loves Gilda, George loves Tom—though not in quite the same way; but Gilda marries Max Plunkett.

Indecorous Deco: Supernatural screwball heroine Constance Bennett makes herself comfortable atop a gorgeous bookcase in Hal Roach's *Topper* (1937).

Hollywood—the western and the historical drama being obvious exceptions—and it lent the movies its own special brand of sleek and polished elegance. Deco could be used in a more or less straightforward fashion as an expression of wealth and chic, and Busby Berkeley found it to be the perfect background for his cold, spectacularly choreographed musical numbers. But in the screwball world, Art

Deco's crisp, clean lines could be a comic foil for less decorous and decorated goings-on. The fine luster of Deco sets, crossed with the idiotic behavior of the characters who inhabited them, produced a visual clash that matched the kind of mixed-up comedy plots from which the genre took off. For instance, the ghostly form of Constance Bennett lounges atop a white lacquer and polished burl wood bookcase in *Topper* (1937). She strikes a classic pose and looks very content, but there's something farcically out of step about the fact that she's up there to begin with.

Art Deco, as well as the other less style-specific furnishings and set designs of the period, suggests an elegant life-style, the most obvious aspect of which was seemingly unlimited money. Cash has tended to play a big role in defining the screwball comedy; the standard critical line is that comedy undercuts the characters' wealth. But perhaps the conflict was mutual. The childish insanity of the Irene Dunne–Cary Grant marriage in *The Awful Truth,* for instance, is incessantly redeemed

by their superb surroundings, not to mention the extraordinary sensual appeal of the stars themselves. Rarely has the ridiculous been so inextricably linked with the sublime. Part of the reason Dunne's and Grant's bickering is so funny is that it occurs between two of Hollywood's best-looking stars in the context of a huge, dreamily elegant apartment. It is difficult, at times, to decide exactly what is undercutting what.

Look at Dunne, standing in the vaguely gaudy two-story living room set, nervously flipping the loose, draping shoulder of her sequined evening gown while discussing the proper etiquette to use in divorce proceedings. And what about the black, cone-shaped, feather-tipped hat she wears on the witness stand, or the bizarre tripartite number that completes her nightclub outfit—the one capped by black bunny ears? And how about the way she clomps through the house in geometric lounging pajamas that have so much excess material they drag on the floor behind her, forcing her to lift her knees just a little too high when she walks, as though she were treading through a swamp? Like so many other screwball women, Dunne is literally encumbered by luxury; in the case of the pajamas, she can't even walk right.

The visual clash between good taste and bad manners is only one of the oppositions on which screwball comedies turn. This is a world of rampant conflict, an uneasy social vision that fills the gap between lofty goals (love and marriage) and warped reality (love and marriage). Trapped by sex and society, screwball couples' antic adventures make fun of a greater cultural distress. Although their discontents are often masked by charm, screwball characters reflect a sense of literal dis-ease, inner turmoil that is often made physical in manic gestures and attitudes. In the middle of *Bringing Up Baby,* for example, Katharine Hepburn's dowager aunt, curiously named Mrs. Random, and her elderly friend Major Applegate decide to follow Hepburn and Grant outside. "Shall we run?" the major

asks, and the two of them trot out the door. There is *no* motivation for them to sprint their way through the dining room other than to bring themselves up to the film's governing speed, to mimic the anxiety of the younger protagonists, and to give that suppressed nervous energy a liberating release. In a world animated by sex but dominated by sexual repression, the energy level has a way of getting out of hand.

Since sexuality itself was kept in check by the Production Code, screwball comedies sometimes turned to sex *roles* for inspiration. Flipping social imperatives upside down provided endless amusement, though innumerable men felt the pinch. The trend toward tailored suits in women's fashion in the late thirties and forties gave "boss lady" movies (*Honeymoon in Bali,* 1939; *Third Finger, Left Hand,* 1940; *Take a Letter, Darling,* 1942; and the like) a certain visual urgency. But clothes weren't the only factor. The stars themselves were powerful personalities whose commanding screen personalities lent themselves to screwball's interest in sex-role farce. Rosalind Russell, Bette Davis, Carole Lombard, Katharine Hepburn, and Irene Dunne all conveyed images of strong, competent women who weren't going to let themselves be pushed around. As Mme Olge Celeste, the professional leopard trainer who managed the feline costar of *Bringing Up Baby,* put it at the time: "If Miss Hepburn should ever decide to leave the screen, she could make a very good animal trainer. She has control of her nerves and, best of all, no fear of animals."

In screwball comedies, the heroine's relative independence is countered all too often by punishing, resentful heroes whose punching fists, spanking palms, and generally threatening mouths serve as the forces of masculine reaction. Women tend to get a raw deal throughout the genre; they were allowed and even expected to be a little footloose as long as they learned to behave in the last reel. But there can be a strangely liberating value to the violence, even when it makes us flinch. The results may not be especially encouraging, for many of the best screwball comedies are pretty pessimistic in what they conclude about humankind's pathetic struggle for happiness in love and marriage. Screwball freedom lies instead in the release of anxiety and tension within the repressive walls of the forcibly happy home, explosions of hostility that in their own peculiar way become irrefutable evidence of intimacy.

All this articulate screaming can inspire a bit of nausea as well as delight. Both Sarris and Everson have noticed that some screwball comedies end up giving their audiences headaches. It's a fair admission, one that the films themselves seem to make. We can hear it, for instance, in the dialogue of *Twentieth Century,* when Oscar's assistant refers to Lily, saying, "O. J., suppose—just hypothetically, of course—that you, Mr. Bromo, could get together again with Miss Seltzer," an event that would presumably cure all the bystanders of the heartburn the relationship has sparked. We can also hear it in Paramount's *True Confession* in a line that is so thoroughly generic, so perfectly suited to its context, that we might be forgiven if we see it at first as being banal. Fred MacMurray says it to Carole Lombard, who is driving him more or less berserk. "I'm not mad," he says. "I was just thinking I could wring your neck, that's all."

It might be difficult, but a true appreciation of screwball comedies requires us to forget almost four decades of TV sitcoms and fluffy throwaway lines and think back to a time when irritation could be, and was, an exhilarating sign of love. In looking at screwball comedies in the following pages, we will hear this line over and over, with variations and embellishments, in better-turned phrases and even cruder threats, but the sentiment will remain more or less the same: "I was just thinking I could wring your neck, that's all." Those who cannot feel a spark of recognition or a little stab of humor have probably never been in love.

Screwball's Words of Love

"*T*he love impulse in man frequently reveals itself in terms of conflict."

Fritz Feld in *Bringing Up Baby*

"I wish someone would tell you what I *really* think of you."

Claudette Colbert to Gary Cooper
in *Bluebeard's Eighth Wife*

FREDRIC MARCH: You mean to say you stood there and let me beat up a defenseless woman?
WALTER CONNOLLY: I did, Mr. Cook.
MARCH: Where's your sense of chivalry?
CONNOLLY: *My* chivalry? Aren't you just a trifle confused, Mr. Cook? *You* hit her!
MARCH: That's entirely different. I love her.

Nothing Sacred

"Yes, I love him. I love those hick shirts he wears with the boiled cuffs and the way he always has his vest buttoned wrong. He looks like a giraffe, and I love him."

Barbara Stanwyck in *Ball of Fire*

"I need you as much as I need a giraffe."

Jimmy Stewart to Claudette Colbert
in *It's a Wonderful World*

Enough to curl your hair: Only moments before freaking out in the beauty parlor, Jean Harlow patiently gets a permanent wave in *Libeled Lady*. Spencer Tracy looks pretty dubious.

Part One

Marriage for Moderns:
The Pleasure of Screwball Pain

CHAPTER I

Brace Yourself: Adultery, Bigamy, and Simple Playing Around

SCREWBALL COMEDIES PLAY WITH A FUNNY CONTRADICTION: THEY tantalize us with sumptuous romantic ideals even while they horrify us with the farce lurking underneath. Old Hollywood's reputation for ceaselessly hyping marital bliss is thoroughly undeserved as far as the screwball era is concerned. In screwballs, unmarried people are put through a sort of courtship by ordeal. The ability to have sex—legal, off-screen, code-sanctioned sex—is the implicit but ultimate goal. But what makes the genre strange, what gives it lasting punch, is that the ordeal continues for married people as well. One could even say that in screwball comedies people's lives deteriorate terribly under the strain of conjugal love.

The ruthlessness with which these films warp the institution of marriage is clear from some of the titles alone: *Are Husbands Necessary?* (1942), *The Awful Truth, Bluebeard's Eighth Wife* (1938), *The Bride Walks Out* (1936), *Day-Time Wife* (1939), *Don't Tell the Wife* (1937), *Hired Wife* (1940), *Married Bachelor* (1941), *My Favorite Wife* (1940), *Our Wife* (1941), *That Uncertain Feeling* (1941), *Too Many Husbands* (1940), *Wife, Husband and Friend* (1939), and *Unfaithfully Yours* (1948).

In each case, of course, marriage endures, though often in a less tradition-bound manner. Popular art can't be expected to overturn concepts the rest of the culture, not to mention the code, enthusiastically endorses. But no less routine is the revelation of an awful

OPPOSITE: Getting a grip. Gary Cooper and Claudette Colbert in a publicity shot for Paramount's *Bluebeard's Eighth Wife.*

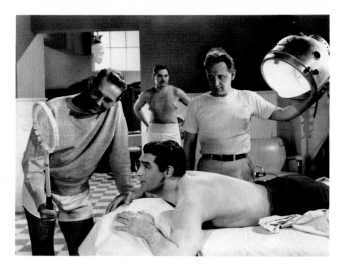

tension beneath the patina of conformity. "I've been to the movies," says Rex Harrison in Preston Sturges's late screwball comedy *Unfaithfully Yours*. "I saw a very long picture about a dog, the moral of which was that a dog is a man's best friend, and a companion feature which questioned the necessity of marriage for eight reels and then concluded it was essential in the ninth."

These last-minute turnarounds notwithstanding, screwball films work on a sense of endless struggle and titanic endurance. Men and women never really come to terms with each other, but neither do they find themselves broken down beyond repair. What's amazing is the lack of resolution to the battles, the sense that nobody ever wins. But what makes their world so hostile? A partial answer can be found in the 1938 guide for young husbands, *Brides Are Like New Shoes,* in which author Anne B. Fisher offered words of caution for the men of America: "Never take any woman seriously when she starts talking about her independence." Fisher's advice was a thirties twist on an age-old problem. Women were becoming more visible in the workplace, divorce was beginning to lose its hot glow of scandal, and the nation's burgeoning communications industry was busy keeping an increasing number of people up to date on the latest social trends on a scale never before imagined. For better or worse, the terms of domestic discord were shifting.

THE ILLOGICAL TRUTH

*I*ncompatibility was a springboard for laughs in many films of the thirties. November 1937 saw the release not only of Columbia's very elegant *The Awful Truth,* but also of MGM's *Live, Love and Learn,* in which wealthy Rosalind Russell finds herself married to bohemian artist Robert Montgomery, and Fox's *Second Honeymoon,* which pitted a frustrated Tyrone Power against ex-wife Loretta Young. As critic and future screenwriter Frank S. Nugent wrote in the *New York Times* in his review of *Second Honeymoon:* "Hollywood used not to take marriage seriously; now the wicked place is refusing to take even divorce seriously. If this sort of thing continues, people are apt to stop believing that di-

IRENE
DUNNE
CARY
GRANT

The Awful Truth

A COLUMBIA PICTURE

COLUMBIA PICTURES

An eye for an eye: Irene Dunne and date Ralph Bellamy take in a nightclub act at Cary Grant's expense. (The dreadful performer is Cary's new girlfriend.)

vorce is a sacred institution, like the Constitution."

The Awful Truth, one of the most enduring film comedies ever made, is the story of how a failed marriage can become a romantic success. The film, directed by Leo McCarey, begins with dashing, handsome Jerry Warriner (Cary Grant) desperately trying to acquire fourteen days' worth of suntan under a New York sun lamp. He's attempting to cover up the massive lie that he has been in Florida doing God knows what for two weeks. Like other cases of screenplays trumpeting adultery without expressing it, the very *lack* of discussion concerning Jerry's whereabouts reveals that he's been staying in New York with another woman— or maybe more. "What wives don't know won't hurt them" is his motto. But when he arrives home with a group of friends acting as unwitting bodyguards, he finds that his wife, Lucy (Irene Dunne), hasn't been home for a while, either. In fact, she

didn't spend the night there, and *her* whereabouts are unknown.

When she does breeze in, dressed in a swank, white, full-length mink coat worn over a glittering sequined evening dress and accompanied by an archetypically untrustworthy Frenchman named Armand, it's clear that Lucy has disregarded the Production Code of Ethics with equal abandon. She explains that she and Armand had attended his students' junior prom and gotten stranded with a broken-down car on the way home. Jerry doesn't buy the story, and we may assume that most people in the audience didn't, either. The junior prom in a mink? Not likely.

"I haven't any faith in anyone," says Jerry. "I know just how you feel," says Lucy, noticing that the orange he has brought her from Florida is stamped "California." This couple is clearly on the road to divorce court, but not before Jerry utters

With an outfit like this (designed by Robert Kalloch), Irene Dunne can afford to express herself however she pleases in *The Awful Truth.*

the film's governing principle: "There's nothing less logical than the truth." As *The Awful Truth* progresses, Jerry and Lucy Warriner confront what might loosely be called "the truth" with increasing discomfort. This learning process begins slowly from their point of view, though from the perspective of the audience it's clear almost instantly that the Warriner marriage is an impossible but vital union. In *The Awful Truth,* the appeal of divorce is most understandable, but Lucy and Jerry quickly find that legal intervention works better in theory than in practice. The rule of law degenerates into farce as the two adults battle in court for custody of their dog, Mr. Smith (played by the personable Asta of the *Thin Man* series and, later, *Bringing Up Baby*). The judge, unable to decide the custody fight on his own, becomes an effective symbol for empty law and collapsing order when he finally leaves the matter up to the terrier. We see Mr. Smith swiveling his head back and forth between his owners, each of whom is hysterically calling to him in a pathetic bid for affection. The dog chooses Lucy (who has cheated by flashing the dog's favorite toy), and the court of modern behavior is adjourned.

The Warriners' divorce will be final in sixty days, a period that leaves ample time for the couple to enjoy their incessant wrangling as husband and wife. Separation doesn't suit either of them; they can't fight when they're apart, and Lucy quickly tires of the dullness that has surrounded her. Her aunt Patsy has moved in, and even Patsy is bored. "I'm going down to the bar and see Joe. Bartender or no bartender, he's still a man. Maybe he knocks off early." Lucy is shocked. "Patsy, you wouldn't!" she gasps. "I wouldn't, eh?" replies the feisty lady. "You're talking to a desperate woman." As she leaves, Lucy calls Mr. Smith, who runs past Aunt Patsy on his way to the couch. "Too bad he can't wear a top hat," Lucy's aunt remarks perversely.

Sexual frustration pervades *The Awful Truth,* but at least Aunt Patsy knows what to do

Divorce, screwball style: Mr. Smith (Asta), ending the custody battle, chooses Lucy (Irene Dunne) over Jerry (Cary Grant) in *The Awful Truth.*

about it. She gets on the elevator, picks up Ralph Bellamy before the elevator reaches the ground floor, and brings him up to meet her niece. Bellamy's character, Dan, is a poor substitute for Jerry—or better, he's an incredibly rich but ridiculous substitute, one who always remains the brunt of jokes and never has the creative gall to play them out on Lucy in return. Jerry's new flame, an idiotic pseudosouthern singer named Dixie Bell, takes an equally unironic view of life, and this lack of irony makes both relationships inconceivable. (At least Dixie Bell is playful. She seems to know she's outlandish, whereas Dan is too thuddingly sincere to be much fun.)

Lucy and Jerry come to see that their essentially ironic personalities need the kind of stimulation that can be provided only by other ironic people. Throughout *The Awful Truth,* both characters perform routines that are only appreciated—often ironically, of course—by themselves. Jerry does a stupid but wonderful duet with Mr. Smith

OPPOSITE: In *The Awful Truth,* Lucy Warriner (Irene Dunne) arrives home after a late night at the junior prom with some Frenchman named Armand.

37

Some Truths That Weren't So Awful

Although it's now considered to be a classic screwball, as stylistically distinctive as the fabulous white mink Irene Dunne wears in her first scene, *The Awful Truth* was actually the third film version of the property. Filmed twice before (in 1925 and 1929), it had been originally written in the early twenties as a play by Arthur Richman. *The Awful Truth* was also the subject of a number of radio adaptations in the late thirties, featuring various combinations of Cary Grant, Claudette Colbert, Ralph Bellamy, Carole Lombard, and Robert Young in the leading roles. But it's Leo McCarey's treatment that has the most cultural resonance—a sublime tale of two people who have learned through experience to survive on implicit distrust and who destroy their marriage only to find that they can't live without each other. The two twenties versions keep the principals innocent; their jealousies and accusations are ultimately shown to be unfounded. In McCarey's version, there's evidence to the contrary. For instance, the orange Jerry Warriner brings to his wife, Lucy, as a souvenir of his trip to Florida is clearly stamped "California," a detail that tells her not only that he's lied about his whereabouts, but also that he has good reason to have done so. The sexual tension between these two vital, blithe, scheming individuals is strangely enhanced by its own suppression under the code. That paradox is the essence of screwball comedy.

early in the film (Jerry on piano, the dog on vocals), and Lucy does a marvelous impersonation of Dixie Bell later on, but in nearly every scene they play together, they speak in a double-edged language of shared ironies and double entendres.

By the end, the couple's language, closed and intimate, amounts to a dialect spoken only between themselves. Ending up at Aunt Patsy's house in Connecticut with only minutes to go before their divorce becomes final, they attempt to sleep in separate bedrooms, but the door between them keeps opening, as if blown open by the force of their mutual attraction. Jerry finally finds himself in Lucy's room and absently closes the door behind him:

Jerry is standing, Lucy is lying in bed. The two are never seen together in the same shot.

LUCY: You're all confused, aren't you?
JERRY: Uh-huh. Aren't you?
LUCY: No.
JERRY: Well, you should be, because you're wrong about things being different because they're not the same. Things are different, except in a different way. You're still the same, only I've been a fool. Well, I'm not now. So, as long as I'm different, don't you think things could be the same again? Only a little different?

Except for the audience, who has been encouraged to learn this meaningless, perfectly romantic language throughout the course of the film, nobody but Lucy could possibly understand what Jerry is saying. Even Jerry himself seems confused by it. She gestures to a chair, which Jerry uses to wedge the door shut. And having locked himself in his wife's room, Jerry appears to be even more perplexed. As Lucy settles into bed laughing, the clock strikes midnight. This couple is now officially divorced, so the Production Code prevents a final embrace. But a resolution can be seen in miniature on the wall: two mechanical figures on the clock march out of their separate doors to signal midnight. Instead of turning around and returning to his proper place, the mechanical boy takes off after the mechanical girl and triumphantly follows her home. The door shuts behind them. There is no indication that the toy couple is married.

Jean Renoir once said that no other Hollywood director understood people better than Leo McCarey, whose great talent lay in the precision and subtlety with which he viewed human behavior. Harry Cohn, the head of Columbia Pictures, chose McCarey to direct *The Awful Truth* partly on the strength of his earlier comedies, which included Laurel and Hardy's *We Faw Down* (1928), the Marx Brothers' *Duck Soup* (1933), and *Ruggles of Red Gap* (1935). But there's another McCarey film, a melodrama, that makes an oddly appropriate contrast to *The Awful Truth. Make Way for Tomorrow,* released only a few months before *The Awful Truth,* is the story of an elderly couple (Beulah Bondi and Victor Moore) who are forced to separate because their children, bourgeois beasts, decide that they can no longer fend for themselves. Although they are inexorably torn apart—the man sent to live with one child, the woman with another—they eventually manage to arrange an excruciatingly bittersweet evening together. They sit together in an enormous dance hall, remembering their youth and enjoying each other's company while delicately postponing their inevitable and final separation.

The Awful Truth is the comic flip side of *Make Way for Tomorrow.* In *Tomorrow,* a married couple struggles to stay together; in *Truth,* a husband and wife fight to get divorced. There are great contrasts between the respective couples—Bondi and Moore are expressly ordinary, while Dunne and Grant are anything but—yet the underlying emotional appeal of both films is remarkably similar. Bondi and Moore endure tremendous hardship by drawing on their shared past, an understanding that Dunne and Grant learn to appreciate in the course of the film. By the end of *The Awful Truth,* when Dunne's Lucy reclines in bed, her arm thrown back languidly on the pillow, there's little reason to think

that Grant's Jerry would ever willingly give her up again. In no other screwball comedy is the intimacy generated by conflict cast in such a warm, affectionate light.

MARRYING YOUR WIFE

*I*n 1940, Grant and Dunne were reunited in another marriage-divorce screwball, RKO's *My Favorite Wife.* Produced by Leo McCarey and directed by Garson Kanin, the film opens with one of the loveliest, most appropriate credits sequences in Hollywood history: the title, stars' names, and production credits are meticulously embroidered on a stack of satiny linens, which are carefully plucked away one by one by a manicured hand. It isn't fake. These credits are not drawn but *sewn,* a superfluous bit of luxury that suggests a marvelous wedding gift or a society woman's trousseau, the perfect connotations with which to open a comedy about bigamy.

My Favorite Wife casts Dunne as Ellen Arden, who returns from seven years on a deserted island on the very day that her husband, Nick, marries a cold shrew named Bianca (Gail Patrick), having had poor Ellen declared legally dead. Like Columbia's *Too Many Husbands,* also released that year, *My Favorite Wife* picks up on what is often called the "Enoch Arden theme," named for Tennyson's famous bigamy poem. In such stories, one spouse sails away, gets shipwrecked, and is presumed drowned, only to return to find the other remarried. (In *Too Many Husbands,* it's Fred MacMurray who "drowns," with Jean Arthur as the bigamist and Melvyn Douglas as the usurper.)

For Tennyson, tragic fate is the point of the *Enoch Arden* tale, but in *My Favorite Wife* it's pure farce. Instead of wrecking the couple's life, casting one into misery and death and the other into guilt and shame, the lurid imbroglio of bigamy winds up making them happier. The screwball era was drawn to bigamy as a comic sexual issue rather than a moral or melodramatic one, and it wasn't just

Embroidered credits: what a trousseau!

Columbia's 1940 bigamy comedy, *Too Many Husbands*, starring Jean Arthur as the poor soul who finds herself married simultaneously to Fred MacMurray (*left*) and Melvyn Douglas (*right*).

Wife, husband, wife, boyfriend, and judge: Gail Patrick, Cary Grant, Irene Dunne, and Randolph Scott face Granville Bates in *My Favorite Wife*.

limited to films like *My Favorite Wife* and *Too Many Husbands*. Bigamy jokes abound in thirties comedies. Under the Production Code, bigamy became a handy sexual problem; the idea of someone ending up with two mates pushed seemingly clean farces to the furthest reaches of propriety. By using unintentional bigamy as a figurative way of working promiscuity into the picture, filmmakers were able to cover a much broader range of intimate behavior than they were otherwise permitted. There's pain, jealousy, humiliation, pleasure, and scandal, all in one:

ELLEN: You're sure you don't love her?
NICK: The moment I saw you downstairs, I knew. . . .
ELLEN: Oh, go on—I bet you say that to all your wives.
NICK: I could strangle you.

My Favorite Wife switches the genders of *Enoch Arden,* in which the man disappears, and the reversal makes the film especially modern. Dunne's Ellen is the wanderer, a woman who leaves on an anthropological expedition to Indochina, specifically, as Nick tells the judge, because she was "having a tough time with the children." ("Teething," he explains vaguely.) The original Enoch Arden ventures out to sea to make money because his fishing business has gone sour and his wife and children are living in squalor. Ellen Arden, in telling contrast, leaves because she's sick of her family. The two men shipwrecked with Enoch die, leaving him lonely and isolated. Ellen is luckier, for *My Favorite Wife* adds an extra player to the tale—Stephen Burkett (Randolph Scott), a muscleman–nature boy with whom Ellen has spent her lost years. She's nicknamed him "Adam." He calls her "Eve." "Adam" says, "We have nothing to reproach ourselves for," a disavowal that simply means they feel no guilt. It's assumed by everyone, particularly Nick, that Ellen and Burkett had a swell time.

Apart from telegraphing the idea that housewives had good reason to escape the home in

All shook up: Cary Grant needs a drink after learning that he's a bigamist in Garson Kanin's *My Favorite Wife*.

41

favor of a faraway sexual idyll, *My Favorite Wife*, like a number of other screwball comedies, spins proper behavior around by playing with sex-role reversals in blunt physical terms. When Ellen shows up at her house, for example, she is dressed as a merchant marine. Her children, the chirpy-voiced Tim and the strangely named Chinch, haven't seen their mother since they were babies, yet they greet her with a different sort of skepticism:

CHINCH: Are you a lady or a man?
ELLEN: Well, I used to be a lady.
TIM: Are ya a sailor?
CHINCH: A lady sailor?
ELLEN: Well . . .
TIM: My mother was practically a sailor. She went down in a shipwreck.
CHINCH: Oh, he's always boasting.

Later, a psychiatrist hired by Bianca, Dr. Kohlmar, visits the house in an effort to discover why Nick repeatedly refuses to consummate his second marriage. At that moment, Nick and Burkett have rushed to the Ardens' house to pick up several of Ellen's dresses to take to the posh Pacific Club, where Ellen has plunged fully dressed into the swimming pool in an obvious physical enactment of her emotional state. ("I can get along without either one of you," Ellen declares moments before missing the edge of the pool. "I'm perfectly able to take care of myself.") Dr. Kohlmar watches in fascination as Nick gathers the woman's outfits together, holding them up to himself in the mirror and studiously judging them for style. "It's for a friend of mine," Nick snaps, meeting the doctor's rapt gaze with irritation. "He's waiting downstairs."

My Favorite Wife is refreshingly open in its treatment of sexuality, sometimes becoming downright smutty in a sly, code-approved way. At the end of the film, Nick, Ellen, and the children have retreated to their country house in the mountains. In a reworking of the final scene of The Awful Truth, Ellen is lying comfortably in bed, happily torturing Nick by refusing to allow him to sleep with her. This time it's under the pretext of waiting sixty days until the annulment is official (though the judge has already called to say, unbeknownst to Nick, that it's a fait accompli). Ellen remarks blithely that they'll get together again around Christmas, and Nick, at his wit's end, departs in frustration. Terrible sounds are heard from the attic, things falling and Nick cursing, but suddenly he reappears at the bedroom door—dressed as Santa Claus! The film's final shot is of a leering Santa shooting Ellen a pair of wickedly raised eyebrows that leave no doubt as to their meaning.

In the case of My Favorite Wife, the sexual underpinnings of screwball comedy drove the censors into a frenzy of indignation. The censors weren't fools; they knew exactly what screwball comedy was driving at. Joseph Breen, the head of the Production Code Administration, repeatedly re-

Sailor drag: Ellen Arden (Irene Dunne) returns from seven years on a deserted island to children (Scotty Beckett and Mary Lou Harrington) who don't recognize her in *My Favorite Wife.*

jected various versions of My Favorite Wife's script, and a series of letters from Breen to RKO shows how far both sides were willing to go in the battle for the hearts, minds, and libidos of the public. Noting "its general offensive sex suggestiveness," Breen singled out in particular the "incredibly offensive" scenes at the Yosemite hotel, the whole story of the desert island, and the many scenes in which Bianca waits for Nick to come to her marital bed. A subsequent letter detailed further demands: Get rid of all references to the Y.M.C.A. (several did survive); "eliminate Nick's line, 'I was born under the sign of Taurus—the bull,' and Bianca's line in reply, 'Live and learn' "; and, in regard to the introduction of Dr. Kohlmar, "change the flavor of this scene to indicate that Bianca is of the opinion that her husband is insane." It's difficult to imagine how else the scene could have been played, but as it was originally written, Bianca was much more direct, telling the doctor that Nick was "a sexual introvert." Regardless of what was meant exactly by "sexual introvert," the interchange is fascinating in that it gives one of screwball comedy's most essential conventions the specific seal of approval of the Production Code. Don't make them sexual—make them crazy instead.

Screwball comedy simply couldn't have developed without people like Joseph Breen, a man

43

who would permit audiences to see Cary Grant modeling a woman's dress but forbade the specific verbal expression of Grant's character's putative neurosis. Had the period been less repressed, moviegoers might still have seen Grant holding a gown up to himself and nodding approvingly, but the underlying tensions would have been made far too obvious. In *My Favorite Wife,* as in the rest of the films that make up the genre, what makes comedy *screwball* is the palpable clash between what can be done and what cannot be said.

Screwballs wouldn't have been screwy if their sexuality had been laid bare. As a result, *My Favorite Wife* revels in the exquisite beauty of repression. When Nick first encounters Burkett, he sees him at the side of the Pacific Club swimming pool. The scene has the quality of a spectacle being played out expressly to humiliate Nick, who watches it from a distance. "Well," says the handsome blond Burkett to his two female companions, "I feel it's about time for a dip!" He stands, stretches, strips to his trunks, and darts athletically toward the diving board. Two older women watch him with breathless excitement. "Young man," says one to Nick, "is that Johnny Weissmuller?" "No," Nick responds glumly. "I wish it were." Kanin then crosscuts between Burkett, looking tremendous on the diving board, and Nick, looking sick on the sidelines. Burkett, in complete command of the situation, walks toward the edge of the board and gracefully jumps to some gymnastics rings that are conveniently suspended over the pool. Nick mops his brow; Burkett swings; Nick looks ready to vomit; Burkett dives perfectly into the water as the crowd applauds. The sequence ends with Nick in abject misery, forced to applaud right along with everyone else.

The poolside sequence is peculiar in that it makes the ethereally handsome Cary Grant seem awed by a lesser star's good looks. It also conveys in an entirely visual manner the nature of his character's imagination. Watching this perfect physical

Her favorite husband.

specimen execute an elaborate gymnastic routine, Nick is immediately drawn to consider the routines Burkett executed with Ellen on the island. No amount of dialogue about Ellen's purported faithfulness is able to overcome the sexual suggestiveness of Burkett's diving and Nick's reaction to it.

Later, Nick is back at his desk, talking on the phone, when Burkett arrives on the scene—courtesy of process photography. At the top left of the image, a miniature Burkett does a gymnastic routine in fast motion; Nick turns around to escape, but the tiny Burkett shows up again, this time on the right. Nick then turns his back directly to the camera and faces the wall, but the muscular little sprite reappears right over his head, swinging and somersaulting frantically.

It's a wonderful image of mental torture, one to which every potential adultery victim can relate. But what makes it so appropriate to screwball comedy is that it's at once maddening and ridiculous, pathetic and terribly funny. Like any number of paranoid film noir heroes, Nick Arden can't escape the madness induced by female deceit. But it's only in screwball comedy that such agony could be expressed in the debonair form of Cary Grant trying to carry on a conversation while mentally fleeing a midget Adonis doing flip-flops in thin air.

FOR LOVE AND MONEY

*I*n a way, courtship and marriage comedies can be true screwballs only when money permits, for wealth gives the characters both the arena and the means to act out as broadly as they please—like hurling a bottle of champagne when necessary or tossing a fur coat off a roof. It's doubly funny because they're doing it in style. The moneyed milieu of most screwball comedies often makes the upper class seem lovable in a time of economic hardship by giving its madcap characters a lot more room to *play*. This constant amusement is some-

Cary Grant wants to know why he has to wait until Christmas to sleep with Irene Dunne in *My Favorite Wife*. They're at their house in the mountains; note that the cabin boasts a satin quilt.

45

times just plain fun, but it also provides the players the freedom and wit to turn social expectations upside down. Too often mistaken for simple craziness, screwball comedy is much more profoundly, essentially playful, a sensibility that in the thirties and early forties seemed to be reserved for people who could pay for the privilege.

The role of money in love-triangle comedies might best be illustrated by looking at two RKO movies that *don't* exploit wealth for laughs—*The Bride Walks Out* (1936) and *A Girl, a Guy, and a Gob* (1941). *The Bride Walks Out* is a Depression comedy of marital disruption that ends with the bickering couple reunited; *A Girl, a Guy, and a Gob* is a wartime courtship comedy that ends in marriage. Both films play on the tensions of love triangles, and both are firmly grounded in what passes in Hollywood for economic reality.

In *Bride,* Barbara Stanwyck plays a moderately wealthy woman, Caroline, who marries a struggling engineer, Mike (Gene Raymond), then falls in love with a rich playboy named Hugh (Robert Young). Mike can't find a job because of the Depression; Hugh owns a department store but spends most of his time drinking himself to death. The film encourages its audience to see Caroline and Mike, who argue bitterly, as nonetheless meant for each other, although Hugh, the dashing aristocratic drunk, appears at times to be an attractive alternative to bourgeois anomie. *A Girl, a Guy, and a Gob* also centers on a triangle, with Edmond O'Brien as a rich suitor, George Murphy as a poor sailor, and Lucille Ball as the working girl forced to choose between them.

In both films, comedy results from argument and romantic disarray, yet the very *lack* of money and class intrudes into each one with such force that the films' screwball potential collapses. These two films suppress screwball comedy in favor of a different, more overtly *logical* kind of humor.

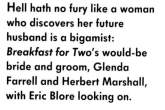

Hell hath no fury like a woman who discovers her future husband is a bigamist: *Breakfast for Two*'s would-be bride and groom, Glenda Farrell and Herbert Marshall, with Eric Blore looking on.

The characters do what is expected of them and little more; their options are terribly limited. No one in these movies possesses the alarming wherewithal of, say, Katharine Hepburn in *Bringing Up Baby,* a woman who is so delightfully confident of the vast amounts of money at her disposal that she can wreck Cary Grant's car without worrying about how to pay for the damages.

Genuine screwball couples (no matter what they might actually say) have enough economic freedom to be able to fight about love. After all, having money means not having to care about it. *Bride*'s Caroline and Mike, in contrast, are forced by circumstance to bicker about paying bills, an issue saddled by the weight of blunt material fact. Look at what these tragically normal people argue about: He doesn't want her to work, she wants to go out more, he doesn't want to live on her money, the furniture gets repossessed. . . . In *Gob,* the situation is even more depressingly down to earth as Lucille Ball's Dorothy labors to find humor amid the strident ordinariness of the middle class. Worse, George Murphy, never one of Hollywood's most appealing leading men (but interestingly its second-most successful politician), is stuck with the aggressively homespun nickname "Coffee Cup," not to mention dialogue that forces him to address Dorothy as, yes, "spindle shanks." This paste-up "reality," phony and strained, doesn't feel anything like the slick, stylish worlds of *The Awful Truth* or *My Favorite Wife,* the latter appearing all the more authentic in contrast.

There are, however, certain moments in *The Bride Walks Out* and *A Girl, a Guy, and a Gob* in which screwball's comic disturbances erupt, bringing playfulness out in the open. *Bride* plays the Robert Young character's alcoholism broadly as a comic means of destroying reason, a generic use of drinking that depicts a debilitating disease in the guise of personal rebellion. In *Gob,* the great character actor Franklin Pangborn's outrageously effete presence as a fussy pet shop owner serves as a wel-

come reminder that everyday life need not be so lackluster. In terms of actual fighting, *Gob* keeps the brawling limited to the two men, but in *Bride,* when Caroline asks two incessantly battling friends why they ever got married, the husband's explanation is purely, irrationally screwball: "Well, it was raining, and we were in Pittsburgh."

Finally, there's *Bride*'s romantic resolution, which, true to form, leaves the couple's emotional future up in the air: the film's final shot is of a moving police van, with Mike being arrested and Caroline kissing him through the bars. The idea of lovers having to be put away somewhere for their own safety or for the good of society is one of screwball comedy's more bizarre leitmotivs. Here it's jail. In even more extreme cases, it's an insane asylum, where the ties that bind two people in love are literalized in the form of straitjackets. One imagines that this obsession with torture isn't exactly what the Legion of Decency had in mind when they forced Hollywood to clean up its act.

Ordinary people: Lucille Ball and George Murphy (embracing) are known as "Spindle Shanks" and "Coffee Cup" in RKO's *A Girl, a Guy, and a Gob.*

CHAPTER 2

The Ties That Bind:
Mad Love and Straitjackets

CONSIDER THIS: WILLIAM POWELL SHUTS MYRNA LOY INTO A CLOSET IN
After the Thin Man (1936); Robert Montgomery locks Carole Lombard into a pair of skis
in *Mr. and Mrs. Smith* (1941); Barbara Stanwyck ties up Henry Fonda in *The Mad Miss Manton*
(1938); Brenda Joyce and George Murphy chain each other to a bed in *Public Deb No. 1.* . . .

Images and threats of confinement appear so often and with such urgency in the
screwball comedy that the genre develops what might be called a bondage motif. Men and
women even threaten to put each other in straitjackets as a way of achieving some sort of
control. In two films, both from Paramount, they actually go through with it.

The Moon's Our Home (1936) ends with Henry Fonda and two men in white coats carting
a straitjacketed Margaret Sullavan away in an asylum ambulance, while Ernst Lubitsch's
Bluebeard's Eighth Wife (1938) reverses the gender pattern by having Claudette Colbert drive
Gary Cooper into an institution, where the experience of being rendered helpless in a straitjacket
helps the temperamental roué understand true romance.

The Moon's Our Home is one of the most vastly underrated films in the genre. Directed
by a Paramount contract director, William A. Seiter, the film suffers unjustly from its director's
lack of a critical reputation. Beautifully written and intelligently shot, *The Moon's Our Home* is a

**OPPOSITE: William Powell and
Myrna Loy are battered but
content in this publicity shot
for MGM's *Double Wedding.*
The film follows painter
Powell's attempts to woo
businesswoman Loy, whose
rebellious sister is trying to
stage an affair with Powell.**

Margaret Sullavan

model studio-era film, yet it's dismissed or forgotten for some of the very reasons that make it worth reconsidering. In a manner that could reasonably be called industrial, Paramount produced in *The Moon's Our Home* a truly classical motion picture. Neither the direction nor the writing aims to subvert contemporary conventions. The conventions themselves—contentious love and, of course, the straitjackets—are subversive enough on their own.

Dorothy Parker and Alan Campbell are credited with contributing to *The Moon's Our Home* that marvelous Hollywood bonus, "additional dialogue," but their contribution was probably more substantial. The credited screenwriters, Isabel Dawn and Boyce DeGaw, adapted the story from Faith Baldwin's *Cosmopolitan* serial, but Parker and Campbell's acerbic influence is strong. *The Moon's Our Home* is about two people who possess a total of four identities: the movie star Cherry Chester, who was born an heiress named Sara Brown (Sullavan), and the famed travel writer Anthony Amberton, who is really an aristocrat named, believe it or not, John Smith (Fonda). Each failing to recognize the other's celebrity persona, they fall rapidly in love, fight continuously and furiously, marry, and separate abruptly, still not knowing anything at all about each other or, for that matter, themselves.

An odd sidelight is that the stars themselves had actually been married and divorced by the time the film was made, a pause-giving historical accent shared the same year by *My Man Godfrey*'s William Powell and Carole Lombard. In the case of Fonda and Sullavan, the real-life marriage was fraught with tension and verbal violence. "Living with Sullavan was like living with lightning," Fonda remembered in his autobiography. "Her tantrums struck at any hour and on any subject." The couple's battles were legendary, so raucous that their Greenwich Village neighbors asked to have them evicted. Fonda later described the affair as having "completely destroyed me." The horrifying details of the Fonda-Sullavan marriage are fascinat-

ing not only because of their undeniable interest as behind-the-scenes gossip, but also because they prove something about screwball comedy: while it might be possible to make a comedy out of *explicit* sexual frustrations, jealousies, and brawls, it probably wouldn't be very funny. Even if it were, it wouldn't be *screwball* comedy, which distorts and sublimates sex in order to make a point about it.

The Moon's Our Home opens in a Hollywood studio bungalow as the temperamental Cherry becomes enraged at her grandmother's telegrammed request that she visit New York. Shrieking at the top of her lungs, the obstinate Cherry responds by hurling a vase at the head of her aging companion, Boyce (Beulah Bondi), who knows enough to duck. The darkness of this comedy is obvious from the beginning as Cherry impulsively apologizes for nearly wounding her closest friend: "If I ever did," Cherry shouts, "I'd blow my brains out!" "I know," Boyce responds sympathetically. "And then I'd have to tidy up afterward."

In an interview with a movie magazine writer who quickly tires of Cherry's pompous discussion of contemporary Soviet literature, Cherry —who happens to be swathed in a satiny white dressing gown with abundant white mink trim— declares with equal pretense that "marriage should be like a ski jump—sudden, swift, reckless! Starting on the heights, leaping into the void! Never knowing the end, never caring!

"There's only one way I could ever fall in love," she continues after a proper theatrical pause. "Not as Cherry Chester the actress—but as a plain, ordinary girl." In one of the genre's most explicit expressions of alienated desire, she sums up her dreams by commenting pensively, "I'd only fall in love with a man I didn't know."

On a train to New York, having succumbed to her grandmother's invitation, Cherry is outraged to see scores of screaming women attempt to attract the attention of a new male passenger, Anthony Amberton. In one sequence, Cherry and

Anthony are seated in adjacent train compartments; separated by a cutaway wall, which creates a split-screen effect, they viciously run each other down without ever having met. Anthony asks his valet-sidekick whether Cherry Chester is "some new kind of soft drink," adding that "marshmallow-faced movie stars make me sick." Cherry, on the other side of the screen, is reading Anthony's latest travel guide with no small degree of irritation. "Mr. Amberton and his camel," she reads; "Oh, I see! *He's* the one with the hat on!" "Give me the simple, primitive woman with a small, high chest," the world traveler declares rather too exactly, only to have Cherry follow through with a fairly vulgar joke sneaked by the writers past the censors: "Mr. Amberton has conquered the highest peaks known

In *The Moon's Our Home*, missing actress/heiress Cherry Chester (Margaret Sullavan, at table) hides out incognito in a Vermont inn with famous author Anthony Amberton (Henry Fonda). Nobody knows who anybody *really* is.

From *The Moon's Our Home*

$\mathcal{F}$amed travel writer Anthony Amberton (Henry Fonda) has just pulled temperamental movie star Cherry Chester (Margaret Sullavan) out of a snowbank, an act that resolves a bet and forces them to marry each other.

CHERRY: Wait a minute! Have I told you about my temper?
ANTHONY: I've had complaints about mine.
CHERRY: We'll fight every day!
ANTHONY: We'll make up every night!
CHERRY: I'll leave you over and over again!
ANTHONY: I'll always find you!

They kiss and fall with a crash onto the snow. Dissolve to a sign reading JUSTICE OF THE PEACE.

to travelers," she reads. (And speaking of vulgar, consider the character's name.) Seiter then flips the characters to the opposite sides of the screen by cutting across the axis, effectively putting them in each other's place. The sequence ends with their two companions departing, leaving the stars looking very lonely in their individual compartments.

The Moon's Our Home is filled with comic scenes informed by a nervous and crazy kind of courtship. Cherry and Anthony—still unaware of each other's true identities—flee to a secluded New England inn, where Cherry is repeatedly dumped headfirst in the snow with violent slapstick used to break down her independence. She agrees to marry Anthony only if she fails to stand up by herself with a pair of skis on (a comment on matrimony?). She fails, but later, on their wedding night, she vengefully but unwittingly makes him sick to his stomach by dousing herself with Cherry Blossom, her own personally endorsed brand of musk. The fragrance, we've already learned, reminds him of the way an African village once smelled in the throes of the bubonic plague.

This seemingly random coupling is still another in a string of absurd events. The couple's wedding ceremony, presided over by Walter Brennan's "deef" justice of the peace, is completed only because the Brennan character mistakes their urgent decision to call off the ceremony for an affirmation of their wedding vows. "I certainly do!" they each shout (really meaning they don't), before being shocked into matrimony by Brennan, who screams, "I now pronounce you man and wife!" over the din of yet another row.

For an image of what a lifetime of married life can do to a person, there's also the hilarious presence of Margaret Hamilton as Mitty Simpson, the pickled innkeeper, whose husband (Spencer Charters) has been rendered virtually mute from the relationship. In a voice that would later achieve epic status in *The Wizard of Oz,* the hook-beaked Mrs. Simpson introduces Cherry to a poor, fat guest, saying (as she marches right in front of her), "This is Miss Hambridge, our schoolteacher boarder from up Barrington way—she's between nervous breakdowns." Mrs. Simpson then leads Cherry to a floral-printed room: "This is the Rose Room. We call it that on account of the roses." Cherry comments favorably on the peaceful quality of a New England winter, to which Mrs. Simpson bluntly responds: "You get pretty used to it after you've had nothin' else for forty years."

From wedding rings to straitjacket, Cherry and Anthony proceed to an eventual reconciliation, one that conforms so strictly to Hollywood convention on the level of plot that it might justifiably be called inevitable. In its actual expression, however, a better description would be *fatal*. After a brush with bigamy, Cherry flees to the airport in a doomed effort to maintain her independence. There she is met by Anthony, two men in white coats, and the straitjacket, one of the most horrifying symbols of marital bliss Hollywood ever concocted. Her arms strapped tightly against her body in an apparatus designed to subdue the victims of extreme psychosis, Cherry finds herself being kissed against her will by a man she both loves and detests. She struggles vainly before giving up her freedom; with twisted logic, she sighs, "I'm tired of having my own arms around me." "Oh, darling!" Anthony cries as he embraces her, eager to join her binding discomfort if only in the realm of emotion.

BECAUSE SHE LOVES HIM

A comedy of fits, starts, and anxieties, Ernst Lubitsch's *Bluebeard's Eighth Wife* asks the question, "Why do you think a woman puts a man in a straitjacket?" Phrased by screenwriters Billy Wilder and Charles Brackett and spoken by Claudette Colbert to Gary Cooper, the answer to the question is self-evident: "Because she loves him!"

One of the greatest humorists of the American cinema of the thirties and early forties, Lubitsch nonetheless made only two true screwball comedies, *Bluebeard's Eighth Wife* (1938) and *That Uncertain Feeling* (1941). Although his other films, most notably *Trouble in Paradise* (1932) and *Design for Living* (1933), play on the irritation that erupts between two (in the latter case, three) people in love, Lubitsch tended to weave the threads of screwball style and substance into a more personal comic fabric, a complex vision less determined by genre than by the storyteller's own sense of humor. Arising out of their author's generous sensibility, Lubitsch's films rarely subject their characters to open ridicule. Nowhere in a Lubitsch film can one find the harsh, accusative laughter that Howard Hawks hurls against Cary Grant in *Bringing Up Baby* or John Barrymore in *Twentieth Century*. At the same time, the day-to-day social observations in a film by Frank Capra or Leo McCarey would be as out of place in a Lubitsch film as a wagon train. Even in his two screwball films, Lubitsch's strong artistic personal-

OPPOSITE: *The Moon's Our Home* director William Seiter (foreground) tells Margaret Sullavan what to do with the snow in her mouth as Henry Fonda listens earnestly. It's an especially brutal scene, with Sullavan being repeatedly pounded into various snowbanks.

53

ity gives this fairly abusive genre an aura of gentle theatricality and quiet satire.

In *Bluebeard's Eighth Wife,* Colbert is Nicole de Loiselle, the daughter of a marquis (Edward Everett Horton). In the course of the film, Nicole meets, falls in love with, marries, divorces, and recaptures Michael Brandon (Gary Cooper), a humorless multimillionaire whose vast success in the business world is balanced by his many failures at marriage.

Michael, who claims not to believe in the institution of marriage, has been married seven times. (One wife died, the others divorced him.) By the end of the film, driven mad by Nicole's schemes to make him jealous, Michael has been committed to an insane asylum after suffering a nervous breakdown. He sits staring blankly into space, quickly and horribly repeating, "I feel fine, I feel fine, I feel very fine. . . ." He's obviously in love.

In the film's opening scene, Michael and Nicole meet at a department store, where Michael is vainly attempting to buy not a pair of pajamas but a single pajama—the top. Michael Brandon is a man who stands by principles. Embracing a puritanical vision of wastefulness as sin, he refuses to purchase the whole pair and simply discard the bottoms. The store clerk, equally stagnant, declines to break up the pair. Michael persists, and in a classic Lubitsch sequence of successive cuts to grander and grander doors and offices, the question is forwarded all the way to the president of the company, who declares, "Never! Never! That is communism!" though he is at that moment wearing only the tops himself. Mercifully, Nicole steps in and offers to buy the bottoms, and the dispute is resolved with an (almost) explicit sugggestion of cohabitation. "Voilà!" the shopkeeper cries. "A lady in love!" Snaps Brandon, "You Frenchmen think the worst."

In this opening scene, Lubitsch, Wilder, and Brackett manage to suffuse the mundane act of buying pajamas with a healthy dose of suppressed eroticism. They insist that the audience think about

Nicole (Claudette Colbert) gently tortures her straitjacketed, institutionalized ex-husband, Michael (Gary Cooper), in *Bluebeard's Eighth Wife.*

what both Cooper and Colbert would look like in their respective halves, focusing especially on the image of Cooper without his pants. This is pure Production Code sex comedy, and in terms of its prurient appeal, it's a big success. At the same time the scene is disturbing, even offputting, since it pushes Cooper's comically taciturn quality far beyond the point at which the character can remain sympathetic. Cooper's Michael Brandon is introduced as a selfish, stuffy skinflint, an impression only partially dampened throughout the film. It's difficult to imagine anyone, let alone someone as cheerfully life-affirming as Claudette Colbert, who would be willing to put up with such a dud, no matter if he's topless, bottomless, or completely undressed.

OPPOSITE: Multimillionaire Michael Brandon (Gary Cooper), the essence of American pragmatism, insists on trying out his most recent acquisition, an antique bathtub, in *Bluebeard's Eighth Wife.*

Unfortunately, the script of *Bluebeard's Eighth Wife* is too programmatically abrasive, Cooper is too stiff, and there's little sense that the two characters ever achieve a recognizable romance. Nevertheless, there are a number of wonderful moments, many of which involve Edward Everett Horton as Nicole's father. By 1938 Horton had mastered the art of playing craven, morally dissolute older men (especially in Lubitsch's *Design for Living* and *The Merry Widow,* 1934). Here, Horton's Marquis de Loiselle becomes hysterical over the concept of premarital financial settlements for his daughter. Given the extraordinary failure rate of Michael's marriages, the marquis rushes around calculating figures and gloating until Aunt Hedwige, the family matriarch, finally bellows, "Are you a father or an auctioneer?!" And no matter what one feels about the rest of the movie, the ending of *Bluebeard's Eighth Wife* works astonishingly well as bizarre marital slapstick. Nicole and Michael engage in a brisk little brawl on the asylum floor—with

Burgess Meredith and Merle Oberon falling in love in a psychiatrist's waiting room in *That Uncertain Feeling.*

Brandon at a distinct disadvantage because of the straitjacket—until the moment she kisses him, at which point he bursts Superman-like out of the jacket and embraces her. They lurch onward to what we presume is the next phase of romantic duress.

ON THE COUCH

Lubitsch began his career as a broad farceur, but by 1941, with *That Uncertain Feeling,* his comic style had evolved toward increasing tonal grace and depth of character. From the evidence on the screen, it appears that Lubitsch could no longer fully commit himself to the kind of comedy in which couples hit each other as an expression of passion.

In *That Uncertain Feeling,* Mr. and Mrs. Lawrence Baker (Melvyn Douglas and Merle Oberon) have been married for six years, a tour of duty considered heroic by their society friends as well as by the magazine *Town and Country,* which has publicized them in a photo spread under the saccharine label "The Happy Bakers." There's only one thing wrong: Jill suffers from uncontrollable hiccups, a neurotic condition from which she reluctantly seeks psychiatric relief. "Doctor, I'm going to be frank with you," she confidently tells Dr. Vengard (Alan Mowbray), a stock period psychiatrist. "I'm absolutely certain there's nothing really wrong with me." "I'm sure you'll feel differently when you leave this office," says the doctor.

The social world of *That Uncertain Feeling,* like those of other Lubitsch films, is governed by an overriding sense of manners—not the stiff moral imperatives of a socially insecure middle class, but the charming inanities of a self-willed aristocracy. Lubitsch's characters maintain their savoir faire even when they're schizophrenic, as the following bit of dialogue demonstrates:

Burgess Meredith, Sig Rumann, Merle Oberon, and Melvyn Douglas in Ernst Lubitsch's *That Uncertain Feeling*, in which Oberon seeks psychiatric help when the mere mention of marriage causes her to fall into an uncontrollable fit of hiccups.

DR. VENGARD: Now what I'm trying to do is to introduce you to your real self. I want you to get acquainted with yourself. Wouldn't you like to meet you?

JILL: No! You see, I'm a little shy.

Despite Jill's bashfulness, Dr. Vengard presses on, zeroing in on her marriage as the source of her anxiety, a diagnosis she resists vehemently. "You could go through all of Park Avenue and not find a happier couple," she declares, to which Dr. Vengard replies, "I'm sorry, but it's my duty to explore every avenue. Especially Park Avenue." The doctor finally manages to engage Jill on the subject of her husband; she launches into a torrent of complaints and promptly begins to hiccup violently.

Disturbed by the revelation of her under-lying marital misery, Jill stops seeing Dr. Vengard in a vain attempt to deny the problem. But when her friend Margie witnesses a typically dull scene between Jill and Larry, Jill realizes glumly that the marriage is in dire straits:

MARGIE: Now I don't want to cause any trouble, but cold facts are cold facts. If Mr. and Mrs. Cooper come —that big awful-looking Mrs. Cooper!—he shaves.

JILL: And if he has dinner alone with his wife, he doesn't shave!

MARGIE: And if anyone should shave, it's Mrs. Cooper.

To which Jill responds with another fit of hiccups. Further exacerbating Jill's frustration and anger is Larry's cute habit of poking her rudely in the stomach and crying "Keeks!" whenever she's in a bad

Melvyn Douglas

mood. "Larry," she says, obviously at the end of the line, "please don't 'keeks' me anymore."

It's back to Dr. Vengard's office, where she meets a distraught musician named Sebastian (Burgess Meredith), who introduces himself with a diatribe about the ugliness of the human race. Having been deadened by the ceaseless loveliness of her Park Avenue marriage, Jill is immediately charmed by Sebastian's misanthropic pronouncements:

> Sebastian: Let me warn you, I say what I think. I'm a complete individualist. I'm against communism, capitalism, fascism, nazism. I'm against everything and everybody. I hate my fellow man, and he hates me!
> Jill (brightly): Sounds rather amusing!

They fall in love. Her hiccups stop. She finally gets a good night's sleep. And before too long everyone is standing in a lawyer's office talking about divorce.

The setup for *That Uncertain Feeling* is more successful than its resolution, though Burgess Meredith is consistently funny as the malcontented Sebastian. At least part of the film's failure to carry through with its initial promise may be due to Lubitsch's discomfort with the breadth of screwball comedy. Such a brutal scene is played between Jill and Larry, but the result veers away from screwball comedy toward bittersweet romance. In the lawyer's office, Jill, Larry, and Sebastian are desperate to find acceptable grounds for divorce, so they stage an act of marital violence in front of a convenient witness, the legal secretary Sally (Eve Arden). But Larry cannot bring himself to hit Jill, even as an otherwise emotionless theatrical stunt, and he repeatedly interrupts the scene to pour himself drinks. Finally, after a series of excruciating rehearsals, he slaps his wife and exits.

The sequence is notable for the expressive conviction with which Lubitsch films it. By giving such weight to Larry's discomfort, Lubitsch concentrates on the underlying sadness of the scene rather than on its more raucously passionate generic roots. To put it another way, Lubitsch could be endlessly amused by the annoying "keeks" of a frustrated couple, but when their relationship degenerates into slaps, even false ones, laughter becomes an inexcusable breach of ethics, an act of raw rudeness that no civilized man or woman could ever tolerate.

That Uncertain Feeling ends with Larry sweeping Jill back into their bedroom and banishing the usurping Sebastian from the apartment, thereby reestablishing the sense of chivalry and romance that had evaporated from the marriage. It is a particularly lovely conclusion. Suffused as it is with unqualified warmth and regenerated compassion, the final shot of a descreetly closed bedroom door is as far from being a classic screwball ending as could be imagined. Couples simply shouldn't be quite so secure.

IN THE BIN

*I*t's certainly de-*light*-ful to be married. . . ." sings William Powell in the opening moments of *Love Crazy* (1941), and as usual, good cheer is a bad omen. Far and away MGM's most energetic screwball comedy, *Love Crazy* mixes high-pitched physical comedy with an ingenious plot in which Powell's character, Stephen Ireland, pretends to be insane in order to prevent his wife from divorcing him. He succeeds so well that she has him committed.

Love Crazy teams Powell with his *Thin Man* (and *Manhattan Melodrama*, 1934; *The Great Ziegfeld*, 1936; and *Double Wedding*, 1937) co-star Myrna Loy. It was their tenth film together. But since *Love Crazy*'s comedy springs directly out of the discomfitting comfort of several years of marriage, the two stars' ease with each other—not to mention their joint image—works to particularly

OPPOSITE: After being repeatedly choked and bashed by a disorderly elevator, Stephen Ireland (William Powell) suffers further indignities at the hands—and tongue—of a dog in *Love Crazy*.

In *Love Crazy*, after assuming the identity of Abraham Lincoln and "freeing" a black butler, Stephen Ireland (William Powell, in top hat) caps his insane performance by pitching his mother-in-law (Florence Bates) into the swimming pool.

good effect. As MGM's highly successful "Exploitation Department" put it in the film's ad campaign, "From blissful kisses to sizzling hisses, they're Mr. and Mrs. again!"

Today is Mr. and Mrs. Ireland's fourth wedding anniversary, and Stephen arrives at their grand New York apartment with a large bunch of red roses. The apartment, designed by MGM's art director Cedric Gibbons, is extraordinarily gorgeous even by Hollywood standards. Since it is inhabited by such an elegant couple, it's almost shockingly ideal—the polished floor, the striped couch, the crisp lighting, the roses. . . . And the Irelands treat it all so matter-of-factly. There's an airy complacency to this household that is really quite beautiful, and Stephen and Susan break into a

William Powell barely keeps his head above water in MGM's *Love Crazy*, in which he plays a man who's forced to get himself diagnosed as insane in order to hold on to his wife.

casual little waltz to celebrate. It is the only moment of serenity in the film.

For the Irelands, the celebration of their anniversary entails what Stephen describes as a "rigmarole." They must do exactly what they did on their wedding day, a lengthy affair that included among other activities a four-mile hike to the justice of the peace and a strenuous stint in a rowboat. To accommodate their advancing age, and to alleviate the tedium of repetition (a quality we can't help but attribute to the marriage itself), Stephen suggests that they perform the ritual backward. Director Jack Conway, together with screenwriters William Ludwig, Charles Lederer, and David Hirtz, focus on the fact that this plan would include serving dinner in reverse order, but lurking underneath all the gastronomic fuss is an implicit understanding that sex, not dessert, is Stephen's primary goal. Following the usual plan, the couple would have to go through one ordeal after another in order to wind up in bed together. Under the new plan, they'd get to the good part first and most likely bag the rest of it.

In classical comic fashion, one thing after another gets in the couple's way. Stephen cracks his foot violently against the bedpost. "Oh, darling, you must be furious!" Susan cries. "No," says Stephen, "just terribly, terribly hurt." Susan's mother (Florence Bates) arrives; Stephen meets his sirenlike old flame Isobel (Gail Patrick) in the elevator and learns that she has just moved into the apartment

Despite the goofy tassle on Myrna Loy's hat, it's William Powell who's supposed to be nuts in *Love Crazy*. In this scene, Powell attempts to prove his dementia to psychiatrist Vladimir Sokoloff, as mother-in-law Florence Bates looks on skeptically.

OPPOSITE: William Powell adds a new angle to his suave screen persona in *Love Crazy*.

below; the elevator gets stuck; when Stephen tries to climb out, the elevator doors close on his head, leaving him grotesquely suspended, at which point the elevator begins to go up and down, bashing Stephen's skull repeatedly against the top of the doorway. When he returns to his own apartment, he mentions Isobel to Susan. "She's married now—got a husband," he says. "Yeah?" Susan asks. "Whose husband she got?"

Through a series of errors, lies, and unlikely twists, Susan and Stephen each come to believe that the other is having an affair—Stephen with Isobel, Susan with an athletic archery champion named Ward Willoughby (Jack Carson). Susan, outraged at Stephen's perceived deceit, de-

mands a divorce. Proceeding on the theory that the divorce couldn't be granted if he was found to be insane, Stephen, dressed in top hat and tails, disrupts a high-class party by running around assaulting all the guests and pretending to be Abraham Lincoln. He "frees" the black butler, grabs men's top hats, floats them in the pond, and finally shoves his mother-in-law into the water for good measure.

Susan, now in the position of having to prove that Stephen is in fact sane, testifies that his actions were simply "private jokes," citing the backward dinner to prove that his oddities are habitual and can only be fully comprehended by her. After being examined by an august group of psychiatrists known as "the lunacy commission," Stephen is found to be certifiably mad. He is then placed in the custody of Susan, who promptly has him committed.

Like most good comedies, *Love Crazy* has to be seen to be believed, for the hilarious twists and turns of its outrageous plot can't be described without straightening them out and ennervating them in the process. Let it be enough to say simply that *Love Crazy* proceeds to that inevitable point at which the Irelands recognize their undying love for each other, a moment that occurs while William Powell is in drag. His signature mustache shaved for the first time in memory, Powell cuts a matronly figure—gray wig, lacy blouse, and busty tailored suit filled out with two skeins of yarn. Ward Willoughby, who is trying to protect Susan, and the police, who are trying to protect the populace (for Stephen has now been labeled "homicidal"), actually come to believe that Stephen is his own sister. The ruse works fairly smoothly until one end of the yarn gets caught on a record player's revolving spindle and Stephen's breasts collapse. But that's the way it should be for a comedy—and a genre—that places such enormous emotional value on the process of coming unraveled.

Remarriage According to Screwball

HENRY FONDA: Haven't I seen you somewhere before?
MARGARET SULLAVAN: Possibly—I'm the girl you married once.
HENRY FONDA: I knew it! I never forget a face!
The Moon's Our Home

"Perhaps it offends my vanity to have anyone who was even remotely my wife remarry so obviously beneath her."

Cary Grant in *The Philadelphia Story*

"I'm more or less particular about whom my wife marries."

Cary Grant in *His Girl Friday*

CHAPTER 3

Out for Blood:
The Intimacy of Violence

ONLY THOSE WHO ARE TRULY MEANT FOR EACH OTHER MAY
rightfully enjoy their partner's pain.

Alfred Hitchcock's *Mr. and Mrs. Smith* (1941) is a comedy of American manners—
specifically, a look at how badly a man and woman behave when they find out that their
marriage is illegal. Although it's as elegant, funny, and perverse as any screwball comedy in this
book, *Mr. and Mrs. Smith* hasn't fared very well in the annals of film history. The first of only
two comedies Hitchcock made in a career that spanned fifty-one years and fifty-three films, *Mr.
and Mrs. Smith* is on the surface so dissimilar from Hitchcock's other work that most film critics
don't know how to deal with it. Hitchcock himself later denied interest in the project, saying in
his book-length interview with François Truffaut that he had made his third American film
purely "as a friendly gesture to Carole Lombard." According to Hitchcock's notoriously
accommodating memory, Lombard had asked him to direct the film, and, "in a weak moment,"
he accepted. Since the director "didn't understand the type of people who were portrayed in the
film, all [he] did was to photograph the scenes as written."

It's true that *Mr. and Mrs. Smith* isn't as fully realized as Hitchcock's best suspense films.
But it's still a classic screwball comedy—faithful to the genre's spirit, rich in expressive detail,

64

witty, and commercially successful. In fact, given the apologetic tone of subsequent film criticism, one would hardly guess that *Mr. and Mrs. Smith* played to sellout crowds at Radio City and became, if not a total smash, a solid commercial hit around the country.

Mr. and Mrs. Smith began as an original script by Norman Krasna, purchased for Carole Lombard by RKO in 1939. Megaproducer David Selznick once expressed some interest in the project, but as it turned out, Lombard herself acted as the film's uncredited producer. Lombard, who was looking for the right project with which to fulfill her four-picture, six-figure-per-picture deal with RKO, saw in *Mr. and Mrs. Smith* an excellent vehicle with which to return to screwball comedy. She was a shrewd businesswoman. Her RKO contract was reportedly one of the first—if not *the* first—instances of a star demanding and getting a percentage of the film's profits as part of the deal. When *Mr. and Mrs. Smith* came along, she correctly sensed that audiences wanted to see her back in screwballs after a succession of darker pictures. Lombard's choice of Hitchcock also shows an astute critical sensibility, for she perceived from his earlier films an implicit comic aspect to the director's tension-fraught sense of romance. Her enthusiasm for *Mr. and Mrs. Smith* altered the course of film history. Asked to star in *Smiler with a Knife,* a melodrama by a fresh face at RKO named Orson Welles, Lombard opted for *Mr. and Mrs. Smith* instead. Welles refused to do *Smiler* without her, and he turned his sights instead on *Citizen Kane.*

Screwball comedy owes so much to Carole Lombard's looks and gestures that one could almost say she defines the genre—the way clothes fall on her body, the color of her hair, the way she laughs, the confident manner with which she delivers ridiculous lines. In the effortlessly hilarious Carole Lombard, queen of the screwballs, Hitchcock found a prototype for the cool blondes who reappear throughout his later films. He emphasizes the air of

detachment in Lombard's screen persona that other directors tended to pass over, but he does so without suppressing her breathtaking physicality.

Despite his own assertions, Hitchcock was enthusiastic about directing *Mr. and Mrs. Smith.* Donald Spoto, the director's biographer, reports that during the first week of shooting Hitchcock had declared, "I want to direct a typical American comedy about typical Americans." For American comedies of the period, "typical" means Park Avenue, and sure enough this street of absurd dreams appears under the credits in the second shot of the film. Abundance reigns on Park Avenue, in particular the mythical Hollywood version, and when the film proper begins, the first thing we see is a bedroom *full* of dirty dishes—stacks of them piled all over chairs, tables, and carpet. Hitchcock's moving camera tracks back and pans to a game of solitaire, the card game for rejected lovers, being played on the floor. The bedraggled player, David Smith (Robert Montgomery) looks up from his bored misery, glances to the left of the screen, and shivers. What he sees, it seems, has given him the creeps, though it's nothing more than the spectacle of his wife, Ann, in bed, her body completely submerged under rumpled sheets and blankets. The camera tracks quickly forward toward the body, the shot ending with a close-up of Lombard's face that is one of the most sweetly domestic visions of marital hostility in the entire genre.

There's some sort of siege taking place in this expansive bedroom, but it's unclear at this point what the nature of the combat really is. The hostility that erupts between screwball couples is, in *Mr. and Mrs. Smith,* a premise; screwball comedy never made a more explicit link between sex and fighting than in this opening sequence. The haggard looks on the faces of both husband and wife imply a sexual marathon as well as an extended war. In either case, it's very unseemly behavior, the kind that brings out one's desire to pry. Everyone wants to know what goes on—for three days!—behind a

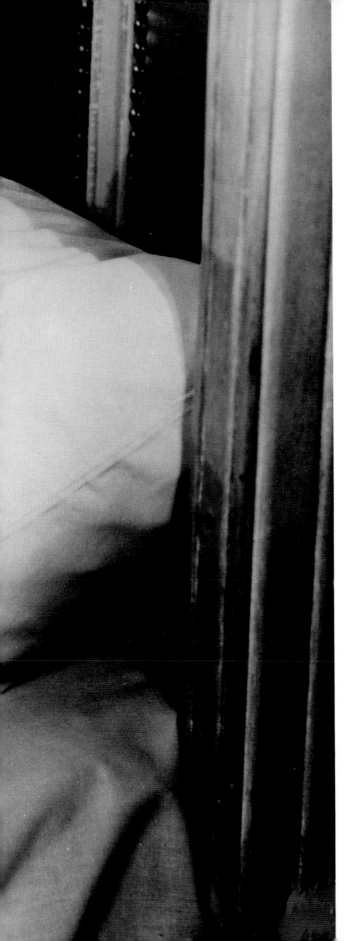

closed bedroom door, including these two curious servants:

MAID #1: Well, what are they doing?!
MAID #2: She's under the bedclothes, and he's playing cards!
MAID #1: You didn't look through the peephole?!
MAID #2: You can't see anything anyway. . . . *(She stops short.)* I only listened.

It's the third day of the Smiths' isolation, and not only the household but David Smith's office is in an uproar. Whatever is happening inside this bedroom is causing some kind of systemic breakdown. David's legal partner, Jeff Custer (Gene Raymond), has sent Sammy, the firm's clerk, to get a paper signed, and the young man's air of determination intensifies the martial quality of the Smiths' bedroom campaign. "Take me to the room!" he commands. Sammy succeeds, and Smith signs the paper, an event that serves in a roundabout way to end the stalemate. David rushes to Ann and embraces her, and we discover that the couple's marriage owes its survival to an essential, unbreakable rule—never to leave the bedroom until an argument has been resolved. "As long as we live, we must never change that rule," says Ann. "You know, if every married couple had it, there'd never be a divorce."

Dr. Belle Wood-Comstock, the author of *Is Love Enough?,* a 1940 how-to book on marriage, found that "attitudes at breakfast often determine the degree of happiness between married people." According to Dr. Wood-Comstock, "this of all times in the twenty-four hours is the greatest test of one's personality." Breakfast at the Smith residence bears out her claim. At first, Ann sweetly sticks her bare feet up David's cuffs under the table, an action Hitchcock photographs in close-up. But after Hitchcock tracks back to a two-shot of the couple seated opposite each other at the breakfast table, the coziness of the scene begins to dissipate. A chill is evident; it becomes apparent, all too quickly, that

OPPOSITE: Cause for alarm. Carole Lombard peeks out cautiously from under the covers at the beginning of *Mr. and Mrs. Smith.*

At the end of *Mr. and Mrs. Smith*, Jeff (Gene Raymond) realizes that he'll never be able to come between such an obviously well matched couple (Robert Montgomery and Carole Lombard).

this marriage is held together by a whole set of rules that Ann rigidly enforces and David silently despises. For one thing, she demands total and absolute honesty: "If we told a lie, we'd have to admit we failed." As if bent on destroying the sense of harmony her ordinances are designed to compel, Ann asks the fatal question: "If you had it to do over again, would you have married me?" "Hon-

estly, no," says David. Ann pulls her feet out of his cuffs, and everything begins to fall apart.

Hitchcock and Krasna follow through nicely on their comic premise by dissolving the Smiths' marriage with a patently ridiculous plot twist wherein Mr. Smith learns that due to some foolish mix-up he is not legally married to Mrs. Smith. Ann, discovering the illegitimacy of her marriage, hurls a bottle of champagne at David (an event that occurs behind closed doors, mercifully out of sight). Later, after she changes the name on the door to "Miss Krausheimer" and insists that he spend the night elsewhere, she slams the front door of their apartment in his face and says pleasantly, "Good night, dear, your nose is bleeding."

This kind of cool and triumphant line can only arise out of intimacy, and its power is such that when we hear it, we know something fundamental is being expressed about human behavior. At the end of the film, for instance, after Ann becomes immersed in an expressly pointless relationship with David's partner, Jeff, the three of them wind up at a ski lodge, where Jeff is proven to be inadequate to the task of screwball romance. David gets Ann clumsily into a pair of skis, which function much like straitjackets do in *The Moon's Our Home* and *Bluebeard's Eighth Wife*. She's unable to walk away or even stand up, a constriction that enables David to get his ex-wife into a half nelson and lock her legs around a post. "Someday when your back is turned, I'll stab you!" she cries in a fury. The threat signals to her husband, and to the audience as well, that this infuriated, defeated woman does indeed plan to spend her life with the one man who enrages her like no other.

IT'S NOT FUNNY

*T*wo postwar screwballs, *Unfaithfully Yours* (1948) and *Monkey Business* (1952), take the screwball motifs of paranoia and physical abuse to its extreme but logical conclusions.

It's accurate to say that screwball comedy declined during and after World War II, but only if the "decline" to which we refer is a matter of quantity rather than quality. A central critical commonplace about screwball comedy is that the war brought on a cloud of narrative darkness, a taste for gritty realism that made screwball's sparkle obsolete. Boiled down to its essence, the shellshock the-

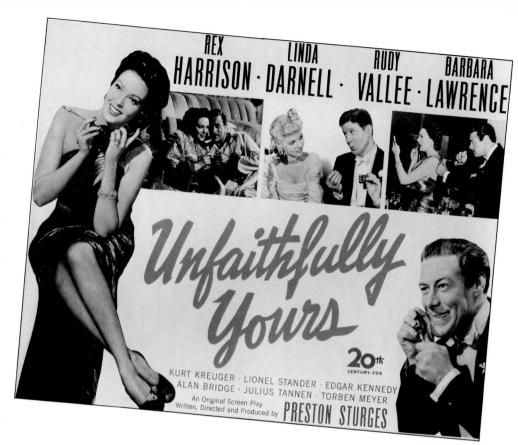

ory of screwball's demise states that people who witnessed the obliteration of Hiroshima and the liberation of Auschwitz could no longer be amused by divorcing couples, dizzy heiresses, and humiliated grooms. But what the truism implies beneath its superficial appearance of common sense is that while the Depression forced audiences to escape from their misery, the war somehow caused them to wallow in it.

The war's impact on screwball comedy was more indirect. Perverse though it may seem, the greatest, most painful influence World War II had on comedies about love and marriage didn't have to do with new ways to kill people but rather with the dramatic increase in real-life marriages at the war's end. America's marriage rate hit a peak in 1946, a fact that literally brought home to larger numbers of men and women the natural tension that evolves from romance, the sense of routine bondage on which screwball comedy plays. And as the baby boom boomed, screwball comedies no longer rep-

Lobby card for Preston Sturges's dark, paranoid comedy *Unfaithfully Yours*, in which Rex Harrison plays a conductor who mistakenly believes that his wife (Linda Darnell) is having an affair with his secretary (Kurt Kreuger). Harrison proceeds to revel in three fantasies about murder, suicide, and the blissful revenge of guilt.

Behind the Camera

Screwball comedy is profoundly social, but it's also personal. For some directors, the genre has very intimate meanings. Above, director Ernst Lubitsch, who characterized *Bluebeard's Eighth Wife* as "mental slapstick," supervises Gary Cooper and Claudette Colbert.

"In those days, the butter was on the toast and not the ass, but there was more eroticism in one such breakfast scene than in all of *Last Tango in Paris.*"
Billy Wilder on morning-after scenes

"Well, it was pretty sad for Cary Grant going around on his hands and knees looking for a bone."
Howard Hawks talking about *Bringing Up Baby*

"You can't really direct it; you've got to feel it. . . . And Carole was a great help in that. She'd get him down on the floor and sit on his chest and say, 'Now be funny, Uncle Fred, or I'll pluck your eyebrows out!' "
Mitchell Leisen describing Carole Lombard and Fred MacMurray in *Hands Across the Table*

resented marriage in the same light. In the late forties and early fifties, television comedy picked up the slack in the domestic department by showing everyday married life in its most comically humdrum aspects. But in films, which had the benefit of not being viewed on the battlefield—which is to say right in people's houses—the tone of romantic comedy became substantially grimmer.

The way these late forties and fifties comedies aggrandize everyday panic may justifiably be linked to postwar perceptions of what is sometimes called the quality of American life, but it's the horror of the home rather than the threat of nuclear war that makes them so upsetting. The dark, sinister tone of late screwball comedies like Preston Sturges's *Unfaithfully Yours* and Howard Hawks's *Monkey Business* is simply a more overt expression of what had always been present—in other words, the genre ripened. These films reveal in some of the clearest, most expressive ways the late flowering of screwball's marriage cycle. More disturbing, more agitated, and certainly more violent, they edge even closer to pure terror than anything that had come before.

Unfaithfully Yours is the story of a man who fantasizes about slitting his wife's throat; *Monkey Business* is about a husband and wife who are reduced to infantilism after ingesting a fountain-of-youth drug invented by a chimp. While the set decoration of *Unfaithfully Yours*—elegant, polished rooms filled with fashionable accoutrements—looks back to the many money comedies of the thirties, its dark cinematography and cramped compositions remain in step with stylistic conventions of the late forties. The light, placid, early-fifties suburban look of *Monkey Business,* in contrast, is strictly of its time and place, yet the film reflects the intellectual elegance of well-wrought scripts from the waning studio era even while wallowing in the giddy hysteria of its moment.

Although a few others were made later, *Monkey Business* (1952) is the last great screwball comedy. By the fifties, the genre was ripe for re-makes, and the studios seized the opportunity: *Nothing Sacred* became *Living It Up* (1954); *The Major and the Minor* (1942) became *You're Never Too Young* (1955); *The Miracle of Morgan's Creek* (1944) became *Rock-a-Bye Baby* (1958); and Jerry Lewis starred in them all, in each case taking what had been the female role. Much later, Peter Bogdano-vich made the manic, romantic *What's Up, Doc?* (1972) in a style that is nothing if not pure screwball. But *Monkey Business* remains well within the classic screwball tradition rather than standing apart from it and looking back, as the others do. It was directed by Howard Hawks, who had made *Twentieth Century, Bringing Up Baby, His Girl Friday,* and *Ball of Fire* (1941). It was co-written by Ben Hecht, who wrote *Twentieth Century, Nothing Sacred,* and *His Girl Friday* (the latter uncredited); Charles Lederer, the credited writer of *His Girl Friday* as well as *The Front Page, I Love You Again* (1940), and *Love Crazy;* and I. A. L. Diamond, who went on to become Billy Wilder's frequent collaborator. It stars Cary Grant and Ginger Rogers, two of screwball comedy's biggest stars. These credits alone make it a classic.

The buoyancy of the screwball genre gives way in *Monkey Business* to flat resignation, a scary sense that not only the genre but the characters' own lives have become routine. The film's precredits sequence makes fun of this repetitive bind by having Cary Grant coming persistently out of his character's front door before his cue, only to be ordered back by the methodical off-screen voice of Howard Hawks gently correcting him—"Not yet, Cary."

Monkey Business is an oddly frightening depiction of maturity being undermined. There's a painful quality to this film, but it's completely intentional; it's unlikely that the director and writers hadn't wanted to ridicule these familiar, middle-aged protagonists, given what they put them through.

A typical screwball couple, Barnaby and

Edwina Fulton are prone to gnashing their teeth in anger or grinding them in rampant anxiety, but more than any of their predecessors, they spend much of the film simply gritting them. Barnaby is a pharmacologist trying to develop a youth-inducing drug, "B-4." His wife, Edwina, is a for-

"Red Eagle" Fulton (Cary Grant) supervises the scalping of his wife's old flame (Hugh Marlowe) in *Monkey Business.* Hilarious frog-voiced child actor George Winslow is the one with the fancy holster.

The Screwball Insult

"You're a newspaperman. I can smell 'em . . . The hand of
God reaching down into the mire couldn't elevate one of them
to the depths of degradation."

> Charles Winninger to Fredric March
> in *Nothing Sacred*

"Waiter, will you serve the nuts? I mean, will you serve the
guests the nuts?"

> Myrna Loy in *The Thin Man*

"The madcap heiress—isn't that what the papers call her?
Millions of dollars and no sense."

> Irene Dunne in *The Awful Truth*

"He's sort of a cross between a Ferris wheel and a werewolf—
but with a lovable streak, if you care to blast for it."

> Fredric March describing Walter Connolly
> in *Nothing Sacred*

mer zoologist (her specialty: the fish world) who
has given up her career to be a housewife. Their
marriage is seen to be rocky from the start, with
petty snipes and jabs revealing the couple's underlying boredom. But when a lab monkey escapes
from his cage and mixes up a successful batch of B-
4 (unwittingly, we hope) and dumps it into the
water cooler (again, we hope, without knowing exactly what it is he's doing, though his actions have
an unsettlingly determined quality), the stage is set
for Barnaby's and Edwina's suppressed fury to find
release.

B-4 unleashes all kinds of hostility in those
who ingest it, and it does so by turning the subjects
first into bratty adolescents and finally into nasty,
unruly children. Barnaby first gets a crew cut and
buys a new roadster, but later, after yet another
dose, he winds up putting war paint all over his
face, transforming himself into "Red Eagle" Fulton,
and joining a bunch of kids in a game of cowboys
and Indians that culminates in the scalping of Edwina's lawyer, who also happens to be her old
flame. Things get so bad that Edwina, who has become quite obnoxious herself while on B-4, comes
to believe that an innocent baby who has wandered
into her bedroom is, in fact, her husband. Finally,
by regaining their youth in as catastrophic a way as
possible (Barnaby describes youth as "a series of
low-comedy disasters"), Barnaby and Edwina learn
that what their marriage needs is less stability, not
more—that farce, by bringing out the worst in people, can also be invigorating.

At its best, screwball comedy is an open
celebration of discord, a comic glorification of the
ugly little annoyances that bubble up between two
people in love. These squabbles sometimes lead to
domestic warfare, but even the combatants must
agree: such distress is certain—and certainly unnerving—evidence of rapture. In no other film is
this passion played out as violently as in *Unfaithfully
Yours*. Rex Harrison stars as Sir Alfred de Carter,
an aristocratic orchestra conductor who makes the

In Howard Hawks's *Monkey Business*, a chimp named Esther *(inset)* gets her revenge on Darwin by inventing a fountain-of-youth drug that regresses adult human beings (particularly Cary Grant) into unruly children. As Cary tells Ginger Rogers, youth is "a series of low comedy disasters."

OPPOSITE: Hattie McDaniel dutifully throws a pitcher of water in Henry Fonda's face in *The Mad Miss Manton*.

"An appalling little game of Russian roulette": Rex Harrison demonstrates the proper technique for Kurt Kreuger and Linda Darnell in *Unfaithfully Yours*.

mistake of telling his brother-in-law, the obscenely wealthy August Heckscher (Rudy Vallee), to look after his wife while he's away. The dull-witted Heckscher takes him at his word and hires a private detective to tail the woman, an eminently sweet-tempered model of grace named Daphne (Linda Darnell). Upon his return, Heckscher promptly—and falsely—reports to Sir Alfred that his lovely wife is having an affair.

Sir Alfred's outrage, delivered with bravura by Harrison, is initially directed toward Heckscher and then to the private eye. He storms into the detective's office and ruthlessly squelches the poor music lover's praise, saying, "Spare me your compliments! The flattery of a footpad is an insult in itself!" ("You mean a flatfoot, don't you,

Sir Alfred?" is the stunned man's helpful reply.) Later, however, he takes his frenzy out on his wife. In a series of three overwrought fantasies followed by a humiliating attempt to put those dreams into action, Sir Alfred pushes screwball comedy to its most horrible—though logical—end.

The pain starts early. In the beginning of *Unfaithfully Yours,* Heckscher and his delightfully ostentatious wife, Barbara (Barbara Lawrence), watch Sir Alfred greet Daphne with a passionate kiss. "You see," says Barbara, "some men just naturally make you think of brut champagne. With others, you think of prune juice." Heckscher laughs —the only time he even cracks a smile in the entire film—but Barbara cuts his enjoyment short with a line that might have had a special resonance for many unfortunate postwar viewers: "You have nothing to laugh at." She's right—it's always harder to laugh at a screwball put-down when the insult's experience is your own.

The letter of the code was still in effect in 1948, but Sturges and the rest of Hollywood had moved sufficiently away from its repressive spirit to allow a little light wife killing to be graphically depicted on screen. Of course it's unfair to reduce the entire film to two literally bloody scenes, but in the context of screwball's marriage comedies, those scenes are simply flabbergasting. At one point, the camera tracks forward on Sir Alfred as he conducts the first work on the evening's program. The camera movement *seems* typical in that it brings us smoothly, progressively closer to the character's emotions at an appropriate moment. But the camera keeps going, venturing farther and farther toward Sir Alfred's face, proceeding beyond even the tightest close-up until it bizarrely singles out Sir Alfred's left eye, which at such intense proximity makes him look utterly deranged. Sturges concludes by dissolving from the enormous eyeball to an absurd little music box in his apartment, and the first of the film's three fantasy sequences begins.

With this jarring, hilarious shot and dissolve, Sturges disrupts convention; romantic comedies don't usually get so visually, physically close to their heroes' innermost passions. But he's also setting his audience up to see another tightly held expectation destroyed. Sir Alfred's fantasy is as logical an extension of screwball conflict as might be imagined: he dreams up an elaborate plot to kill his wife and then, to the audience's horror, does so right there in front of us all.

In this daydream, Sir Alfred throws Daphne onto the bed and rips her throat open many times over with a straight razor. Were it not for the absence of spurting blood, this murder scene, hideous in conception and funny only because of its shock value, might be mistaken for an early psycho-slasher movie. Later, in a somewhat more subdued but no less graphic suicide fantasy, Sir Alfred alludes to his earlier dream by saying, bluntly, "I cut your throat with a razor. Your head nearly came off." In the later scene, Sir Alfred turns the tables—and the weapon—on himself by spinning the pistol barrel in what he calls "an appalling little game of Russian roulette. . . . Then," he says, "with a rigidly steady hand and without any sniveling yammerings—I would ask you to notice, Daphne—I place the muzzle here, and with a simple 'Godspeed,' in case I should be unfortunate, I pull the trigger . . ." and swiftly blows his brains out, a fact Sturges drives home with a shot of a black, bleeding hole in Sir Alfred's head.

It's probably scenes like this that lead people to credit World War II for comedy's shifting perspective, but as this chapter ought to have made clear, it's simply the end product of screwball's history of violent antics. It was only a matter of time before the implied or threatened violence that appears in nearly every screwball comedy became literalized in the form of murder. In *Libeled Lady* (1936), Spencer Tracy asks Jean Harlow, "Do you want me to kill myself?" and Harlow replies with a hardheadedness typical both of her persona and of the genre, "Did you change your insurance?" In *The Mad Miss Manton,* a furious Henry Fonda tells Barbara Stanwyck, whom he has grown to love almost as much as he hates, "You are a nasty creature, aren't you? But in time, *I'll beat it out of you!*" Couples actually punch each other out in *The Moon's Our Home, Breakfast for Two* (1937), and *Nothing Sacred,* and men turn women over their knees and spank them in *Public Deb No. 1* and *Bluebeard's Eighth Wife.* And while *My Favorite Wife* doesn't celebrate violence openly, the critic Otis Ferguson was horrified at the way it treated Cary Grant and Irene Dunne. "It forces its best people," Ferguson wrote, "to treat each other with an aimless viciousness that even Boris Karloff might hesitate to reveal to his public." In terms of physical assaults, *Unfaithfully Yours* is the end of the line.

"Art Direction By…"

In the screwball era—and indeed until the studio system collapsed—the major studios helped maintain their "house style" by employing a single art director to supervise nearly all productions. Two of the most famous and talented of these studio art directors were Hans Dreier at Paramount and Cedric Gibbons at MGM. Even when the art director wasn't head of the studio's art department, as Gibbons and Dreier were, he most likely did not design each and every detail in the film but rather orchestrated the work of other set designers and decorators toward a unified style, for which he can be considered responsible. Here is a selected filmography for screwball art directors, listing their best and most representative films.

LIONEL BANKS
(Columbia)
Holiday (with Stephen Goosson, 1938)
His Girl Friday (1940)

HANS DREIER
(Paramount)
Design for Living (1933)
Easy Living (with Ernst Fegte, 1937)
Bluebeard's Eighth Wife (with Robert Usher, 1938)
Cafe Society (with Ernst Fegte, 1939)
Midnight (with Robert Usher, 1939)
The Lady Eve (with Ernst Fegte, 1941)

ERNST FEGTE
(Paramount)
Easy Living (with Hans Dreier, 1937)
Cafe Society (with Hans Dreier, 1939)
The Lady Eve (with Hans Dreier, 1941)
The Palm Beach Story (with Hans Dreier, 1942)

PERRY FERGUSON
Ball of Fire (Goldwyn, 1941)
Bringing Up Baby (RKO, with Van Nest Polglase, 1938)

CEDRIC GIBBONS
(MGM)
The Thin Man (1934)
After the Thin Man (1936)
Libeled Lady (1936)
Double Wedding (1937)
Ninotchka (1939)
Another Thin Man (1939)
The Philadelphia Story (1940)

ALEXANDER GOLITZEN
That Uncertain Feeling (United Artists, 1942)

STEPHEN GOOSSON
(Columbia)
It Happened One Night (1934)
Mr. Deeds Goes to Town (1936)
Theodora Goes Wild (1936)
Holiday (with Lionel Banks, 1938)

CHARLES D. HALL
(Universal)
The Good Fairy (1935)
My Man Godfrey (1936)

VAN NEST POLGLASE
(RKO)
Bringing Up Baby (1938)
The Mad Miss Manton (1938)
Bachelor Mother (with Carroll Clark, 1939)
Fifth Avenue Girl (1939)
My Favorite Wife (1940)
Mr. and Mrs. Smith (with L. P. Williams, 1941)

ARTHUR I. ROYCE
Topper (Hal Roach/MGM, 1937)

ALEXANDER TOLUBOFF
The Moon's Our Home (Universal, 1936)

CARL JULES WEYL
(Warner Brothers)
It's Love I'm After (1937)

LYLE WHEELER
Nothing Sacred (Selznick/United Artists, 1937)
The Young in Heart (Selznick/United Artists, 1938)
Unfaithfully Yours (Twentieth Century-Fox, with Joseph C. Wright, 1948)
Monkey Business (Twentieth Century-Fox, with George Patrick, 1952)

LEFT: Jean Arthur's immense and gaudy suite at the Hotel Louis in *Easy Living.*

RIGHT: To make the Borden family of *Fifth Avenue Girl* seem even more miserable and out of step, RKO's art director Van Nest Polglase and set designer Darrell Silvera built this mammoth, stuffy Victorian living room. In this scene, the Bordens (*left to right on the couch:* Kathryn Adams, Verree Teasdale, and Tim Holt) call in the family lawyer.

OPPOSITE TOP: Nick and Nora Charles's stylish living room in *After the Thin Man*, designed by Cedric Gibbons for MGM.

OPPOSITE BOTTOM: MGM's Cedric Gibbons designed this elegant living room for businesswoman Myrna Loy in *Double Wedding*. Note the curvilinear wall and banquette, echoed by the upholstered chairs.

ABOVE: Set design of the absurd. Paramount's art directors Hans Dreier and Ernst Fegte engaged in flights of organic fancy for the Hotel Louis set in *Easy Living*.

LEFT: Hans Dreier and Ernst Fegte supervised the design of this deceptively simple nightclub set in *Cafe Society*. Note the exotic murals.

Jean Arthur raids her piggy bank in Paramount's *Easy Living* (1937); little does she know the good fortune that awaits her.

Part Two

Cents and Sensibility:
The Uses of Screwball Cash

CHAPTER 4

Heiresses in Overdrive:
Poor Little Rich Girls Running Wild

IN ONE SCREWBALL COMEDY AFTER ANOTHER, THE OLDER GENERATION maintains the notion of money's paramount importance while the younger generation—especially the glamorous, scatterbrained heiresses—learn to reject it, only to wind up keeping it anyway. This screwball precept rears its blithely duplicitous head in Frank Capra's landmark comedy *It Happened One Night.* The story of this movie's success has been repeated often, but it bears one more go-round (with a few corrections) since it's about a movie that helped make not only a great director's career, but also the entire screwball genre, thanks to its immense and unexpected popularity. Money talked, and Hollywood listened.

In February 1934, a film starring Clark Gable and Claudette Colbert opened at Radio City Music Hall to mild reviews. It was called *It Happened One Night,* and the critics found it diverting but undistinguished. Gable played a newspaper reporter who follows Colbert, a flighty heiress, as she sneaks her way to New York on a bus to marry a playboy her father despises. *It Happened One Night* left Radio City after only one week. But within a month, audiences all over the country were swarming to it, and the film created a sensation. The Greyhound Bus Company, near bankruptcy, was thrilled that Gable and Colbert chose their line. Underwear manufacturers were aghast when Gable removed his shirt to reveal his bare chest. Many women

OPPOSITE: Swinging-Door Susie—Katharine Hepburn as Susan Vance in *Bringing Up Baby.* Hepburn's screwball heroine pushed the genre's airy romantic irritations to an extreme, perhaps more than audiences of the day could appreciate.

were delighted. At the Oscars the following February, *It Happened One Night* made history: the film swept the awards, winning Best Picture, Best Director, Best Screenplay, Best Actor, and Best Actress, the first film in history to win all five of the top awards.

Now for the corrections. It makes a good yarn for Frank Capra to claim in his autobiography that his popular film had been embraced by the public after being dismissed by the critics, but in fact most of the New York reviews were positive. Its departure from Radio City wasn't unusual; most films left the Music Hall after a single week's run. And it wasn't the critics but rather industry analysts for the trade paper *Variety* who were most widely off the mark about *It Happened One Night*. *Variety* called it an "odd holdover" at one New York theater and went on to declare that if the film ended up doing better than predicted, "it will be due to Connie's 'Hot Chocolate' tab," the "colored show" on the theater's stage.

No doubt that *It Happened One Night* made money—lots of it. It ranked among the top ten grossing films of the year and raked in still more when it was rereleased the following year after the Oscars hoopla. But what made this money interesting was that it all went pouring into the coffers of a studio on Poverty Row. *It Happened One Night* was made at Columbia Pictures, which along with United Artists and Universal, comprised the so-called Little Three studios. (The Big Five were MGM, Paramount, Fox, Warner Brothers, and RKO.) Columbia was run by Harry Cohn, who liked to keep costs down, and although *It Happened One Night* was one of Columbia's more expensive projects, it is said to have cost less than $300,000 despite its two big stars. (As a point of comparison, when Darryl Zanuck took over the reins as head of production at Fox in 1935, his *average* budget was $400,000 per feature.)

The extraordinary profits of *It Happened One Night* are the stuff from which legends spring. Fondly repeated are stories about Louis B. Mayer punishing an uppity Clark Gable by dispatching him from his berth at MGM's luxurious headquarters in Culver City to Columbia's more pedestrian lot on Gower Street. "I got an actor here who's being a bad boy," Mayer is reported to have said to Cohn, "and I'd like to spank him." The same tele-

phone call is also alleged to have contained one of those pithy summations Hollywood types often regret having uttered after the film in question turns out to be a box-office bonanza. Capra had originally wanted Robert Montgomery, another star in the MGM stable, for the role of the reporter, but as Mayer conveyed it to Cohn, "Montgomery says there are too many bus pictures."

If we can forget for a few moments the nostalgic raves of film critics, the Oscars on Frank Capra's bookshelves, and the many times we've seen clips of what are supposed to be the film's best scenes, *It Happened One Night* may come into clearer view for what it really is and was—an unpretentious, unusually leisurely screwball comedy about a

mismatched couple who meet and fall in love on the road. It's about an heiress who travels by Greyhound Bus and a cynical reporter who happily marries into the richest family on Wall Street. And it's about the Depression, which is to say that it's about money.

Capra and screenwriter Robert Riskin introduce Ellie in the midst of a big fight with her father, a fat financier played by Walter Connolly. They're on the family yacht moored in the waters off Florida. Ellie claims to have married the notorious playboy King Westley, and she threatens to go off with him; her father is holding her against her will, an action to which she has long grown accustomed. "You've been telling me what not to

Clark Gable

do for as long as I can remember!'' she shouts. Ellie is obstinate. She dumps his tray of food all over the floor, and he slaps her. Ellie appears to be used to mental cruelty, but her father's violence drives her to revolt: she dives—fully dressed—into the water and swims away to what she thinks is freedom.

Capra is sometimes said to be corny and sentimental, too mush-headed to be a great artist, but the yacht scene—never chosen as representative of Capra's work in the way the later doughnut-dunking and hitchhiking scenes inevitably are—is a fine example of how he works against obvious emotional tugs. What we see is a spoiled, rich young woman who has married a man with an obnoxious name, and we might expect to find her attitudes to be annoying in the extreme. They are, yet when she dives off the yacht—an action Capra characterizes as quick, effortless, and graceful—the director manages to turn everything around. Suddenly her marriage to Westley—and more specifically her escape from her father—seems a stroke of genius, an impulsive lunge toward glorious freedom. In an instant, Capra makes Ellie real and likable, not so much by the fact of the dive—which could have looked clumsy, rude, silly, pathetic, or insane, according to the director's wishes and talents—but by his sharp sense of visual characterization.

Ellie, on the lam from her father, heads back to New York to meet Westley; Peter meets her, discovers her identity, but decides to help her for purely mercenary reasons—so that he can publish as a newspaper exclusive the chronicle of her desperate flight toward love. Perhaps because the very notion of the madcap heiress has lost its cultural appeal, *It Happened One Night* can't be experienced with the same excitement that surrounded it in 1934. In fact, it's nearly impossible even to think about the famous doughnut-dunking scene in anything approaching its real context, since it has been used so often as an example of Hollywood charm and romance. Looking at it as a screwball scene, however, something else emerges. Peter and Ellie

are seated at the breakfast table in their room at a roadside camp, where they've been forced to spend the night in the same room—as "husband and wife" —because their bus has been stopped by a bridge washout.

They have erected between them a makeshift wall (clothesline, blanket), which Peter insists on calling "the wall of Jericho," an allusion that suggests rather too coyly both sexual combat and the inevitability of its collapse. (In fairness to Capra and Riskin, the Jericho image is one of the few important plot devices taken directly from Samuel Hopkins Adams's "Night Bus," the *Cosmopolitan* short story on which *It Happened One Night* was based.) In the morning, in their room, Peter and Ellie are seated at a small table eating breakfast. Peter teaches her how:

> PETER: Hey, where'd you learn to dunk? Finishing school?
> ELLIE: Aw, now don't you start telling me I shouldn't dunk.
> PETER: Of course you shouldn't—you don't know how to do it. Dunking's an art. Don't let it soak so long. Dip, and then *slock*—in your mouth. Let it hang there too long it'll get soft and fall off. It's all a matter of timing. Aw, I oughta write a book about it.
> ELLIE: *(laughing)* Thanks, professor.
> PETER: Just goes to show you—forty millions, and you don't know how to dunk.
> ELLIE: Oh, I'd change places with a plumber's daughter any day.

Having seen it so often, it's difficult to block from consciousness the most obvious aspects of the scene. We know Peter is trying to topple Ellie from her aristocratic perch by showing her how real folks eat, and we also know that the domesticity of the scene is so irresistible that Peter and Ellie will eventually have to become a couple. Yet there's something irritating about Peter's manner. There can be no antietiquette etiquette; you either abide by the rules or you don't, and you certainly can't teach

someone the right way to be wrong. Isolating the scene from the rest of the movie, as the Hollywood-tribute clips do, not only puts the focus on Gable's character, since he's the one with the punchy lines, but it also makes it seem like a great Depression-era bit of Hollywood realism—real guy teaches heiress how to live like the hoi polloi. But the scene is actually slanted toward revealing Peter's character flaws and playing with them. It's more screwball than cornball.

We can see, after all, that Ellie is not a snob. Capra and Riskin have previously slipped in a few lines to show us why:

ELLIE: You think I'm a fool and a spoiled brat. Well, perhaps I am, although I don't see how I can be. People who are spoiled are accustomed to having their own way. I never have. On the contrary. I've always been told what to do, how to do it, and when, and with whom. Would you believe it? This is the first time I've ever been alone with a man! It's a wonder I'm not panic-stricken.

Still more succinct is what we *see*. Ellie is not too proud to dunk the damn doughnut to begin with, and she does it without *thinking* it to death the way

89

Peter does. Besides, if it did fall apart, there is little doubt that this strong-willed, independent young woman wouldn't be above digging the soggy remnants out of her cup with a spoon. After all, what would she care?

What emerges from the scene, finally, is the sense that Peter's insecurity is greater than we thought. He's threatened by this attractive woman and in the persona of Clark Gable it's jarring to see. It can also be gratifying, if one is prepared to accept it, to watch Peter begin to make a fool of himself.

There's a sense, too, that Ellie isn't the kind of woman who will put up with too many of Peter's lessons; this suggestion becomes explicit in the equally famous hitchhiking scene. After being forced to leave the bus in the middle of nowhere, they attempt to bum a ride. Peter, ever the man of the people, insists on demonstrating the three correct methods to use when hitchhiking, but this time the teacher loses the student's faith entirely and humiliates himself in the process. Ellie lies down on the top rail of the fence on which she has been sitting—clearly an uncomfortable position, but it's worth it to her to show how little she thinks of his lesson. Peter remains oblivious to her more or less silent critique (she does toss in a few words of sarcasm), and he attempts to put his teachings into action when the next car comes by. He misfires badly, not just once but repeatedly. Car after car goes racing by, and none of his three tricks causes even so much as a slowdown. Ellie then assumes control. She confidently declares that she can do better, and with the very next car that appears, she does—by raising her skirt provocatively above her knee, causing the car to screech to a halt.

The scene works well as a war of wills and skills, though Ellie's mercenary use of her sexuality comes off tragically in retrospect. There is no reason to think that she would have failed had she simply used her thumb rather than her leg, and the way in which Capra cuts to a closer shot of the skirt being raised compounds the problem, since it disembodies the leg at exactly the moment when Ellie ought to be triumphing with her wit and integrity. The cut contradicts what we have already seen: a strong woman who can succeed on her own is reduced to a posed leg, a moving hand, and a piece of skirt.

It Happened One Night works itself around to a grand conclusion. Ellie, under the mistaken belief that Peter has used and abandoned her, decides to marry King Westley officially in an elaborate outdoor ceremony, but she disrupts her own wedding by racing from the altar and into a waiting car. Ellie's exit from the wedding is, as a number of critics have said, very brisk and gratifying, especially as a repetition of her original escape from the yacht. And the sheer physicality of her exit is a fine setup for the film's final scene, which takes place in a tourist camp: we see the exterior of a cabin and hear a trumpet signaling the fall of Jericho's walls.

Apart from its self-evident symbolism, the film's ending also demonstrates what screwball comedy sees as the virtues and limitations of cold cash. One can only imagine the ambivalent emotional effect a pomp-filled wedding scene must have had in the middle of the Great Depression. There must have been a mixture of contempt and awe in those run-of-the-mill neighborhood theaters in which *It Happened One Night* became a hit.

The split sensation of desire and distaste toward wealth is an emotional paradox screwball comedies exploit. In this context, it's important to remember that *It Happened One Night* made its reputation—as well as its money—not in the big urban movie palaces like Radio City Music Hall, with their ornate lobbies and expensive seats, but in the smaller, ordinary theaters where it played out its extended runs. There, where audiences weren't surrounded by the trappings of luxury, is where the film touched a nerve, and its success probably had something to do with a similarity between the audience's perspective about money and that of the film. After all, Capra made an heiress comedy that takes place largely outside the world of wealth, fea-

Claudette Colbert

turing a heroine who literally dives out of her moneyed background.

Yet she never gives up the cash. Neither does Peter renounce it when he marries her. Peter tells Ellie's father that he is uninterested in the reward money, preferring instead to submit an itemized list of expenses that totals exactly $39.60. It's not an effort to be noble. If you buy the fact that Peter loves Ellie, surely you buy his desire not to capitalize on her, even after her apparent rejection of him. But the intrusion of integrity in the face of money serves ultimately to insure Peter's financial security, since it impresses the financier-father enough to tell his daughter to reject the real gold digger, Westley, in favor of Peter. No one who has witnessed the fabulous mansion and its grounds, the food, champagne, dresses, and tuxedoes that money can buy—especially after tracing the couple's arduous, impoverished trip on and off a bus—can forget the fact that Peter Warne has married big, big money in the end. His obliviousness to it only makes him more appealing.

In the case of *It Happened One Night,* it's clear that while money may define Ellie as one of the Great Depression archetypes, the infamous "poor little rich girl," it actually *propels* Peter. First he has to beg for work, then he has to stick with Ellie despite any reservations he might have about her personality because he needs to sell her story. Finally, in the twist, his rejection of the reward secures his place as a new American aristocrat, a man Ellie's father can trust will never whittle away the family fortune the way King Westley obviously would. What better honeymoon could there be in times of economic hardship than one that guarantees the preservation of capital?

At the same time, movie money means liberation. It buys characters like Ellie enough confidence to knock down an old, repressive social order and to do so without fear. With so much cash, Ellie and her heiress cohort can afford to be their own women alongside the men who love them.

POOR LITTLE RICH GIRLS

It Happened One Night didn't spark America's obsession with heiresses, but the popularity of Capra's film certainly breathed new life into the conventional rich-girl character, leading to a slew of movies about madcap heiresses and the more or less helpless men who loved and hated them. The thirties were full of heiresses running amok: from Barbara Stanwyck's heiress-turned-communist in United Artist's *Red Salute* (1935) to Myrna Loy's litigious clothes horse in MGM's *Libeled Lady* (1936); from Stanwyck's rock-'em sock-'em corporate pirate in RKO's *Breakfast for Two* (1937) to Katharine Hepburn's irresistibly aggravating Susan Vance in RKO's *Bringing Up Baby* (1938). Heiresses survived into the early forties, as in RKO's *Cross Country Romance* (1940), in which Wendy Barrie runs away from a bad marriage only to wind up in a trailer with Gene Raymond, and Warners' *The Bride Came C.O.D.* (1941), in which Bette Davis finds "happiness" in the form of flyer James Cagney.

The presence of an heiress doesn't guarantee that a film's comedy is screwball. It's as much a question of when the film was made as how the heiress is treated. Look at the difference between, for example, RKO's *The Richest Girl in the World* (1934) and Paramount's *Cafe Society* (1939). Made before *It Happened One Night* had had a chance to rack up its Oscars and spur the production of like-minded comedies, *The Richest Girl in the World,* with a script by Norman Krasna, has little in common with the many comedies about frazzle-brained heiresses that followed. It takes its title very seriously; it's a film about the emotional problems of the world's wealthiest woman, though the title does have a built-in irony. The heroine, Dorothy (Miriam Hopkins), has remained single due to the decidedly unromantic burden of her wealth. Dorothy doesn't believe in love, mostly because she's convinced that men could only desire her for her money and not for herself. She then exacerbates the problem through the odd habit of masquerading as her own secretary at public functions, while her compliant friend Sylvia (Fay Wray) takes over the millionairess's role.

Dorothy's insecurities are simultaneously challenged and tantalized by the arrival of Anthony Travis (Joel McCrea), a man of modest means whose naked interest in becoming the world's richest husband coincides with his self-evident attraction to the real Dorothy. Faced with potential romance, Dorothy turns ever more neurotic, repeatedly pushing Anthony toward the phony Dorothy as if to prove her own lack of personal worth.

The Richest Girl in the World isn't a bad film, with Hopkins and McCrea each adding a nice hard edge to their characters, but it isn't a screwball comedy. For one thing, there's little abrasion between the two leads. Their fights arise circumstantially rather than out of any kind of deeper, more intractable passion. Add to this the sheer reasonableness of their behavior, and screwball comedy becomes impossible. "I wish I hadn't started this thing," Dorothy says, referring to her dual role, "but now I have to find out. All my life I'd feel that maybe he liked her better, that I was second choice. I couldn't stand that." No one could argue with such ingenuous good sense, especially since it corrals her apparently illogical behavior within the confines of personal honor. It's not difficult to imagine accepting a certain amount of doubt in a marriage —especially when your husband looks like Joel McCrea—but Dorothy makes that option seem positively immoral. Moreover, the McCrea character maintains his interest in pursuing an incredible amount of money as long as he thinks he has a chance, a perfectly reasonable course of action given the character's honesty about it. Within the terms of the film, both Dorothy and Tony act precisely as they ought to, an artistic strategy that makes them

Miriam Hopkins and Joel McCrea in *The Richest Girl in the World*, a 1934 RKO comedy about the romantic tribulations of a neurotic heiress and an ingenuous gold-digging lothario.

seem normal, understandable, and terribly unscrewball.

Lovers in screwball comedies are much more profoundly contentious, irritable, and emotionally unruly, a convention that *Cafe Society*, a comedy made five years later, takes for granted. *Cafe Society*, like *It Happened One Night* (and MGM's *Love on the Run*, 1936; Fox's *Love Is News*, 1937; and Hal Roach's *There Goes My Heart*, 1938), once again pits two of the great cultural powerhouses of the thirties—the heiress and the reporter —against one another in a struggle for love and authority. Power is really the key here, for *Cafe Society* assumes that the two central characters, the heiress Christopher West (Madeleine Carroll) and the reporter Chick O'Bannon (Fred MacMurray), are able to oppose each other (in the beginning of the film, at least) as equals despite their class differences. Chris has the power of money, but MacMurray has the power of thirties character

convention: he's a tough and streetwise reporter who doesn't *need* anything in the way McCrea's mercenary wife seeker did.

Cafe Society forces Chris and Chick into a marriage that occurs solely to get Chris's name into the society column of the newspaper, though both husband and wife dislike each other intensely. Forced to stay married for reasons that remain fairly obscure, the two characters get the chance to inflict various abuses on one another and discover the depth of their love. In the best, worst, and most literally painful sequence, Chick and Chris conclude an idiotic party on her yacht, complete with all of her dreadful friends—and the film is pretty nasty about these rich deadbeats, too—by having a huge fight and falling overboard into the water. Chick climbs into a speedboat and Chris grabs on to the surfboard tied to the back, but when she refuses to join him and go home, he takes off, forcing Chris absurdly to water-ski for five miles while they periodically scream at each other through the surf. Being a classic screwball sequence, the event prompts them to face their emotional needs: "Your hands hurt a lot?" Chick asks. "Those ropes certainly cut them up, didn't they? I'm a great guy." Chick may seem guilty, but Chris has fallen in love: "Yes!" she says, nearly swooning with joy. "I never met a man before who'd do a thing like that to me!"

Such violence, of course, is all of a piece in terms of proper romance in the screwball genre. At one point, after Chick has slapped Chris, Chris's grandfather actually apologizes—to *him:* "You see, if I had started smacking her earlier, maybe it wouldn't have been necessary for you to do it." Later, after the brutal speedboat scene, he reiterates: "You know, Christopher's grandmother was never any good 'til one night I spanked her with her own hairbrush—you remember that, Watkins!—and so after that she was all right. We had no more trouble with her at all."

Unlike some other notable screwball comedies, in which such punishment is meted out in a

more sexually balanced manner, *Cafe Society* comes down far more fiercely on the woman than on the man. Not only is Chris slapped, ridiculed, insulted, and rope-burned, but she's also dismissed as just another looney fad. "Oh, you must've had yourself a time with that little screwball of a Christopher!" declares busty Mrs. DeWitt (Jessie Ralph), the commonsensical mother of the city's preeminent gossip columnist. "You know, she's a screwball because girls all over the country are screwballs this year. She thinks she has to be one, too." Never mind that this is 1939, "girls" having been depicted as screwballs for five years already. It's the spirit of the remark, not its historical accuracy, that's telling. *Cafe Society* sees screwball's anarchic energy, here and elsewhere, as being women's fault, an inherent character defect for which they have to pay. And in the end, Chris does pay: she apologizes for being who she is, cries remorseful tears, throws herself on Chick's mercy, and agrees to live forevermore as a plain and ordinary wife.

Cafe Society is more unsparingly bitter toward wealth than most other screwball films, but even here the assault is duplicitous. Chris's grandfather, true to his patriarchal type, is the film's real

Joel McCrea

financial nexus, and he's treated with great respect. It's Chris, the spoiled young female heir, who bears the brunt of the film's ire, as though it would be intolerable for a woman to inherit the fruits of male labor without a working man there to tame her. The film's final moments are about as grim as could be. Chick and Chris are seated on a forgettable couch in Chick's drab apartment. The camera has tracked slightly forward to a tight two-shot, the kind that tells us the end is near:

CHRIS: You hit a cop for me!
CHICK: Sure—nobody's gonna get tough
      with my wife but me.
They look at each other lovingly.
CHICK: Do you want a cigarette?
CHRIS: Yeah.
CHICK: Do you want a drink?
She shakes her head no.
CHICK: Too warm?
She nods. Chick helps her remove her beautiful white mink stole. One senses it's gone for good.
CHICK: Do you want a bean sandwich?
CHRIS: I'd love one.
CHICK: With ketchup?
Chris nods. They kiss. The end.

IN THIS RING, I THEE WED

*I*t's one thing to have a wild heiress tamed by a man of the people, but what happens when an heiress starts picking on an heir? That's the premise of RKO's *Breakfast for Two* (1937), a film described by one critic as "a piece of arrant foolishness" with a "wretched plot." It would be tough to defend *Breakfast for Two* as great art or even good art, but what the film lacks in style it more than makes up for in animosity between the principals, tension that spills over into physical violence when the two lovers engage in a boxing match.

Herbert Marshall is an irresponsible, alcoholic playboy named Jonathan, whose fortune derives from the family steamship line, a company

that is now going under because Jonathan has abandoned his birthright and ignored the business. For reasons that remain unclear, a Texas heiress (Barbara Stanwyck) with the terrible name of Valentine not only has fallen in love with the impoverished New York drunk, but has decided to supervise his rehabilitation as a corporate leader. She does so by humiliating him back to manhood.

Comparing men to horses, Valentine declares, "Sometimes they both need a whip to put some sense into them." She presses the point further: "First you have to slip a bit in his mouth"— she smiles coolly and with a trace of malice—"and make him *like* it." Valentine swiftly takes over the company, secretly buying up all the stock she can under the belief that Jonathan will learn how to fight for what's his. He becomes enraged but remains helpless. "You're the type of woman who wants to wear the pants!" he shouts, but he does nothing to stop her.

"The whole plot is undermined," says Valentine dejectedly in one of screwball comedy's more self-conscious moments. "He's not going to fight."

She takes over his household, seizing everything he owns except for his wardrobe. Looking him straight in the face, she calmly informs him of his emasculation: "You need your clothes in order to *look* like a man." Tension escalates. Valentine picks up a handy boxing glove, puts it on her fist, and hauls off and slugs Jonathan in the face. True to screwball form, Jonathan finds his own pair of gloves, and the two of them proceed to punch each other out.

Breakfast for Two may be rough going in terms of art, but it's certainly pure screwball. Not only is there a fight scene, but there's a classic bigamy joke uttered when Jonathan's butler, played broadly and hilariously by Eric Blore, "discovers" a marriage license in his boss's pocket just before Jonathan attempts to marry his rattle-brained fiancée, Carol. "That's bigotry!" Carol cries. Of course no marriage has occurred; Valentine has planted the

Fred MacMurray

THAT SCREWY RED MENACE

Strange as it may seem, the presence of big stars, great directors, wild costumes, and over-blown sets often confuses matters in some films, while the very lack of style in others may allow meaning to spew forth without restraint. This is certainly the case with two bizarre anticommunist screwballs, *Red Salute* (1935) and *Public Deb No. 1* (1940), a matched set of cautionary tales of how the red menace could infiltrate cafe society and turn gullible heiresses into mouthpieces for the Kremlin.

The first of the two, *Red Salute,* was made independently by the producer Edward Small, who released it through United Artists. It stars Barbara Stanwyck and Robert Young, and it was one of the first films made specifically to capitalize on the success of *It Happened One Night,* a fact not lost on most of the reviewers. Stanwyck plays Drue Van Allen, the spoiled daughter of an army general, who falls in love with an exceptionally villainous radical student (Hardie Albright). Drue's father arranges to have her kidnapped to Mexico, where she meets a sturdy soldier named Jeff, played by Young. Jeff promptly goes AWOL to help her sneak back to the radical, fighting about politics and falling in love along the way.

Writing about the film, *New York Times* critic André Sennwald blasted the film's depiction of left-wing politics as having "the subtlety of a steam roller and the satirical finesse of a lynch mob." Sennwald also hit upon the film's explicit anti-intellectualism, citing one of Young's most egregious speeches to Stanwyck, the turncoat heiress:

> JEFF: You aren't kidding me. You aren't as red as you make out. You're just shooting off your face to those longhairs because you haven't found out yet what you want. You're not such a heavy thinker. Do you know how I know? Because a thinker is a dodo on the dance floor and you aren't!

fake license in order to prevent Jonathan from making the mistake of his life. And in a patently idiotic conclusion, Valentine knocks Jonathan out with a weighted boxing glove in a big slapstick scene that leads them inexorably to marriage. In the final scene, Donald Meek, the celebrant, hastily pronounces the couple man and wife, then throws his hands over his head to reveal yet another pair of boxing gloves.

Made at the height of the screwball era, *Breakfast for Two* simply *assumes* that brawls and nasty insults are the foundation of romance, but it reverses the genre's tendency to cast the heroine as a financial and emotional incompetent. It's Marshall, not Stanwyck, who plays the dizzy fool, though the film substitutes a temporary condition —active drunkenness—for the assumedly more permanent condition of feminine inanity often used to characterize heiresses. As a result, our moneyed heroine uses her wealth and power to help return a man to preeminence. How Valentine will fit into the corporate world after her marriage is a question left unanswered.

If leftist students kept trying to subvert the American way of life, reviewer Sennwald snidely concluded, "not only will Miss Barbara Stanwyck deny them her allegorical caresses, but Mr. Robert Young will punch their noses."

Fox's *Public Deb No. 1* follows a similar course in its depiction of dumb-dumb heiresses who sympathize with the reds. Brenda Joyce is the duped debutante, Penny Cooper, the dizzy blond heiress to the Cooper's Soup fortune whose entrance into the film is literally a riot. She's first seen marching through Union Square in solidarity with the working class in a demonstration that quickly turns ugly. The communists—the film is blunt about this, just as it is about the demonstrators' dark, Eastern European looks—are summarily hauled into court, Penny among them. But just like many movie heiresses before her, this isn't the first time the madcap blonde has found herself in front of a judge. A thrilled reporter, stuck on the night beat and excited to have such a scoop dropped upon him, explains to his editor, "This time it's for being a red!" *Public Deb No. 1* then provides an excellent (though unintentional) rationale for communist uprisings: as soon as the paunchy jurist finds out that Penny is richer than he is, he obligingly lets the young woman and her cohort off scot free.

"Comrade madame!" cries Penny's butler

Grisha (Mischa Auer) as he greets her at the mansion door. The rest of the film proceeds apace. *Public Deb No. 1* doesn't exactly ring with wit, and the screenplay as written is a true Johnny one note of bad political humor. The story, however, is pure screwball. Penny is vaguely attached to a dull boyfriend, Bruce (Ralph Bellamy), an aspiring politician. One evening soon after the riot, the couple goes out for dinner—to a place called the Red Samovar, naturally—where an incompetent waiter named Alan (George Murphy) picks an olive off the *zakuska* platter, pinches it, and sends it flying down Penny's décolletage.

The inevitability of a romance between Penny and the bumbling waiter is sealed when the two get into a fierce argument about communism: "A bunch of lazy people trying to get something for nothing!" is how Alan describes Penny's comrades. "What you need is a good spanking," is his pragmatic and generically imposed solution. A man of his word, Alan immediately turns Penny over his knee and, to the tune of "Ta-Ra-Ra-Boom-Dee-Ay," begins to paddle her furiously.

By subjecting Penny to violent public humiliation, Alan carries out the express command of *Public Deb*'s political muse, Elsa Maxwell, the real-life party-giving powerhouse. The film is actually introduced in the opening credits as "Elsa Maxwell's Public Deb No. 1," and indeed the portly Maxwell, who appears as herself, clomps through the movie as if she owned it. Maxwell tells Penny's uncle Milburn that he ought to take that girl "out to the woodshed," presumably to teach her a thing or two about the American dream. Later, when Penny declares that Maxwell's way of life is "as dead as the Incas," Maxwell responds with the movie's most singularly idiotic line. "I once met an Incan boy at a dude ranch, and there was nothing dead about him!" Maxwell lewdly asserts, apparently unaware of the ancient Peruvian tribe's extinction at the hands of the conquistadors.

Like *Red Salute*, *Public Deb No. 1* demands

Take that, you dirty red: Penny (Brenda Joyce), reacting badly to the Soviet invasion of Finland, finally sees the light and socks her communist butler (Mischa Auer) at the end of *Public Deb No. 1*.

97

Street Scenes

Producer Edward Small's 1935 madcap heiress movie *Red Salute* has one great distinction: it was the only screwball comedy ever to have provoked a political street riot. "It's fight at first sight with them," one reviewer admiringly wrote about the film's stars, Barbara Stanwyck and Robert Young. But the brawling wasn't confined to the screen. When *Red Salute* premiered at New York's Rivoli Theatre in late September 1935, members of the leftist, antiwar National Students League stood outside the theater with leaflets urging a boycott of the comedy. "Spotted along the theatre front," *Variety* reported matter-of-factly, "was a squad of cops." The situation was livelier inside, with "contending rounds of applause, hissing, and booing" during the show, culminating in "several fist fights" between some students and a group of outraged patriots. Eighteen people were arrested. The following week there was a riot, with at least 125 people hauled off to jail.

that Penny finally reject her leftist politics, which both films mercilessly deride as the whims of brats, and embrace what the film sees as traditional American values—industrialism, canned soup, heterosexual union, and Elsa Maxwell. The final two items are a particularly odd match-up, since Maxwell herself was a lesbian and rather openly so in society circles. Yet with perfect duplicity, it's Maxwell who conspires—both as the film's nominal producer and as one of its central characters—to give the girl what every heiress needs: a storybook romance with a working-class he-man. In an effort to counter the bad publicity that Penny is giving to Cooper's Soup as a result of her political agitating, Maxwell insists that Penny find true love and publicize it in the gossip columns. What better candidate could there be than Alan, who has become America's hero for giving Penny the whipping she deserved? "Love at First Slap" is the newspaper's catch phrase description of their affair, a strained but no less characteristic screwball courtship that goes so far as to include the two "lovers" leashing each other by the ankle to a bed.

The unyielding power of money, an idea that screwball comedy sometimes subverts by portraying those who possess it as nitwits, is taken so for granted here that the film isn't ashamed to make its hero as mercenary as possible. In *It Happened One Night,* Gable's Peter Warne successfully marries money in part because he doesn't seem to care about it. In *Red Salute,* the film's uncritical equation of military and money may be outrageously prescient, but it also serves to make Young's capturing of Stanwyck's heart seem like an act of patriotism. But in *Public Deb No. 1,* George Murphy's Alan runs on simple naked greed, a motivation the film enthusiastically endorses. Alan vies for Penny's affections, but he also vies for her corporation, thereby providing a handy lesson in how a regular working man can become a successful corporate executive if he follows his heart. By the end of the film, the love between Penny and Alan has become self-evident

In *Public Deb No. 1,* Charlie Ruggles gets an earful from society steamroller Elsa Maxwell.

LEFT: Sometime film producer and ubiquitous partygirl Elsa Maxwell tries to get a closer look at soup heiress/communist sympathizer Penny Cooper (Brenda Joyce), who gets booked on rioting charges (*inset*) in *Public Deb No. 1.*

OPPOSITE: "I can't give you anything but love." Susan (Katharine Hepburn) and David (Cary Grant) wonder what's next, having successfully transported a leopard from New York City to Connecticut in *Bringing Up Baby*. The famous intercostal clavicle is in the box.

even to Penny, though it actually takes the announcement of the Soviet invasion of Finland to give her the final push into Alan's arms. "I'm afraid the revolution is over," Penny sighs after kissing her true love. She pauses, then adds: "You're probably just marrying me for my money." "Sure I am," Alan declares with characteristic American aplomb, "but it's nice you're good-lookin', too, cutie pants."

ANYTHING BUT LOVE

Rising up out of the swamp of bad art and hysterical anticommunism, we may now move to the other extreme—that of the ultimate screwball comedy, *Bringing Up Baby*. This brilliant film, which somehow manages to survive countless viewings and critical discussions, is usually approached in terms of romance. But it's almost as

much a tale of money as it is of love, for the unlikely relationship between paleontologist David Huxley (Cary Grant) and heiress Susan Vance (Katharine Hepburn) would make little sense if the issue of money didn't lurk underneath almost every scene. Indeed, its comedy would be nearly unbearable otherwise.

This isn't to say that what the film sees as "love" doesn't play the central role. As the film's most quotable line expresses it, "the love impulse in man very frequently reveals itself in terms of conflict." But since the screwball world depicts love as something that goes well beyond comprehension, there would be literally *no* comprehensible reason for David, an obsessive paleontologist, to endure the abuse he suffers at the hands of Susan, a whimsically self-assured heiress, if large amounts of her family's money weren't at stake.

Money is so integral to the plot of *Bringing Up Baby* that even the heiress Susan pursues it. Most film heiresses don't lack for much in material terms, and it's obvious from the way Susan dresses, not to mention her casual use of the expression "my farm in Westlake, Connecticut," that she's no exception. But Susan doesn't underestimate future needs, either, and she's not about to take her standard of living for granted, as so many other screen heiresses do. Susan Vance is nothing if not calculating. "It's *not* a harebrained scheme!" she declares to David, defending her plan to transport her new pet, a live leopard named Baby, by car from her New York apartment to the Connecticut farm. Susan's rationale, delivered at breakneck speed by Hepburn, explains her economic position in blunt terms: "Imagine Aunt Elizabeth coming to this apartment and running smack into a leopard! That would mean an end to my million dollars!" She continues, stepping right over David's feeble interjection: "If you had an aunt who would give you a million dollars if she liked you and you knew she wouldn't like you if she found a leopard in your apartment, what would you do?"

Lobby card for RKO's 1938 box-office failure *Bringing Up Baby*.

David quickly answers, "I don't know," and tries to flee, but Susan has made her point so successfully that fleeing becomes his only option, aside from admitting (which for all practical purposes he does) that the so-called harebrained scheme makes perfect sense, thereby accepting irrationality as reasonable, a central screwball principle. But here, the leap of faith is made possible only on money's account, for it's David's own financial project —to ensure a grant of $1 million to support his paleontological research—that keeps him going. The trouble is, the grant giver is the same Aunt Elizabeth, a fact that makes it impossible for David simply to act like a scientist and exercise his reason; get rid of Susan, systematically lobby the aunt's lawyer and financial administrator and get the grant in the usual way; marry his stalwart girlfriend, Miss Alice Swallow; and spend the rest of his life up to his neck in bones.

The previous night David had found himself standing in the lawyer's front yard watching in horror as Susan threw fistfuls of pebbles at the poor man's bedroom window, insisting all the while that she always had "Boopie," her old family friend, wrapped around her finger. Here as elsewhere, Susan exudes an emotional and physical pull that forces David to remain by her side, but there's also the subtle suggestion that David stays with her simply because he wants to get the money the quickest way possible. "Oh, I know we ought to go," says David tragically as he stands transfixed on the lawyer's lawn with Susan hurling stones toward the window, "but somehow I can't move." Given the circumstances, *who would?* We've already witnessed, in the first scene of the film, the drab and methodical Alice Swallow in action—particularly the fierce determination with which she exhorts David to forget about their honeymoon and work instead. Alice's tightly done hair and dull clothes, together with the clinical way she fights off David's embrace, makes her own interest in fossils seem almost like wish fulfillment. When David exits that

scene, it's no wonder he cries, "Good-bye, Alice!" while extending his hand to his skinny, beak-nosed, and unambiguously male colleague. "I mean, Professor," he fumblingly corrects, making his frustration all the clearer.

If Alice is David's sex life, Susan is a big relief. She's athletic, free, irrational, and well dressed. She's also exceedingly rich. And rich as she is, she knows people who are even richer—people like Aunt Elizabeth.

Ironically, although the characters in *Bringing Up Baby* expend a great deal of energy in the pursuit of money, the film itself was a flop at the box office. In fact, it's one of Hollywood's most famous flops, not because it got terrible reviews and lost a lot of money in a big, dramatic way, but because it came and went without making much of an impression on the public whatsoever. Hawks,

who had gone over budget, was held partly responsible, with Hepburn, who had just placed first in the Independent Theater Owners Association's list of "box-office poison" stars, taking the rest of the blame. One reviewer went so far as to say that the film had obviously been designed with the idea of brutalizing Hepburn for laughs.

This was, of course, the era of the ditzy heiresses, but Hepburn wasn't ditzy even when the genre called for it. In *Bringing Up Baby*, she works against her character's type so thoroughly that audiences found themselves faced with an heiress who paid nothing for the sin of being rich. Moreover, she doesn't forfeit her brain in the process. As a result, Hepburn's Susan Vance has everything— money, clothes, an apartment in New York, and a farm in Connecticut. Most of all she has complete command of every situation. Susan is impervious.

She's not a lucky pawn of the system, like 1938's number-one glamour girl, debutante Brenda Frazier; she's a manipulator in her own right. She gets her way in every situation, and she does so with the kind of total self-assurance that inspires admiration —when it doesn't provoke rage and resentment, which seems to have been the case in 1938.

For example, when Susan wants David to stay in Connecticut, she steals his clothes and tells the cook to give them to the gardener to take into town to be cleaned and pressed. She then calmly goes about the business of taking a shower, thus humiliating David by forcing him to wear the only article of clothing he can find—her feathered dressing gown. Not until *The Lady Eve* would a comic heroine torture a man with such relentlessness and pleasure. The difference, however, is that Eve's victim is rich, whereas Susan is taking it out on a man whose economic status has already rendered him helpless. David needs Susan's money, whereas Henry Fonda's Hopsie needs only a woman's love.

In a way, David's moment of truth occurs when he becomes aware enough of the consequences of his relationship with Susan to see that his only refuge from her irritating power lies in irony. Suddenly forced to split himself off from his pain when the pain becomes too great, David greets Aunt Elizabeth at the door and responds to her insistent questioning about why he is wearing a woman's dressing gown by dementedly jumping into the air and shouting, "Because I just went *gay!* All of a sudden!"

It's a breakthrough line in a number of ways. First, it's one of the first uses, if not *the* first mainstream use, of the word *gay* in its modern meaning. David knows exactly what the word means, since the line simply doesn't make sense other than as a sarcastic comment on the effect that

Director Howard Hawks. *Bringing Up Baby* might not have been such a flop if Hawks hadn't gone so far over budget; *Baby* was supposed to cost $767,000—an already high figure—but ended up at a whopping $1,073,000.

From Bringing Up Baby

David has first met Susan on the golf course, where she has played his ball as her own. He then follows her to the parking lot, where she is playing bumper cars—with his car. He has been trying to explain, but she simply will not understand:

DAVID: You don't understand—this is *my* car!
SUSAN: You mean, *this* is your car?
DAVID: Of course.
SUSAN: You mean, *your* golf ball? *Your* car? Is there anything in the world that doesn't belong to you?
DAVID: Yes, thank heaven—you!
SUSAN: Now, don't lose your temper.
DAVID: My dear young lady, I'm not losing my temper. I'm merely trying to play some golf.
SUSAN: Well, you choose the funniest places. This is a parking lot.

A quiet dinner in the country: Major Applegate (Charlie Ruggles) and Aunt Elizabeth (May Robson) are perplexed at the bizarre behavior of Susan (Katharine Hepburn) and her guest, "Mr. Bone" (Cary Grant) in *Bringing Up Baby*.

Susan, who has been knocking olives into her mouth with her fist, has discovered that the man whose olives she has been knocking is in fact a psychiatrist. She seizes the opportunity to learn something about another man she keeps running into:

SUSAN: What would you say about a man who follows a girl around. . . .

DR. LEHMANN: *(following her intently)* Follows her around! . . .

SUSAN: And then when she talks to him, he fights with her?

DR. LEHMANN: Fights with her! . . . Is he maybe your fiancé?

SUSAN: Oh, no, I don't know him. I never even saw him before today. *(blithely)* No, he just follows me around and fights with me.

DR. LEHMANN: Well, the love impulse in man very frequently reveals itself in terms of conflict.

Psychiatrist Dr. Lehmann (Fritz Feld) and Aunt Elizabeth (May Robson) get much more than they bargained for in *Bringing Up Baby.*

OPPOSITE: The human condition, according to Howard Hawks. Susan causes David's life's work to collapse at the end of *Bringing Up Baby.*

Baby

the obnoxious Susan Vance has had upon his sexuality. Given the representations of women in the film thus far—a sexless puritan who cringes at his embrace and a rich, castrating tyrant who renders him powerless by stealing both his clothes and his will—David's turning gay might not be such a bad idea. In any case, David's athletic leap is a sensational physical gesture, the first real sign that this paleontologist isn't just a walking brain. Having finally been pulled out of his stultifying life in a museum, David is literally stripped and given a radical new identity, and he responds by jumping into the air as if for joy.

Classical psychoanalysis liked to call homosexuality "inversion," a term whose connotations help explain the incidence of cross-dressing in screwball comedies. "Susan," says David with a touch of fear as he finds himself being caught up in her world in an earlier scene, "you look at everything upside down." It's not a question of hidden homosexuality here, but the sense that Hawks and writers Dudley Nichols and Hagar Wilde went looking for ways to dramatize David's inversion at Susan's hands and found just the right one—a visible symbol of humiliation and pleasure in the form of a man in women's clothes. Hawks, whose comedies are unusually logical even when the activities in them are not, understood the conceptual comedy of inversion so well that he inserted moments of inverted sexuality in a number of his screwball films —Barrymore acts out the role of the girl "Emmylou" in one scene in *Twentieth Century.* Grant does a momentary impression of Rosalind Russell flirting with him in *His Girl Friday,* and he wears at least one article of women's clothes not only in *Bringing Up Baby* but in *I Was a Male War Bride* and *Monkey Business* as well.

David's emerging sense of self may be gratifying to the audience, and his humiliation is certainly gratifying to Susan, but there's a price to be paid for all the fun, and in this instance it's Susan who pays it. David, Susan, Aunt Elizabeth (May Robson), Aunt Elizabeth's friend Major Applegate (Charlie Ruggles), and the dog, George (Asta), are all standing in the entrance hall screaming at one another. David is fighting for attention, and Susan won't shut up, so he stomps on her foot in an obvious effort to cause her as much physical pain as possible—a good way, he thinks, of distracting her from her compulsion to speak. It works. David is reduced to using the most childish method to silence Susan, and Susan is reduced to agony.

The word *inversion* works just as well to describe this comic moment, too, for sexual connotations are only part of the screwball meaning of the word. It's not just sexuality but all of behavior that's being inverted in screwball comedy: not only are men forced to look like women, but adults are forced to act like children. Later in the film we see David chasing the dog around a tree, David and Susan getting up from the dinner table to run around the yard, and Major Applegate and Aunt Elizabeth scampering (for no logical reason) onto the patio. In the final analysis, what's being inverted is the expectation, conditioned by culture, that whole groups of people—rich old ladies, paleontologists, fuddy-duddies, and heiresses—have somehow had the human elements of ridiculousness and childishness bred out of them. On the grandest scale, this is what makes screwball so liberating— the sense that rules of behavior can be shattered.

The ending of *Bringing Up Baby* works toward a kind of inversion as well, but it's one that many critics haven't been especially pleased to see. After the whole lot of them ends up in jail, after Susan does a patently idiotic imitation of a gangster's moll and escapes, and after the return of both Baby and the fierce circus leopard with whom Baby has been confused, David is reunited with Alice, only to say to her, "Oh, Alice, I just can't explain it, it's just one of those things, and here I am." Clearly, it's not a good enough explanation, and she leaves him. After all, he has ruined his chance to get Aunt Elizabeth's grant by landing her behind bars.

"You're just a butterfly!" cries Alice as she exits.

Back in the museum, David is working on his brontosaurus skeleton. Susan marches in with David's lost intercostal clavicle—which George had buried—and announces that Aunt Elizabeth has given her the million dollars and that she is going to give it all to the museum. She climbs a rickety ladder to get closer to David, who is on the scaffold behind the skeleton. A number of critics have complained about the obviousness of the skeleton's eventual collapse; we know it's going to happen, and it does. But if there is a lack of freshness, it's intentional. It would be comforting to think that romances always concluded happily, but in Hawks's world, the terms are reversed. Susan's treatment of David throughout the film suggests that love isn't just inevitable—it's *awful,* in its own gratifying way.

In the final shot, Susan and David are locked in an embrace, the nature of which is well described by David's final words: "Oh dear, oh my." The fear of inevitable collapse into meaninglessness, literalized in the form of the skeleton's fall, is not a new idea in this film; most of the second half of *Bringing Up Baby* is played in darkness—at night and in jail. And the portents for this relationship, as voiced in David's final line, aren't good. What meaning can money have in such a distressed universe? It pays, of course, for a beautiful apartment, a farm, gorgeous clothes, all the food one can eat, and years of unlimited research. But as Hawks had demonstrated with equal force and viciousness in *Scarface,* acquired wealth cannot make meaning out of chaos. The darkness of *Bringing Up Baby* may look out of sorts with screwball's putative sparkle, but it's really the single screwball comedy that brings out most fully the genre's implicit skepticism and frantic despair. In a world where nobody can relax, where love is literally maddening and happiness simply the brief absence of calamity, money doesn't really amount to very much at all.

Oh dear, oh my.

Department store scion David Niven (shown here with E. E. Clive) finds himself stuck with an orphaned little bundle of joy in *Bachelor Mother*. Niven's dad, played by Charles Coburn, mistakenly believes that Niven is the real father, while Niven wrongly thinks Ginger Rogers is the real mother. Eventually, three other "real fathers" show up.

Ginger Rogers

the wayside. There were other kinds of chain letters sent during the era—letters protesting the New Deal; letters urging Coolidge to run again, a plan that was especially well suited to the something-for-nothing mystique of the chain letter format; and even "send a pint" letters for big-time whiskey drinkers. But the most popular draw, naturally, was the promise of a cash flood.

In certain screwball comedies, a similar kind of ludicrous, greedy pleasure wins the day by turning good individuals, almost always women, into modern-day Cinderellas. These comedies play on a sense of sudden freedom: our heroines are plucked out of the working world and sent soaring into clouds of luxury, and all without *earning* a dime. In *Midnight* (1939), the most literal Cinderella update, Claudette Colbert arrives in Paris flat broke. Before the night is through, she's been transformed —by fairy godmother John Barrymore!—into the gracious but fraudulent Baroness Czerny of Budapest, complete with a suite at the Ritz and thousands of dollars of mad money. "Every Cinderella has her midnight," she nervously notes just before things start to go awry. In *Easy Living* (1937), Jean Arthur has the good fortune to be sitting in an open-air double-decker Fifth Avenue bus at precisely the moment Edward Arnold hurls his wife's latest $58,000 sable coat out the window in a fury. It descends from the heavens like manna—or pennies,

the thirties equivalent—and lands right on top of Arthur.

The Cinderella myth was tailor-made for Ginger Rogers, especially insofar as it suited the infantilization of women under the Production Code. As critic Molly Haskell has noted, "The demarcation line between films of the early thirties and those made afterward, between films with satin and Freudian slips and explicit sexuality and films in which sex took cover under veils of metaphor, is particularly important in its effect on women's roles. It is the difference between Ginger Rogers having sex without children—*Gold Diggers of 1933*, *Upper World* (1934)—and Ginger Rogers having children without sex—*Bachelor Mother* (1939)." Rogers, who opens *Gold Diggers of 1933* with a production number in which she's clad only in strategically placed gold coins, becomes in *Bachelor Mother* a cross between Cinderella and the Virgin Mary. Rogers's route to riches is much more roundabout than either Colbert's in *Midnight* or Arthur's in *Easy Living,* but she does end up with millionaire merchant David Niven, and that's what counts. Shopgirl Ginger finds a baby on her doorstep, gets fired by Niven for being an unwed mother, falls in love with the suave moralist anyway, and eventually winds up as Mrs. Department Store.

In *Having Wonderful Time* (1938), Rogers is cast once again as an earnest young woman from the lower middle class—the honest, humble kind we're supposed to think deserves better. She escapes from the crowds and heat of a New York summer to an upstate camp, where she meets, fights with, and eventually falls in love with Harvard man—counselor Douglas Fairbanks, Jr. Here, the Cinderella transformation occurs in an almost money-free context, since the Fairbanks character doesn't have a steady job. But he's no less of an aristocrat, and his Ivy League self-assurance lets us know he's a step up for Rogers. In Garson Kanin's *Tom, Dick and Harry* (1941), Rogers finds herself torn between three suitors—the auto salesman preoccupied by his

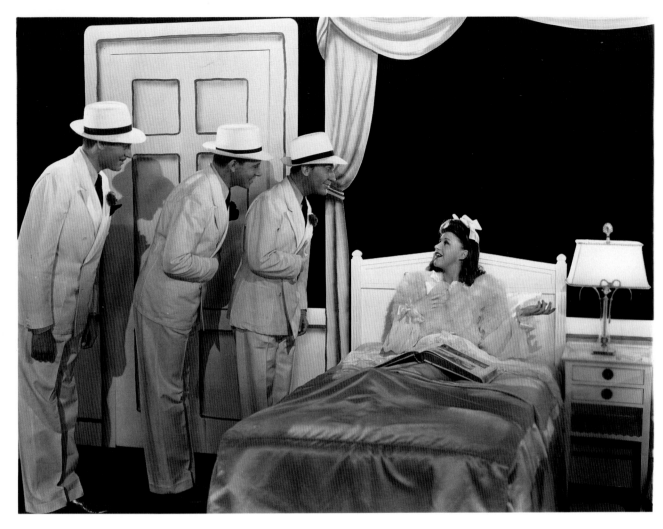

business (George Murphy), the poor mechanic who doesn't believe in "success" (Burgess Meredith), and, of course, the ubiquitous rich playboy (Alan Marshal) who enables her literally to throw money out the window of his private plane. At one point, she fantasizes about marrying all three of them, the minister intoning, "I now pronounce you the only solution," thereby providing a kinky (if momentary) variation on screwball's polygamy leitmotiv as Rogers hugs Marshal and Murphy hugs Meredith. Poor, dizz-brained Ginger finally picks the millionaire, only to run off with the mechanic in the final shot.

Moviegoers were primed for such vicarious getting-ahead-in-the-world fun, even if love conquered cash every once in a while. They paid less than a quarter to see extravaganzas costing hundreds of thousands of dollars, and thus each patron was given the satisfaction of having turned two bits into an expensive spectacle. They paid, of course, for many different kinds of films, but screwball comedies in particular worked to enhance this sense of magical transformation by being about people who *do* relatively little but nevertheless *get* a lot in the end. The fairy-tale quality is overt, but it's a mistake to see these films—especially the best ones—as naive feel-good comedies cranked out by the dream factory for the gullible masses. The best screwball comedies are too wise to the outlandish fortune on which they play. The opiate joy of easy money cannot be denied, but neither can the facetiousness with which screwball comedies depict it.

PENNIES FROM HEAVEN

The setting is Paris, the scene a working-class cafe. Eve Peabody (Claudette Colbert), dressed in a shimmering gold evening gown, is discussing her career as a gold digger with Tibor Czerny (Don Ameche), her taxi driver. He is buying her dinner. The gold digger is penniless:

> EVE: I landed a lord—almost.
> CZERNY: Almost?
> EVE: Well, the family got between us. His mother came to my hotel and offered me a bribe.
> CZERNY: You threw her out, I hope!
> EVE: How could I, with my hands full of money?

Directed by Mitchell Leisen from a script by Charles Brackett and Billy Wilder, *Midnight* is one of the great gems of the studio era. With its visual light touch and its fluid storytelling, the film is as sprightly as anything Hollywood ever produced. But like so many other slick comedies set on the back-lot Continent, *Midnight* has been unwittingly belittled by critics whose enthusiasm never rises above the pastry shop praise usually reserved for the films of Ernst Lubitsch. For them, *Midnight* is "a confection," "a concoction," "frothy," "delectable," and so on, ad nauseam. What these critics miss is the movie's hard edge, particularly the breathtaking resilience of Colbert—a sublimely confident actress who in this case plays a mercenary woman who cannot be flustered. Except, that is, at the moment when reality abruptly exceeds her wildest dreams of wealth, at which point she goes briefly mad.

Colbert's Eve is tremendously elastic. She plays whatever cards she's dealt, and she does it with style. Her train has arrived from Monte Carlo. The door of her compartment is open, and we first see her curled up asleep—in gold lamé—on a bench. "So this, as they say, is Paris, huh?" she says, look-

ing out at the station through the open door. The porter asks where her luggage is. Her reply: "The municipal pawn shop, Monte Carlo." This young woman has obviously seen better days, but she takes her decline in stride.

Outside the station, Eve meets Czerny, the cabdriver. It's raining, and she's direct:

> EVE: Here's how things stand. I could have you drive me all around town and then tell you I left my purse home on the grand piano. There's no grand piano, and no home. And the purse? Twenty-five centimes with a hole in it. That's what's left of the Peabody stake. . . . I need a taxi to find myself a job, and I need a job to pay for the taxi. No taxi, no job—no job, no soap.

Colbert delivers this speech with an enviable effortlessness. The lines are slangy enough to be relaxed but rhythmic and well worked enough to be stylized. Her command of the situation is reflected by her command of the idiom, a linguistic sign that tells us that the speaker, true to type, is nobody's fool.

Alone and broke in Paris, where she knows no one, Eve Peabody is a woman without much bargaining power, yet she manages to come up with an offer—Czerny will drive her for free through the rainy streets of Paris as she hunts for work, but she'll pay him double if she lands a job. After some hesitation, Czerny relents. "Say, uh . . ." Czerny asks suddenly, as if snapping out of a spell that has made him oblivious to obvious questions. "Do you always travel in an evening dress?"

> EVE: No, I was wearing this in Monte Carlo when a nasty accident occurred.
> CZERNY: What happened? Fire?
> EVE: No, the roulette system I was playing collapsed under me. I left the casino with what I had on my back.

Eve is a blues singer. They drive from club

Millionaire Georges Flammarion (John Barrymore, *left*), cabdriver Tibor Czerny (Don Ameche, *center*) gold digger Eve Peabody (Claudette Colbert, *second from right*), and hostess Helene Flammarion (Mary Astor, *right*) in *Midnight*.

to club, meeting rejection at every turn. "I guess mine is strictly a bathtub voice," she concludes. Czerny is horrified at her pathetic recent history:

> CZERNY: What you went through!
> EVE: How far do you think "through" is for a woman these days?

That's it—there's no follow-through quip after this line, and the subject is dropped. It's a good question, though, for it suggests her hesitation about the future while implying a certain unspoken dirt about her past. Still, she remains buoyant in the face of such desolate confusion. It's raining when they stop for dinner, and Czerny holds the door for her as if she'd been not a deadbeat but a regular paying rider. "Oh, wait!" Eve cries. "I forgot my hat!" Without missing a beat, she reaches for a soggy newspaper, puts it gallantly over her head, and emerges regally from the cab. The real story behind this scene isn't as important as its expressive truth, but it's worth noting that according to Leisen, the bit was Col-

RIGHT: In *Midnight*, John Barrymore looks askance at Claudette Colbert, who's just crashed a party. Gracious hostess Hedda Hopper discovers that she has an unwanted extra guest. Hedda *(above)* is told by mad pianist Eddy Conrad that he is about to play an étude, not a prelude.

bert's idea: she had bad sinuses and was afraid of catching cold in the machine-made rain.

Inside, Eve orders the oysters. She hasn't got a dime, he's buying her meal because he feels sorry for her, and the oysters, of course, are extra. *That's* self-confidence.

Eve and Czerny seem to be getting along fine—she confesses that she has a habit of falling in love with impoverished men who have noses like Czerny's—but as Eve herself puts it, "No woman ever found peace in a taxi." So she dumps him, leaving him driving around in his cab searching for her as she crashes an extravagant party purely as a means of getting out of the rain and away from Czerny. We learn what kind of party this is going to be when a guest comments, "It always rains when Stephanie gives one of her dull parties. Even nature weeps." A soprano is singing some sort of ditty, and the only words one can make out are "la la la la weary . . . weary. . . ." Eve makes her way in, using her pawn ticket as her invitation, and promptly sits on a dog.

The party is dreadful. Stephanie, played by gossip queen Hedda Hopper (née Elda Furry), ceremoniously terrorizes her guests into acquiescence. A madman named Prince Potopienko plays Chopin's Twelfth Étude—a great broad performance by character actor Eddy Conrad—and a strange gentleman keeps leering suspiciously at Eve. As for him, all we know is that he's John Barrymore, and while we therefore know more than Eve, who merely sees him as potential trouble, we don't know *much* more. Eve escapes, more or less, to another room, where a bridge game is forming. Two of the people are obviously having an affair—Mme Flammarion (Mary Astor) and Jacques Picot (Francis Lederer)—and when Barrymore enters, we discover that he is the adulterous woman's husband.

The rest of *Midnight*'s plot, in brief, concerns Flammarion's attempts to break up his wife's affair by hiring Eve (who has been introducing herself as the Baroness Czerny) to seduce Jacques. But it's the *way* Barrymore hires her that makes the film a Cinderella tale, for what he does is to become her fairy godmother, providing her with money, clothes, a suite at the Ritz, and even a chauffeur named Ferdinand. Eve is then whisked off to the Flammarions' immense country house at Versailles. Mme Flammarion thinks she discovers Eve's identity. Czerny shows up just in time to prevent a showdown, and to prove their authenticity, Baron and Baroness Czerny bandy about the name of their invented daughter, Francie, who has come down with an equally fictitious case of the measles. (This causes Mme Flammarion's self-evidently gay friend Marcel, played by Rex O'Malley, to assert his rule of fashion: "Sometimes that polka-dot effect is very unbecoming.") "Aren't children terrifying!" Mme Flammarion comments graciously.

Eve may be in love with Czerny, a fact we glean from her evident irritation with him, but she's almost as obviously attracted by Jacques's money. "Jacques's family makes a very superior income from a very inferior champagne," Flammarion has told her. Since the real prince is a poor cabbie, the specific Cinderella aspect of *Midnight* evaporates as the film increasingly turns into a more typical screwball battlefield. The Baron and Baroness Czerny cause several scenes in front of their fascinated but appalled hosts and friends, and when they're alone again in their palatial room (strangely described by Flammarion as "the bridal suite of the château," as if private estates were like fancy hotels), it finally reaches a head:

> CZERNY: Don't forget—you're married to
> me!
> EVE: I'm *not* married to you!
> CZERNY: Jacques Picot thinks you are.
> You're in a bind, miss. You've got
> to get a divorce from a man you
> aren't even married to!
> EVE: All right, I'll *get* a divorce!
> CZERNY: Just try it!
> EVE: Watch me!

They fly to the nearest courtroom. Judging by his commentary, the bearded jurist, played by Monty Woolley, seems to have been following the development of the screwball genre from a legal perspective:

> JUDGE: There's a very healthy law—in
> Albania, I think it is—that a husband
> may bring his wife back to her senses
> by spanking her, not more than nine
> blows with any instrument not larger
> than a broomstick. What do you say
> to that?

Eve has been following screwball's spanking motif, too, no doubt:

> EVE: I say it's a fine idea! A husband should
> have that privilege, and no wife would
> resent it. *If* she knew he loved her.

Fortunately, it doesn't come to blows. Eve's act of sitting on the dog is the closest the film comes to physical violence against women (though poor Czerny, back at Versailles, is struck in the head with a dish of kidneys). The judge dispatches the frustrated twosome to what he calls the "reconciliation room," and after another series of improbable events, the couple is finally united.

For a film that takes such delight in money, *Midnight* ends on a disconcerting note of poverty and insecurity, since Eve agrees to marry Czerny despite having witnessed her own parents' marriage dissolve under a cloud of poverty. "So many worries, so many quarrels—they just gave up. They didn't even *hate* each other," she has told Czerny earlier. In fact, the easy acquisition of money in *Midnight* is such a delightful animator of the plot that at the end one expects Barrymore's Flammarion to suddenly bestow a sizable fortune on Eve for having succeeded in getting his wife back. Alas, no such luck—M. and Mme Flammarion exit the courthouse without bestowing a check, a bauble, or even a word of thanks.

But there's a hidden outlet for the audience's vicarious greed. Eve tells Czerny, "I won't

OPPOSITE TOP: Joel McCrea, Loretta Young, and David Niven star in the quintessential three-girls-look-for-rich-husbands movie, Fox's *Three Blind Mice*.

OPPOSITE BOTTOM: Gary Cooper is eccentric Longfellow Deeds in Frank Capra's "Cinderfella" comedy, *Mr. Deeds Goes to Town*. Deeds, a tuba-playing volunteer fireman, inherits vast amounts of cash and proceeds to be used, confused, and abused by practically everyone.

promise to manage on forty francs a day," an extremely unlikely pledge even if she'd try. Nothing we have seen of Eve Peabody suggests that she'll do without for long, and Czerny agrees: "Who said forty?!" he cries optimistically. "With you around, I'll make as much as we want! Anything is possible!"

CINDERFELLAS

The closest thing the United States has produced in the way of a male Cinderella myth is the Horatio Alger–style tale of poor boys making good through diligence and honesty. There is, of course, an obvious difference: boys earn their money while girls are simply granted theirs. It would be a mistake to see these Cinderella movies on such simple terms, for Eve Peabody, like many of her Cinderella sisters, is much more actively conniving than her slipper-wearing forebear. And in the case of *Easy Living,* where the heroine is elevated to wealth because of a charmed collision of chance and personal worthiness, her transformation is seen as bluntly farcical. Yet the fact remains that the Depression didn't produce a profusion of Cinderfellas to match the Cinderellas, probably because in America, men richened by magic or extraordinary luck would have come off as gigolos. (Later, when such a comedy was made, the implication was even worse: men came off as Jerry Lewis—*Cinderfella,* 1960). Morally and mentally suspect, men would have seemed emasculated by their inability to *earn,* whereas women were presumed to be needy to begin with and therefore required supernatural assistance. At the same time, increasingly large numbers of women were themselves becoming wage earners; as a class, their financial status was rising, an economic trend that the Cinderella myth pushes to a ridiculous extreme.

As far as the absence of male Cinderellas is concerned, there are exceptions to the rule—like King Vidor's eerily prescient pre-Depression melo-

Gary Cooper

drama *The Crowd* (1928), in which the hero loses all the money he gains. A happier ending is found in Paramount's omnibus comedy-drama *If I Had a Million* (1932), which features individual segments by different directors chronicling various characters' responses to having won a million dollars. The best of all the segments, by Ernst Lubitsch, depicts a male office worker getting word of his fortune at his desk. Without uttering a sound, he gets up and proceeds through innumerable doorways to the head of the company, whereupon he blows the boss a healthy dose of raspberries and exits, a thoroughly satisfied man.

In William Wyler's *The Good Fairy* (1935), adapted by Preston Sturges from the play by Ferenc Molnar, Margaret Sullavan plays Luisa Gingle-busher, an orphan who vows to do a good deed every day. With a name like Ginglebusher, we know she's charmed. She meets Konrad, a wealthy buffoon (Frank Morgan), and in order to forestall his amorous advances, she claims to be married to a man whose name she picks at random out of the phone book—Max Sporum (Herbert Marshall). Konrad then becomes Max's benefactor as a way of showering Luisa with gifts, though of course poor Max hasn't the faintest idea of what's happening or why. Much of the comedy of *The Good Fairy* concerns Luisa's role as the eponymous fairy who finds herself playing out of her league, with lucky Max as Cinderella. Sturges did his best to Americanize Molnar's play, much to the consternation of most contemporary critics. But *The Good Fairy* is still too European-minded to be truly screwball. Even though Universal's back-lot Budapest has its own kind of charm, it scarcely reflects the American sensibility of the great screwball comedies. What saves *Midnight* from a similar Continental fate is its strictly American heroine. Luisa, Max, and Konrad, in contrast, have a different worldview, one that enables Max to accept his strange fortune in a way that a more puritanical American male character might not.

A much more central male Cinderella movie was Frank Capra's *Mr. Deeds Goes to Town* (1936), a film that might be classified as an anti-screwball comedy-drama, in which the hero, an eccentric tuba player from an outlandish place called Mandrake Falls, inherits an immense fortune from a long-lost uncle. Capra clearly asks his audience to see Longfellow Deeds (Gary Cooper) as a screwball. In the words of the two old ladies brought in by the court to testify about Deeds's sanity, he's "pixilated." And Babe (Jean Arthur, in her first big role), the wily newspaper reporter assigned to his story, even refers to him in print as "the Cinderella man." But look at the way gender turns *Mr. Deeds* staunchly away from Cinderella-movie precepts: Deeds *doesn't want* the money and has to be forced into taking it, and when he gets it, it leads to nothing but misery. By presenting the outcome of Deeds's new money in such a harsh and uncompromising light, Capra insists that we understand Deeds's "Cinderella man" nickname ironically. It's an insult, and we feel its sting.

One of the few American comedies to approach male Cinderellaism is Mitchell Leisen's *Hands Across the Table* (1935), in which manicurist (hence the title) Carole Lombard seriously gold-digs her way into the life of disabled heir Ralph Bellamy, though she finally falls for penniless, gold-digging Fred MacMurray. *Hands Across the Table* was the first film Ernst Lubitsch supervised from script to screen in his capacity as director of production at Paramount. Regi (Lombard) meets Ted (MacMurray), who she thinks is a millionaire, and invites him for a manicure, during which she cuts his fingertips till they bleed. Her use of a nail file as a weapon might be written off to her nervousness—she wants him and his reputed money desperately—but there's an unmistakable screwball viciousness to her actions, whatever their psychological motivation may be.

Hands Across the Table may cast MacMurray as a male gold digger whose drive toward unearned wealth equals Lombard's, but while MacMurray's character may *try* to be a male Cinderella, he can't succeed because of two built-in qualifications: he *was* rich once but now is poor, and he doesn't end up getting the money. Ted's fortune, it seems, was wiped out by the stock market crash, a fact that would give any newfound money the quality of a restoration of birthright. "I suppose you heard about the Crash, haven't you?" he asks. "Well, that was us." More important—and this is something that applies to a lot of other purported thirties Cinderellas, too—he doesn't enjoy even the trappings of big money at any point in the film. Eve Peabody may wind up with a taxi driver, but she gets to be Baroness Czerny along the way. Not so with Ted in *Hands Across the Table;* he may be courting "the daughter of the pineapple king," Vivian (Astrid Allwyn), but he doesn't find himself awash in luxury as part of the process. In fact, one of the film's best-remembered scenes plays precisely on the split between the fantasy he lacks and the reality he's stuck with. Ted, playing the rich playboy, tells Vivian he's calling her from Bermuda, but Regi has to pretend to be a phony long-distance operator in order for the ruse to succeed. He eventually has to get sun lamp treatments to simulate the effects of the trip, an idea picked up by Leo McCarey in *The Awful Truth.*

Finally, there's a big difference between gold-digging and Cinderellaism, between going out in search of money—like Joel McCrea in *The Richest Girl in the World*—and having money land on your head. Eve Peabody starts out in the former mode but quickly plunges into the latter, whereas the countless women in the popular *Gold Digger* musicals and other film comedies never reap the benefits of screwy fairy-tale happenstance. Ruby Keeler gets that big, impossible break in *Forty-second Street* (1933), but the sense of farce accompanying her transformation is unintentional. It's the outrageousness of fortune in the best Cinderella comedies, the self-conscious celebration of unlikelihood and fan-

ABOVE LEFT: In Paramount's *Hands Across the Table,* disabled millionaire Allen Macklyn (Ralph Bellamy, *right*) lives in the kind of style to which male gold digger Theodore Drew III (Fred MacMurray, *left*) would like to grow accustomed.

ABOVE RIGHT: Regi (Carole Lombard) and Ted (Fred MacMurray) becoming a team in Mitchell Leisen's *Hands Across the Table.* The film was a big hit, and Lombard, who was always a tough businesswoman, advised MacMurray to go on strike for more money. Her judgment proved sound; the bosses caved in.

tasy, that makes them screwballs. But paradoxically, it's precisely this improbability that keeps them honest.

A NICE PLACE TO FLOP

> JOHNNY: You know, there's something awfully phony about all of this.
> MARY: You're just beginning to figure that out?
>
> Ray Milland and Jean Arthur in *Easy Living*

There's posh, and then there's *posh*. There's making it big, and then there's making it *big*. That's one of the messages of *Easy Living* (1937), the manic Cinderella comedy in which Luis Alberni, as the hotel proprietor Louis Louis of the Hotel Louis, utters his immortal line, "Until you have lived in the Hotel Louis, you ain't!" Until a sable coat flies down from the sky and lands on her lucky shoulders, setting off a series of fabulous turns of fate and fortune, it seems that Jean Arthur,

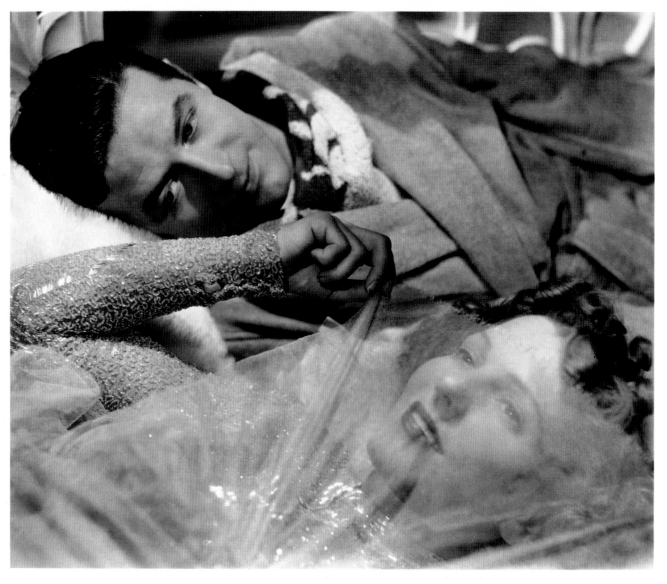

Johnny (Ray Milland) and Mary (Jean Arthur) fall dreamily in love in one of the few genuinely romantic scenes in *Easy Living*.

OPPOSITE: Working girl turned Cinderella. Jean Arthur gets some more of life's little necessities in *Easy Living*.

as our girl Mary Smith, just *ain't*. But now, with the sable and a farcically overwrought suite at the Hotel Louis, Mary, formerly of West 112th Street, can really live.

> LOUIS: Dis is vhere you belong! A beautiful young girl like you has got to have a beckground. Dis is vot you call a beckground!
> MARY: I should say it is!
> LOUIS: No matter vhere you look, you'll never find anudda beckground goes so far beck!

Louis ushers Mary through the first reception room, the second and third reception rooms, the main "saloon" complete with a white grand piano —"Some joint, huh?" Louis preens—the fourth reception room, the kitchen, the fifth reception room, the undressing room outfitted with an insanely ugly bathtub, and the imperial bedroom. "Nice place to flop, eh?" he remarks with pride.

As anyone familiar with Louis's hybrid language must have recognized, *Easy Living* was written by Preston Sturges. No one else in the history of Hollywood could have fused the ersatz with the real to such spectacular comic effect. Like *Midnight* and *Hands Across the Table, Easy Living* was

directed by Mitchell Leisen, who made more box-office hits for Paramount than anyone but that behemoth of vulgarity, Cecil B. De Mille. With *Midnight* and *Easy Living,* Leisen's visual taste was aided greatly by particularly elegant and witty scripts. But because of Sturges's tendency to heighten comedy through amplification—he pushes action and sound past even the exaggerated levels one expects to find in film comedy—*Easy Living* is a far more chaotic movie than *Midnight*. Its sheer *loudness* clashes violently with the relative thinness of the story, but that's its charm. *Easy Living* is a comedy of excess and improbability, from the flying sable coat to the prolonged and riotous food-fight scene in an Automat. Things happen not because of any grand, underlying motivation, but because of Sturges's and Leisen's glorifying appreciation of kismet.

Variety's reviewer didn't get any of the glory. "A trivia of nonsense," was *Variety*'s description of *Easy Living,* and it wasn't meant as a compliment. "Disconcerting is the fact that the studio spared neither expense nor talent in its efforts to make something good out of something that was second-class when it started." Because of the relatively dismissive attitude of this and many other contemporary reviews, it has been reported that *Easy Living* was "a flop," but that's simply not true. It wasn't a hit, certainly, but it did above-average business when it opened and was held over in several cities because of unusually large crowds.

Easy Living begins with Edward Arnold, as J. B. Ball, "the bull of Broad Street," tripping down a flight of stairs. The maid laughs, and the butler snidely comments, "I see you're down early for breakfast, sir." In this short opening scene, we get the humiliation of a gruff rich man and the liberating triumph of a smart-mouthed servant, physical comedy and social comedy, pain and pleasure. Second-class indeed.

We quickly learn that J. B. is not an easy-going guy. True to type, he's something of a miser, but his stinginess may have a point. It's one thing to complain, as he does at the breakfast table, about the cook's liberal use of butter and the outrageous expense of a new garbage disposer ($3.50), but it's quite another to discover the furrier's bill for $58,000 for his wife's latest sable coat. We also see that his son, Johnny (Ray Milland), is a more or less idle and irresponsible son of money, though the astounding volume with which J. B. berates the boy can't help but throw a little audience sympathy Johnny's way. And we learn, courtesy of the furrier's bill and Ball's ensuing rage, that his wife (Mary Nash) is even more extravagant in matters of taste and economy. In fact, as Leisen reveals in one casually opulent shot, she already owns an entire closet full of furs. But like any good screwball matriarch, Mrs. Ball reacts swiftly when her property is threatened: she simply shoves J. B. into the closet and beats a quick retreat with the sable clutched in her hot hands.

There's a great deal of brisk physical comedy in *Easy Living,* not the least of which is this fight scene between husband and wife. Like so many other depictions of long-standing marriage, the Balls' union is seen as mainly terrible, composed as it is of two overgrown spoiled children who have grown tired of each other's company but stick around because there's nowhere else to go. Their antics are light and funny, but only to a point: crashing through doors and wrecking furniture along the way, J. B. chases his wife up a spiral staircase, whereupon she hurls a broom down on his head. But an enraged magnate cannot be stopped (except maybe in a Capra film), and in a total, I'll-teach-you-a-lesson fury, J. B. flings the coat off the penthouse roof and down onto Fifth Avenue, where it lands on Mary. "What's the big idea?" she shouts at the Indian gentleman seated behind her, not knowing who else to blame. "Kismet," he replies quite implacably.

Mary, a stalwart employee of a sappy, true-blue magazine called *Boy's Constant Companion,* walks back in the general direction of the mysterious sable launching pad and meets J. B. on the sidewalk. In classic screwball style, it takes an annoying conversation to clue them in to each other's charm; J. B. argues with Mary about the precise nature of percentages and interest, and neither understands the other's logic. Although J. B., the financier, has the facts and figures straight, one's sympathies still gravitate to Mary, whose sense is as common as her frustration with economics. Something about this young woman affects J. B. deeply. He gives her the sable and escorts her to a hat store, where he plans to treat her to a gift.

The hat store proprietor is played by the great character actor Franklin Pangborn, who elevated effete, proto-gay effeminacy into an art form. Pangborn's character is named Van Buren here, but one gets the sense that his name used to be something a little less elegant—a name and a background from which he needed to escape. (Contrast "Van Buren" with the character he plays in Hal Roach's *Turnabout,* the self-reflective "Pingboom.") Fussy and hilarious, Pangborn is as imperious as he can be, until he finds out who J. B. is; at that moment, he turns perfectly, wonderfully servile. Unlike many of his screen appearances, Pangborn's performance in *Easy Living* had the advantage of a gay director; Leisen was both shrewd and witty enough to construct a proto-gay character who could be endearing even in the face of the contempt to which his stereotype was condemned. Seen in its historical context, Pangborn's comedy—like that of the Rex O'Malley character in *Midnight*—is almost heroic.

Van Buren is so taken with the "bull of Broad Street" that one begins to consider how funny nicknames—and psychoanalytic interpretations—can be. His uncontrollable need to gossip rages. Why else would J. B. be taking a beautiful young woman to a hat store if not to fulfill his role as sugar daddy? "Wherever there's smoke, there must be . . . somebody smoking!" Van Buren reasons breathlessly. At this point, *Easy Living* lunges

Dignified Hysteria

Franklin Pangborn probably appears in more screwball comedies than any other actor. His character type—fussy, flustered, silly, and temperamental—fits perfectly into screwball's world of urban extremism. A deft comedian, Pangborn makes himself an object of mockery in film after film, but he never gives up his dignity. In fact, the comedy of Franklin Pangborn is nothing if not the hysterical preservation of dignity in the face of an endlessly degrading and insulting reality. Pangborn's best roles are the distracted scavenger-hunt registrar in *My Man Godfrey* and the gossipy manager of the hat shop in *Easy Living;* he also appears in *Bluebeard's Eighth Wife; A Girl, A Guy, and a Gob; The Palm Beach Story; Vivacious Lady; Mr. Deeds Goes to Town; Design for Living; Joy of Living; Topper Takes a Trip;* and *Fifth Avenue Girl,* and many other nonscrewball films.

Henry Fonda

remarkable moment when Jean looks at Hopsie and demands, with just a trace of irony, "You'll have to kneel down." She succeeds in getting poor Hopsie down on the floor, ostensibly to have him help her on with her slippers, ideally to make him crawl. Enticed by such an elegant dominatrix, Hopsie has little choice but to gulp back his bursting desire and finally, when the slippers are on and all hope is lost, to bring himself up off the ground and lean forward as if to kiss her. "Why, Hopsie!" she says. "You oughta be kept in a cage!"

Not too long afterward, Sturges shakes his heroine's self-assurance and evens the sexual score. "Would you like to come in and see Emma?" Hopsie asks her outside his stateroom door. "That's a new one, isn't it?" Jean remarks flippantly, but when she sees what Emma is—a long, thick snake —she doesn't have the chance to be glib. She runs screaming down the corridor, down the steps, and into her own stateroom, where she anxiously begs Hopsie to make sure that the snake hasn't climbed into her bed.

For generations raised on popular Freudianism, Sturges's use of a snake as a sexual symbol might seem too obvious. As the philosopher and film historian Stanley Cavell puts it, "We are being clunked on the head with an invitation to read this through Freud." True, but there's something else

If the slipper fits: An innocent Prince Charming (Henry Fonda) falls in love with a crooked Cinderella (Barbara Stanwyck) in *The Lady Eve*.

going on. First, it's important to recognize that this snake may not have seemed quite so obvious to an audience in 1941. It certainly didn't have the encumbering baggage of the last forty years' worth of popular psychology. Second, though we may be getting "clunked on the head," we're not being jabbed in the ribs. By using this snake—a *female,* by the way—as a way of terrorizing his heroine, Sturges is making an appeal to the mind, a gesture of wit more than farce. As Cavell himself continues, "The very psychological obviousness of it serves the narrative as an equivalent, or avatar, of the issue of innocence. It demonstrates that sexuality is for this sophisticated and forceful woman still a problem." The same could be said for the culture at large. I think it's safe to say that Sturges used this "obvious" snake joke as a way of reminding his audience what was missing from contemporary romantic comedy. The high wit and airy grace of screwball comedy wouldn't have been possible without enforced sublimation, an across-the-board refusal to deal with sex in a direct manner. But as Jean's persistent dream about "that slimy snake" shows, the repressed does return. And like Hopsie being hit on the head by Jean's apple, sometimes it takes blunt force to break through the barriers of repression.

Jean and Hopsie—and the susceptible audience toward whom Sturges aims his comedy—are romantic enough to be vulnerable, idealistic enough to be taken for a ride. To further dramatize their ability to collapse under the strain of love, Sturges provides contrasts in the form of two older men, the Colonel and Mugsy. Pure cynics, these two characters act as a kind of chorus reminding the audience of the folly of love, trust, and honesty. "There's as fine a specimen of *Sucker sapiens* as I've ever seen!" is the Colonel's assessment of the man with whom his daughter is falling in love. When the Colonel wins $32,000 from Hopsie during a card game, he broadly feigns discomfort, then says, "This is very embarrassing. Just make it out to cash." Mugsy, less clever but more skeptical than the Colonel, has been nosing around in an effort to protect his boss from the disaster known as romance. "Remember the clergyman you thought was a pickpocket and he turned out to be a bishop?" Hopsie asks. "Well, I still ain't so sure," is Mugsy's reply. And Mugsy does discover the truth: he wangles some photos out of the ship's purser, pictures that reveal Jean and the Colonel to be notorious crooks.

Until now, Jean has ruthlessly deceived Hopsie, speaking a double-edged language of love to a single-minded lover. Hopsie's inability to see the second level has allowed her this freedom, but it suddenly works the other way around. After Mugsy's disclosure, Hopsie sees *only* the deception and not the love behind it. Unable to deal in anything but moral absolutes, he refuses to believe that she is anything other than a crook and a conniver, and he rejects her.

Fortunately for this romance, love turns quickly to hatred. She has conned him, he has destroyed her, and now with increased desperation they play out the passion that binds them. A chance meeting with "Sir Alfred MacGlennon-Keith," a con-artist friend known as "Curly" to the trade, provides Jean with information: Curly is currently working the "Conneckticut" circuit, and he is acquainted with the Pikes. "Do I know them?" Sir Alfred exclaims. "I positively swill in their ale!" Playing—and preying—on Americans' gushing adoration of British nobility, and using Sir Alfred as her entrée, Jean transforms herself into the Lady Eve Sidgewick and descends upon the Pikes' social circle to wreak her revenge on Hopsie.

The Pikes, like lots of other wealthy screwball families, are an amalgam of class values. The unending quality of their grandiose mansion suggests that their money is old as well as big, but with Eugene Pallette cast as the family breadwinner, the Pikes' *richesse* begins to seem somewhat more *nouvelle*. The lumbering Pallette enters singing, his

Irascible Capitalist

It's difficult to believe, but the fact is that tubby Eugene Pallette was once employed as a jockey. Pallette began working in films in 1910, his horse-racing years already behind him. After World War I, he became one of Hollywood's most easily recognized character actors. The arrival of sound film added greatly to Pallette's glory. His extraordinarily deep, grinding voice—sounding rather like an adenoidal foghorn—is itself one of screwball comedy's best jokes; coupled with his immense three-hundred-pound-plus body, Pallette's voice has a kind of comical human excess that stops just short of the grotesque. The essence of plenitude, Pallette was appropriately cast twice in screwball comedies as an irascible capitalist with a heart of gold: Mr. Bullock in *My Man Godfrey* and Mr. Pike in *The Lady Eve*. Pallette also appears in *Topper, The Bride Came C.O.D.,* and scores of dramatic roles.

Falling in love again: In *The Lady Eve*, Barbara Stanwyck gets Henry Fonda's attention by tripping him—twice.

In *The Lady Eve*, William Demarest (*left*), a veteran member of Preston Sturges's stock troupe, plays Henry Fonda's skeptical bodyguard, Mugsy, who here assumes the role of butler in order to check out some dinner guests at close range.

grinding bass voice warbling an old drinking song as he descends the mansion's immense staircase. The household is in an uproar; the Pikes are throwing a party that evening to introduce the Lady Eve to local society. But as usual with Pallette's characters, Mr. Pike is removed from the proceedings. Ingratiated to the audience as a money earner rather than a money spender, Mr. Pike further distances himself from the stilted, stuffy world of wealth by loudly banging two silver dish covers together like cymbals when his servants fail to serve him his breakfast.

For Connecticut society, Eve's entrance is the height of elegance. For Sturges, it is the culmination of arriviste pretensions. For Hopsie, it is the beginning of the end. Pretending to be someone else but remaining the captivating essence of herself, Jean/Eve literally sends Hopsie into paroxysms of neurotic distress. The results are violent. First, Hopsie trips over the back of a couch and lands with his head in a bowl of lobster dip. On his way out the door, humiliated, he compounds the catastrophe by pulling a set of drapes down on his head. Later,

at the dinner table, he causes a huge platter of roast beef to be dumped upon him. As Sir Alfred puts it the next morning, "Entirely disgraceful! I've never seen such a farce in a respectable household."

With his finely tuned knack for extremism, Sturges barrels forward using the film's inner logic as momentum. Hopsie's fall is far from complete, for Eve then succeeds in getting him to marry her, a plot development that would never have worked had Hopsie not been so relentlessly stupid in the first half of the film. *The Lady Eve* returns again and again to deception as an inescapable part of romance, and as the film races toward its climax, Eve's mendacity snowballs out of control. This is a film about fate—the awful, inescapable unfolding of romantic conflict. Jean is compelled to play out her scheme, and Hopsie is compelled to succumb. Like many screwball couples who appear to detest each other, these two people are tracked together with a sense of mutual destiny, which Sturges expresses physically by getting them onto a speeding train. On their wedding night, Eve tells Hopsie an increasingly preposterous set of stories about her previous "marriages." She rattles off names like a racetrack announcer calling a race: Angus, the stable boy; Herman; Herman's friend Vernon; Cecil; John; John's twin cousins, Hubert and Herbert. . . . Hopsie, driven mad by disgust and jealousy, makes an all-too-hasty exit from the train and, as if to clinch his abject misery, promptly lands on his rump in a sea of mud.

With both parties cloaked in loathing, there might seem to be only one solution: the revelation of the truth. But truth isn't exactly what Sturges has been driving at. For Sturges, forcing his characters to relinquish themselves to their joint fate is more important than making them understand it. Jean, triumphant but ruined, refuses to accede to a divorce unless Hopsie asks her for one himself; Hopsie refuses to speak to her, and so the two remain bound to each other in a marriage of despair. By pushing Hopsie toward divorce, Jean becomes divorced from herself, and her insistence on Hopsie's personal request to end the marriage is a way of breaking down the deceptions that have brought her so much pain. It's also an admission that the very self-sufficiency that has enabled her to carry off such an audacious scheme has proved insufficient for happiness. For once, Jean admits that she is emotionally incomplete without a dense, taciturn, ridiculous man by her side.

For Hopsie, the inability to grant Jean her wish also suggests his inability to be a full, whole human being on his own. Even after all the torture, he won't let go of the relationship, though he claims to want to forget it. He embarks on another trip to the wilds of South America. Hopsie's instincts, of course, prove to be more trustworthy than his consciousness. By returning to a steamship, Hopsie makes it possible for the two of them to rediscover each other, a reunion they accomplish quickly and violently. She trips him again. They proceed immediately to her stateroom, where Hopsie proves that he has indeed learned something about love:

> HOPSIE: I don't want to understand. I don't want to know. Whatever it is, keep it to yourself. All I know is that I adore you, that I'll never leave you again, we'll work it out somehow, and that . . . I have no right to be in your cabin.
> JEAN: Why?
> HOPSIE: Because I'm married.
> JEAN: But so am I, darling. So am I!

ABOVE LEFT: Barbara Stanwyck gets her revenge on priggish, moralistic Henry Fonda by marrying him under a false identity. As icing on the cake, she lists for him, on their wedding night, her innumerable past affairs.

Hopsie doesn't comprehend the specifics of their farcical affair, but he does understand something more significant, namely that love entails the acceptance of conflict, ambiguity, and even deceit. Having rejected Jean twice on grounds of immorality and become ever more miserable in the process, Hopsie now makes a leap of faith toward unconditional love. For this priggish man not only to admit ignorance but to embrace it is an enormous step forward; for him to remain in her room with the door closed is an act of profound sexual awakening. The censors are appeased by the fact that they really *are* married, but from Hopsie's point of view he's so much in love with Jean that he's willing to commit adultery. As for our cynical Cinderella, she's been raised out of the ashes by her own selflessness, and thus she becomes worthy of the prize—Prince Charming's colossal wealth is now half hers.

The film's energy spent, the cartoon snake returns, weakly shaking his mariachi and smiling with a look of exhausted contentment. He curls himself around two snuggling apples, happy to have once again engineered a tale of human frailty and knowledge.

131

CHAPTER 6

Screaming Social Significance: The Screwball Family

BELEAGUERED FATHER, HAREBRAINED MOTHER, DAFFY SISTERS, irresponsible brothers, rotten children . . . Craziness in screwball comedies isn't always confined to couples. It often wraps itself around the handiest small social unit available, the family, which by its very nature provided a nicely self-enclosed target for mockery and awe. It would be impossible to depict an entire economic or social class on screen, but individual wealthy families are something else again. In a single shot, there they are—a group of disturbed relatives stuck together in one big house or apartment, bound by common blood to suffer the same space, the same fate.

Audiences in the thirties were fond of prying into the lives of nutty, rich families, whose houses looked like grandiose zoos. There's an oddly ethnographic attitude to the way some of these movies depict silly wealthy white people, and nowhere is this sense of comic anthropology more noticeable than in *My Man Godfrey*, Gregory La Cava's 1936 classic about a forgotten man from the city dump who becomes a butler to a household of spoiled adults.

My Man Godfrey is based on Eric Hatch's short novel *1011 Fifth Avenue*. Hatch, who went on to write the script for the supernatural screwball comedy *Topper*, was a prolific writer and original staff member of *The New Yorker*, and although he was especially pleased with La

OPPOSITE: Family values. Guy Kibbee, Alice Brady, Lucille Ball, and Warren Hymer are the hangers-on in Irene Dunne's life in *Joy of Living*.

132

Cava's treatment of his work, he expressed surprise at what he called *Godfrey*'s "social significance." Seeing *Godfrey* today, one can hardly imagine what it would be like without it—nor can one fully believe Hatch's ingenuousness in crediting others, since he himself co-wrote the script with Morrie Ryskind. La Cava is said to have reworked much of the dialogue, often the night before shooting the scene in question, but *Godfrey*'s basic scenario is so purposefully grounded in social realism (for lack of a better description) that its observations about class and economics can't have been much of a surprise.

It would be wrong to say that *Godfrey* begins in a dump; the credits sequence that leads into the dump scene is so striking that when the hoboes finally appear, shrouded in darkness and dressed in rags, the absence of Hollywood glamour is all the more noticeable. *My Man Godfrey* opens with one of the most gorgeous credits sequences in Holly-

wood history, a vast modernistic cityscape illuminated by the names of the cast and crew in sequentially flashing neon. Designed by Harkrider and Associates, the credits depict an urban landscape that by virtue of its size, style, and glamour could only be New York's. The extraordinary detail of the design and the craftsmanship of its execution—with more and more of this fabulous city being revealed as the camera pans to the right—only add to the sense of absolute and unending luxury, as does the musical score with its confident brass and percussion. Yet at the end of the sequence, the lights suddenly trail away, though the camera keeps panning, and suddenly we find ourselves in what seems like an entirely different city—one without any neon lights or buildings, except for what looks like a shack. It's there that the film proper begins.

Two bums are in the midst of the dump talking about crime and how nice it would be if the cops went after the real criminals and left alone those basically honest guys who were just trying to survive. One of the bums, seen in close-up, turns out to be one of the biggest, classiest male stars of the mid-thirties, William Powell. It's difficult now to appreciate just how radically La Cava introduces Powell against type, the implication being that if the debonair Powell could find himself living in a city dump, such a fate could befall anyone. No sooner does La Cava humanize abject poverty by way of Powell's popular image than he offers a sarcastic attack on Herbert Hoover—Powell puts a pipe to his lips and ironically remarks, "Prosperity is just around the corner." The attack is bitter but a bit out of time; Hoover's remark, made in 1931, had been the subject of criticism and derision for five years already.

As if the politics of dissatisfaction (which *Godfrey* at this point simply assumes are shared by its audience) weren't stark enough, into the scene steps the tall, fashionably dressed, and impeccably coiffed Cornelia Bullock (Gail Patrick), who offers Godfrey five dollars to be the forgotten man she

needs for a scavenger hunt. Patrick's performance is terribly successful, so much so that one despises her character violently on first sight and continues despising her long after the point at which a less self-confident actress would have tried to beg some cheap forgiveness by toning it down. Godfrey agrees with us; he forces Cornelia into a heap of ashes, and she escapes in humiliation and fear.

The dump scene is unusually threatening for a screwball comedy, and the sense of misty terror continues even after the arrival of the romantic lead, Carole Lombard, in the guise of Cornelia's sister, Irene. Irene has been standing in the background, but now she comes forward, a lithe blonde dressed in an outfit even more luminous than Cornelia's. Irene's dress, together with her hair, seems

The beginning of *My Man Godfrey*'s credits sequence, designed by Harkrider and Associates.

Franklin Pangborn (standing next to the goat) presides over the scavenger hunt in *My Man Godfrey*. Carole Lombard (*first row, right*) eagerly presents her most impressive find: William Powell.

OPPOSITE TOP: Mrs. Bullock (Alice Brady, *left*) appears to have some reservations about hiring Godfrey (William Powell), but her air-headed daughter Irene (Carole Lombard) won't be dissuaded. *My Man Godfrey*'s costume designer, Travis Banton, was responsible for both Lombard's glittering gown and Brady's outlandish cape.

OPPOSITE BOTTOM: The morning after. Godfrey (William Powell) presents breakfast in bed to Irene Bullock (Carole Lombard) in *My Man Godfrey*.

to sop up all the light in the vicinity. It's such a brilliant contrast to the dark misery of the dump that the presence of a rich and glamorous woman is a big relief. But La Cava isn't quite through with the fearfulness of poverty, so he has a bum in the background ask Godfrey if he needs any help—presumably in beating up the invading woman. Mercifully, Godfrey declines. Casting Powell as a derelict is one thing; having him physically assault Carole Lombard, his former wife, is something else again.

Godfrey thinks he has the scene under control, and he asks Irene to define "scavenger hunt." "In a treasure hunt," she glibly replies, "you try to find something you want, and in a scavenger hunt,

you try to find something that *nobody* wants!" Irene is completely oblivious to the cruelty of her remark, yet it seems less offensive than it might otherwise have been because of the character's self-evident lunacy, not to mention the subtle suggestion that somewhere under innumerable layers of acculturated stupidity there lies an innocent heart.

As with the rest of *My Man Godfrey*, an appreciation of Lombard's performance in this scene is essential to one's acceptance of the story. In other words, you have to believe not only that Godfrey is attracted to Irene, but also that there is an immutable reason for the attraction, a sense that something of great value lurks beneath her imbecilic words. Otherwise the film can be galling. It's all in the way

Lombard uses her body. Free and athletic, Lombard moves with such breathtaking grace that we see in her what Godfrey is supposed to see in Irene. And if you can't see it—if you can't slip into the pure sexiness of it—you're left with nothing but a rich dumb blonde leading a fake bum around by the holes in his pockets.

My Man Godfrey is less inspired than its reputation suggests, these inordinately tight opening scenes notwithstanding. La Cava's mixing of blunt social observation and airy screwball comedy might have succeeded had he and his screenwriters been able to construct a less amiably complacent plot. Instead, they work quickly to eliminate both the economic and the sexual conflicts implicit in the first few scenes. As a result, *My Man Godfrey* turns the Great Depression into nothing more than a prolonged lapse in common sense. The plot is fantastically tidy: after becoming the Bullock family's butler, Godfrey is revealed to be the heir to an old Boston fortune, a man driven to such despair by an unhappy love affair that he simply gave up and became a bum. By the end of the film, Godfrey has not only restored the Bullock fortune after Mr. Bullock (Eugene Pallette) fritters it away, but he also builds a fabulous nightclub on the site of the old dump—calling it "The Dump"!—thus providing menial-labor jobs for all of his old hobo friends.

It doesn't take a Marxist to see the reactionary slant to this scenario, though a taste for class conflict and economic reality helps. *Godfrey* goes to great lengths to show how farcically degenerate the Bullocks are: the selfish and obnoxious Cornelia, the addle-headed Mrs. Bullock (Alice Brady), her pretentious do-nothing "protégé" Carlo (Mischa Auer), and even the foolish Irene herself. Yet these cartoonish creatures learn how to be human from another aristocrat, the *good* rich man who maintains his own wealth, props up his fellow rich, and gives homeless men hope by making them servants.

In addition, there's little about Irene's character *as written* that suggests she's worth the trouble,

137

The Other Woman

A former dean of women at Howard College, Gail Patrick underwent a drastic career change when she came to Hollywood as a contestant in Paramount Pictures' "Panther Woman" contest. She lost, but no matter; Patrick quickly built herself a cool, cynical, and vaguely dangerous screen persona in a string of sophisticated thirties films. In fact, the expression "the Gail Patrick character" has come to define the type she played so well— the wrong woman, the languorous and worldly brunette the leading man sometimes thinks he loves but doesn't. Patrick's characters exist to be disliked and feared, but in a delicious and enviable sort of way. She's the obnoxiously confident Cornelia Bullock in *My Man Godfrey,* Cary Grant's second wife in *My Favorite Wife,* and the essence of the sultry "other woman" in *Love Crazy.*

and as a result the love relationship in *My Man Godfrey* is one of screwball comedy's worst. Even at the end of the film, when Irene hastily arranges her wedding with Godfrey, there is no sense that this couple is compelled to love each other the way people are supposed to in screwball films. We're left instead with the impression that they simply haven't anything else to do. Godfrey—especially as performed by the take-charge Powell—never loses control in Irene's presence, and Irene is as one-dimensional a heroine as the genre ever produced. There's no tug-of-war between them, and the absence makes their wedding perfunctory.

These criticisms aside, *Godfrey* remains entertaining, not only because of the magnetic images of Powell and Lombard, but because of the richness of the supporting performances. If ever an actor could recuperate a Depression audience's idea of fat capitalists, it was the immortal Eugene Pallette. Granted, La Cava casts him as the sole representative of sanity in a house full of crackpots and creeps, a role that complements his position as an earner rather than a spender. Nonetheless, Pallette's hilarious *basso*-frog voice and air of resignation tinged with suppressed panic elicit feelings of warmth, sympathy, and identification despite his role as a moneybags.

The film's funniest and in some ways most horrific scene belongs to Mischa Auer, the deadbeat pianist Mrs. Bullock has taken under her wing. Obviously Carlo is no more than a gigolo, though the code couldn't allow such goings-on to harbor any sexual implications, and his repeated mooching serves as an amusing reminder that one doesn't have to be rich to be idle. When Irene throws a highly theatrical fit in response to Cornelia's suggestion that Godfrey should be fired, Mrs. Bullock, with sublime superficiality, asks Carlo to perform his wonderful gorilla routine. Carlo obliges; he's evidently gotten used to being a trained monkey in this household as a way of earning his bananas. He screeches and lopes around the living room in a gro-

tesque simian side show. Irene and Mr. Bullock look at him with a mixture of horror and fascination, while Mrs. Bullock laughs lightly and encourages him. Finally Irene screams in phony fear and begs him to stop. "It's not a real gorilla," Mrs. Bullock explains helpfully. "It's only Carlo!"

My Man Godfrey's images of women aren't especially attractive, either, though the actresses are marvelous in their roles. Gail Patrick's Cornelia may be terrifying, but Alice Brady's matriarchal Mrs. Bullock is harmless, too caught up in her own raw idiocy to do much damage. Once again, we're forced by the sheer hostility reflected in these images to notice how Hollywood portrays wealthy women purely in terms of the way they consume the luxury surrounding them—luxury supplied by male "labor." Her contemptible passivity aside, Mrs. Bullock does get to utter one of the film's most resonant lines. When Godfrey brings her breakfast on his first morning at work, Mrs. Bullock, slogging through a terrible hangover, is unable to remember who he is. "I'm the forgotten man," he reminds her gently. "So many people

have such bad memories," she replies in a daze. What an excellent summation of the social anxieties of the era. It's a shame she's too dumb to know what she means.

HIS GIRL GODFREY

These are the lives of the rich, according to screwball's crazy-family films: pass the hors d'oeuvres, mix the martinis, and make room for the monkey routine. As degenerate as the social vision may be, there's still something tantalizing about the insanity of the rich, for they simply aren't *bound* either by bourgeois conventions or by unpaid bills the way normal folks are. That's the attraction of upper-crust madness, but what's behind it? Why were audiences so eager to put themselves vicari-

ABOVE LEFT: Deadbeat gigolo Carlo (Mischa Auer) does his wonderful gorilla routine in *My Man Godfrey*, much to the amusement of Mrs. Bullock (Alice Brady).

ABOVE: In *My Man Godfrey*, spoiled heiress Irene Bullock (Carole Lombard) is prone to staging fainting fits to get her way; how convenient that the butler (William Powell) is there to catch her.

Sugar Daddy

A successful Broadway actor, Walter Connolly repeatedly refused to have anything to do with movies until Columbia Pictures' boss Harry Cohn finally talked him into it in 1932. Although he wasn't nearly as fat as Eugene Pallette, Connolly's girth was considerable enough to get him typecast in screwball comedies as the rich, conservative patriarch who holds himself responsible for spoiling his heiress daughter. Connolly appears as the father of Claudette Colbert in *It Happened One Night,* of Myrna Loy in *Libeled Lady,* and of Kathryn Adams in *Fifth Avenue Girl;* he's also memorably authoritarian as the corrupt newspaper publisher Oliver Stone in *Nothing Sacred.*

ously in the company of such idealized fools?

For La Cava the answer was this—to teach them a lesson. In *Godfrey,* La Cava rehabilitates the Bullocks by having an Ivy League worker show them how to be human. In La Cava's *Fifth Avenue Girl* (1939), a kind of *My Girl Godfrey* with Ginger Rogers in the Powell role and Walter Connolly as Eugene Pallette, heroine Mary is a down-to-earth working-class girl with enough hunkered-down nobility to know that "rich people are just poor people with money." (!) With an awful sense of missionary zeal—an up-'n'-at-'em quality suited particularly to Rogers's screen persona—Mary moves into the Fifth Avenue mansion of a depressed industrialist (Connolly) and his good-for-nothing family and sets about the task of making everything right again for her social superiors, ultimately marrying into the family and thus injecting into it some necessary, new, and staunchly common blood.

Rogers herself achieved political fame several years later as a right-wing zealot whose notorious mother, Lela, cheerfully named as many names as she knew in front of the House Committee on Un-American Activities. Among other things, Lela reported that poor Ginger had once been forced to utter a communist line of dialogue ("Share and share alike—that's democracy") in Dalton Trumbo's *Tender Comrade* (1943). Neither Lela nor Ginger had anything to recant as far as *Fifth Avenue Girl* was concerned. Rogers's Mary is so true blue that she tells off the family's ridiculously communistic chauffeur, Michael (James Ellison), saying, "You haven't the courage to be a capitalist yourself, so you try to drag everyone down to where you are!" Sadly, words aren't enough to convince Michael to change his red ways, so the fanatical Mary charges at him with a knife and shrieks, "You talk too much! I'm going to cut you a new mouth!"

Mary's line is arresting if for no other reason than that it makes no sense—except as a fantastic collision of Freud and Marx. A working-class man threatened with laceration by a knife-wielding

In *Fifth Avenue Girl*, patriotic Mary (Ginger Rogers) threatens to butcher the Borden family's loud-mouthed communist chauffeur (James Ellison), who cowers in the corner, leaving his fiancée, Katherine, to fend off the attack.

petit-bourgeois female: what a radical nightmare! After all, if Michael really does suffer from an excess of revolutionary speech, Mary's best response would be to threaten to truss his mouth shut with a poultry needle and thread rather than provide him a new orifice with which to offend her patriotism. In any case, the moment is unusual for screwball comedy in that Mary isn't attracted to Michael in the least, so her violence is simply that—mindless violence. Generally in screwball films, threats of brutality are slung between people who love each other; in this case, Mary really does detest the shallow red coward, so the moment has no romantic resonance. By the time she finally gets around to hooking up with Junior (Tim Holt), as we know all along she will, we're glad to be done with the whole lot of them.

THE GREAT ESCAPE

*I*n 1936, playwrights George S. Kaufman and Moss Hart opened a new comedy called *You Can't Take It With You.* It concerned an eccen-

OPPOSITE: "Rich people are just poor people with money." Mr. Borden (Walter Connolly) and Mary Grey (Ginger Rogers) reach satisfactory terms in *Fifth Avenue Girl*, in which our Mary shows an upper-crust family the true meaning of life.

tric New York family by the name of Vanderhof, a group of oddballs who have managed to accumulate still more oddballs under their roof. The play was a smash hit, and it captured the escapist spirit of the times better than almost any other play or musical for the simple reason that escapism was explicitly the play's theme. This is a comedy about a group of people who deliberately abandoned the real world outside their doorstep in favor of creative fantasy. Mother Penny is a playwright who couldn't care less about seeing her plays produced and who began her career as an author after a typewriter was mistakenly delivered to her home. Dad spends his time making fireworks in the basement, along with someone named Mr. De Pinna, who had arrived one day many years before to deliver the ice and just stayed on. And old Grandpa Vanderhof, the literal as well as spiritual patriarch, spends his time going to Columbia University graduation ceremonies, refusing to pay his income tax, and doling out nuggets of home-grown philosophy.

THRILL TO THE GREAT PULITZER PRIZE PLAY . . . NOW THE YEAR'S BIGGEST PICTURE!

Frank Capra's
YOU CAN'T TAKE IT WITH YOU

with
JEAN ARTHUR · LIONEL BARRYMORE · JAMES STEWART · EDWARD ARNOLD
MISCHA AUER · ANN MILLER
SPRING BYINGTON · SAMUEL S. HINDS · DONALD MEEK · H. B. WARNER
Based on the Pulitzer Prize Play by George S. Kaufman and Moss Hart
Screen play by Robert Riskin · Directed by FRANK CAPRA
A COLUMBIA PICTURE

That the Vanderhof clan does not work for a living is the premise of *You Can't Take It With You*. Only daughter Alice has a job. This family isn't fabulously wealthy like the Bullocks of *My Man Godfrey* or the Bordens of *Fifth Avenue Girl,* but they do have enough income—nearly all of it unearned—to support themselves in a large house in Manhattan. The Vanderhofs' wealth, modest as it is, is a key element of the comic fantasy. It's much easier to embrace a philosophy of personal fulfillment when you're assured of being fed, housed, and clothed without having to lift a finger.

Both the play and Frank Capra's 1938 film adaptation of *You Can't Take It With You* were full of screwballs, yet neither is actually a screwball comedy in the strictest sense of the term. The difference is critical, for screwball comedy is a particularly *romantic* idea. These screwballs, though prominently displayed for comic effect, frolic around on the sidelines of the central and exceedingly normal love affair that moves the plot along. In both the play and the film, daughter Alice, for all her sparkle, is in fact fairly ordinary, as is her beau, Tony, the ingratiating son of a stuffy banker and his pretentious wife. A number of contemporary reviews of the play went so far as to express relief at this couple's banality. Alice and Tony anchor *You Can't Take It With You* in reality, or some such thing, and thus keep comic anarchy from becoming too threatening.

The drab struggle to earn money—and help keep the government running—is derided by the title itself as well as by most of the play, but Alice (played on screen by Jean Arthur) and Tony (Jimmy Stewart) are the embodiments of good common sense. These are people who accept eccentricity only on a vicarious level, and as a result they're not very different from the idealized and presumably normal you-and-me to whom both play and film are meant to appeal. In other words, it's okay to know a few eccentrics as long as you don't become one yourself. The best screwball

142

comedies ask us to relate personally to the craziness of the central characters and to see the rest of the world as dull and deficient by contrast. But while the Vanderhof household sports an ersatz ballerina, her mad Russian coach, a deposed Russian countess now employed as a waitress—and, in the film, a bizarre extra character named Poppins (Donald Meek) added for obscure reasons by Capra and screenwriter Robert Riskin—these more or less formulaic screwball sensibilities are relegated to the fringe. Alice and Tony are only too happy to be day trippers, and so, presumes *You Can't Take It With You,* are we.

Screwball or not screwball, fun or escapist, *You Can't Take It With You* was immensely popular.

It was one of the few instances in which a Broadway play ran concurrently with its own movie adaptation. Although it doesn't fit the screwball genre very well, it does epitomize the crazy family comedies that were popular during the period. In the theater, Noël Coward got the ball rolling in 1925 with *Hay Fever.* Later there was Rose Franken's *Another Language* (1933) and Gertrude Tonkonogy's *Three-Cornered Moon* (1933), each celebrating familial eccentricity. *Three-Cornered Moon* took the particularly timely twist of being the story of a family reduced to poverty by idiotic investments. The movie version of *Three-Cornered Moon* (1933), directed by Elliott Nugent and starring Claudette Colbert, Mary Boland, and Richard Arlen, led to

You Can't Take It With You, the ultimate screwball family. *From left to right* (more or less): Jean Arthur, James Stewart, Dub Taylor, Lionel Barrymore, Spring Byington, Edward Arnold, Ann Miller, Mischa Auer, Mary Forbes, Lillian Yarbo, Donald Meek, Eddie Anderson, Samuel Hinds, and Halliwell Hobbes. According to director Frank Capra, "This heterogeneous group of 'happies' found the courage to do what most Americans secretly wished *they* could do: consign to oblivion the hammerblows of crisis headlines—depression, wars, Hitler, Stalin. . . ."

The crazy surrogate family: George Cukor's *Holiday* isn't a pure screwball comedy, but it does have its moments. Here, avuncular Nick Potter and his wife, Susan (Edward Everett Horton and Jean Dixon, with puppets), put on a show for disgruntled heiress Linda Seton (Katharine Hepburn) and her brother, Ned (Lew Ayres).

OPPOSITE: Money is an excellent motivation in *The Palm Beach Story,* a film that not only fails to criticize the rich, but wholeheartedly endorses their wealth. Here, the Wienie King ("Invented the Texas wienie! Lay off 'em—you'll live longer!") hands over a wad of cash to needy Gerry Jeffers (Claudette Colbert).

other cinematic tales of wacky families in debt: *We're Rich Again* ((1934) with Edna May Oliver and Billie Burke; *Down to Their Last Yacht* (1934) with Mary Boland; *Blind Date* (1934) with Ann Sothern; *Love at Work* (1937) with that crazy Mary Boland again; and *Rich Man, Poor Girl* (1938) with Robert Young and Ruth Hussey. And from Selznick International came *The Young In Heart* (1938), in which Janet Gaynor, Douglas Fairbanks, Jr., Billie Burke, and Roland Young play an unscrupulous family who move in on a rich old lady (Minnie Dupree) only to find themselves increasingly, dreadfully reformed by her.

By the forties, the crazy-family comedy had been worked over so thoroughly that newer, even more bizarre behaviors were introduced to keep the cycle going. The most famous of these late crazies, of course, is *Arsenic and Old Lace,* Joseph Kesselring's 1941 play about two kindly old maiden aunts who poison lonely men and bury them in the cellar. Frank Capra's film adaptation of *Arsenic and Old Lace* reached the screen in 1944 with Cary Grant in the lead. Unfortunately, it's one of Grant's broadest comedy performances and one of Capra's least resonant films.

THE ROOT OF ALL HAPPINESS

One of the most remarkable things about Preston Sturges's hilarious, delirious *The Palm Beach Story* (1942) is the near total absence of criticism leveled against the big-moneyed family at its heart. Sturges takes the most famous living symbol of American wealth, the Rockefeller family, alters their name by way of a middle-class New Jersey suburb, and turns them into the most marvelous people on earth.

Having money, not having it, trying to get it, trying to get away from it—in the thirties and early forties, money problems were often good for laughs, and the immediate social cause could scarcely be clearer. But there's also a sense of wide-open meaninglessness in the way screwball comedies depict the pursuit of cash, a level of anarchy that doesn't quite jibe with the blunt fact of the Depression. The emotional chaos in these comedies can't be reduced to an economics lesson. The Depression may have spurred interest in money, but the richest comic results are found in films that twist financial panic into a broader, more existential one. And there is no better example of this emotional free-for-all than *The Palm Beach Story* (1942).

The film begins raucously and nonsensically. To the tune of the *William Tell* Overture, we are presented with a rapid montage featuring (among other things) a screaming, fainting maid; Claudette Colbert bound and gagged; Joel McCrea trying to get into a tuxedo; Colbert in a wedding gown racing for a taxi; the same maid screaming and fainting again when she sees Colbert's legs poking through a hole in the wall; and finally the beginning of a wedding ceremony between Colbert and McCrea, after which the camera tracks rapidly back "through" a glass title card that reads "And they lived happily ever after" and yet another that reads "Or did they?"

Like *The Lady Eve, The Palm Beach Story* is

In *The Palm Beach Story*, Claudette Colbert, having lost her clothes, makes do with a pair of pajamas and a Pullman blanket. Suave Rudy Vallee pretends not to notice.

a nearly perfect film that gets better with repeated viewings. It may have more quotable lines than any other screwball comedy—lines that work brilliantly in context but can also be lifted out of the dialogue and thrown at one's friends or enemies at will. Like: "Everybody's a flop until he's a success." And: "Men don't get smarter as they grow older, they just lose their hair." And the classic: "Sex *always* has something to do with it, dear."

This is a tale of imminent divorce. Gerry (Claudette Colbert) can't spend money fast enough, while her husband, Tom (Joel McCrea), can't make any at all. Tom is an inventor, whose latest idea—as yet unfinanced—is a wire-mesh airport runway

system that could be suspended over city streets. Gerry and Tom, who live in a gigantic New York duplex, are so far behind on their rent that their apartment is being rented out from under them. A real estate agent (Franklin Pangborn) escorts an elderly man and his wife through the premises. The strange little prospective tenant, who's almost lost under a ten-gallon hat, finds Gerry hiding behind the shower curtain in the bathtub. "I'm the Wienie King!" the old man weirdly explains. "Invented the Texas wienie! Lay off 'em—you'll live longer." He then pulls a gigantic wad of cash out of his pocket and gives her $700.

This sudden influx of cash is sufficient in

the short run, but it forces Gerry to come to terms with the fact that she's married to someone who can't bankroll her the way the Wienie King could. But Tom and Gerry's financial problems are simply the outward manifestations of a more essential incompatibility. They're like the other Tom and Jerry, MGM's cartoon cat and mouse who were introduced two years earlier in 1940; natural forces keep them together for better or worse. With the human Tom and Gerry, it's mostly a matter of cash, though at the same time we've got to see Sturges's use of the thick roll of cash the Wienie King keeps in his pants pocket as a hilarious covert way of talking about sex.

Coming fairly late in screwball history, *The Palm Beach Story* takes the genre's use of money as a plot motivator and pushes it to a self-conscious extreme: a farcical old capitalist simply shows up and doles out greenbacks, making it possible for Gerry to run away to get a divorce and find another man and, later, for Tom to follow her and win her back. On the street, Gerry asks a cabbie, "Where's the best place to get a divorce?" His answer is certainly well reasoned: "Well, most people go to Reno, Nevada, but for my money it's Palm Beach. This time of year you got the track, you got the ocean, you got the palm trees—three months. You leave from Penn Station." She takes his advice. On the train, while attempting to get into her top berth, she steps on the face of the man underneath (Rudy Vallee), an action that in typical screwball fashion signals the beginning of a relationship. He, too, is a moneybags. Not only does he buy her a seventy-five-cent breakfast and a prairie oyster, he also outfits her with twelve pairs of stockings, twelve pairs of shoes, eight handbags, eight hats, two dozen handkerchiefs, six dresses, two coats, six nightgowns, and three brassieres.

"You're not a burglar or something?" Gerry asks skeptically. "Oh, no, that was my grandfather," the man replies. "I keep feeling that two men with butterfly nets are going to creep up

behind you and lead you away," she says. "You're thinking of my uncle," he answers. When she asks him his name, he replies "Hackensacker." "Not *J. D. Hackensacker*?!" "Oh, I'm not my grandfather, of course," he says. "He's dead, anyway." From the Wienie King to the richest man in the world, literally overnight. "I would step on *your* face," she says, embarrassed. "Oh, that's quite all right," Hackensacker answers in typically gracious fashion. "I rather enjoyed it."

The rest of *The Palm Beach Story* traces Gerry's delirious entry into the world of unimaginable wealth, only in this case it's quite imaginable because we see it in loving detail—Hackensacker's yacht, his mansion, his servants, his clothes, his much married sister, Maude, aka the Princess Centimillia (Mary Astor). . . . Tom, financed by the Wienie King, travels to Palm Beach to convince Gerry to return with him, but she persists in her quest to marry money. She introduces Tom to the Hackensackers as her brother; to top off the indignity, she tells them his name is Captain McGloo.

Even the conventional princess character is delightful; in fact, the only object of mockery in the

Director Preston Sturges makes sure Joel McCrea knows how to unbutton Claudette Colbert's evening gown on the set of *The Palm Beach Story*. For such an uproarious film, nobody looks very happy.

Mary Astor

whole film is poor Toto (Sig Arno), the princess's latest escort. Toto is from an obscure nation, possibly Baluchistan. (As Maude clarifies it, "Toto is a refugee from his creditors.") Toto's favorite word is "nyits," which is evidently negative, since he often uses it to answer the princess when she tells him to go away.

In countless other screwball comedies, there's a price to be paid for wealth—the children are bratty, the wives are selfish, and even when the husbands are full of common sense, as is Edward Arnold or Eugene Pallette, they're still not very happy. In Hackensacker and Maude, however, we find images of bliss. The worst that can be said for Hackensacker is that he's a little stuffy, but under Sturges's direction, Rudy Vallee turns upper-crust pomp into something charming. And Maude, who under a different writer-director's sensibility could have been merely another Gail Patrick–type spoiled bitch, comes off as a self-possessed woman who has the wherewithal—not to mention the money—to keep the world wrapped around her finger. A more moralistic director than Sturges would have punished Maude for her multiple marriages. Listen to her discuss, in the wry language of Preston Sturges, the institution of marriage:

MAUDE: Why don't you marry her? She's lovely!
HACKENSACKER: In the first place, she isn't free yet. In the second place, you don't marry somebody you just met the day before. At least *I* don't.
MAUDE: But that's the only way, dear! If you get to know too much about them you'd *never* marry them! I'd marry Captain McGloo tomorrow —even *with* that name.
HACKENSACKER: And divorce him next month.
MAUDE: Nothing is permanent in this world except Roosevelt, dear.

These two rich, beautiful people are so deserving of romance that the impossibility of their getting together with Tom and Gerry gradually begins to cast a pall over the film. In fact, Gerry rediscovers her passion for Tom while Hackensacker serenades her from the terrace below, a moment Sturges plays as bittersweet. And when Hackensacker walks in on Tom and Gerry as they're packing to leave, we get the strong sense that a grave injustice is being committed against two undeserving rich folks. It's at precisely this moment of tension, then, that Sturges pulls one of the greatest stunts in narrative history, an outrageous plot twist that not only enables the comedy to conclude without inflicting pain on the wealthy brother and sister, but also serves as the final word on the whole crazy-family idea that governs screwball comedy:

HACKENSACKER: I don't suppose you have a sister? . . .
GERRY: Only a twin sister.
HACKENSACKER: A *twin* sister?!
GERRY: Oh, didn't you know about that? How we were married in the beginning— both being twins?
TOM: Of course that's another plot entirely.
MAUDE AND HACKENSACKER: *Both twins?! (Maude to Tom, Hackensacker to Gerry:)* Are *you* a twin?
TOM AND GERRY: Yes!
MAUDE AND HACKENSACKER: Well, what's *(s)he* doing?
TOM AND GERRY: Well, *nothing* . . .
Cut to a triple ring ceremony—Tom figuratively remarrying Gerry (though they've never been divorced), Hackensacker marrying Gerry's twin sister, and Maude marrying Tom's twin brother. The camera tracks quickly back through the same glass title cards:

"AND THEY LIVED HAPPILY EVER AFTER."

"OR DID THEY?"

148

"Gowns By..."

The swank style of screwball comedy is all of a piece with the way characters dress. Here is a filmography for most of the major designers whose taste and talents are greatly responsible for giving screwball characters their inimitable look. The studio listed in parenthesis at the beginning of each entry is the studio at which the designer worked most consistently during the screwball period; other studios for which the designer worked are listed individually within the entry.

FAR LEFT: This extravagant Robert Kalloch and Edward Stevenson number, worn by Irene Dunne in *Joy of Living*, features an endless fur collar and chic turban. **LEFT:** Robert Kalloch's leopard-skin fantasia for Carole Lombard in *Twentieth Century*. **INSET BOTTOM:** More leopard from Robert Kalloch (with Edward Stevenson), this time for Irene Dunne in *Joy of Living*. **INSET TOP:** Jean Arthur's elegant sable clashes with her working-girl bows in *Easy Living*; costumes by Travis Banton.

ADRIAN (MGM)
Double Wedding (1937)
It's a Wonderful World (1939)

TRAVIS BANTON
(Paramount)
The Bride Comes Home (1935)
Ruggles of Red Gap (with Edith Head, 1935)
Hands Across the Table (1935)
The Princess Comes Across (1936)
My Man Godfrey (Universal, 1936)
Nothing Sacred (with Walter Plunkett, Selznick/United Artists, 1937)
Easy Living (1937)
Bluebeard's Eighth Wife (1938)
Eternally Yours (with Irene, Walter Wanger/United Artists, 1939)

BONNIE CASHIN
(Twentieth Century-Fox)
Unfaithfully Yours (1948)
I Was a Male War Bride (1949)

HOWARD GREER
(RKO)
Page Miss Glory (with Orry-Kelly, Warner Brothers, 1935)
Bringing Up Baby (1938)
Holiday (with Robert Kalloch, Columbia, 1938)
Merrily We Live (with Irene, MGM/Roach, 1938)
Fifth Avenue Girl (1939)
My Favorite Wife (1940)

EDITH HEAD (Paramount)
Ruggles of Red Gap (with Travis Banton, 1935)
True Confession (1937)
Honeymoon in Bali (1939)
The Gracie Allen Murder Case (1939)
Cafe Society (1939)
Midnight (with Irene, 1939)
Christmas in July (1940)
The Lady Eve (1941)
Ball of Fire (Samuel Goldwyn/RKO, 1941)
The Major and the Minor (1942)
Are Husbands Necessary? (1942)
The Palm Beach Story (with Irene, 1942)

IRENE
Merrily We Live (with Howard Greer, Roach/MGM, 1938)
There Goes My Heart (Roach/United Artists, 1939)
Vivacious Lady (with Bernard Newman, RKO, 1938)
You Can't Take It With You (with Bernard Newman, Columbia, 1938)
Bachelor Mother (RKO, 1939)
Eternally Yours (Walter Wanger/United Artists, 1939)
Topper Takes a Trip (Hal Roach/United Artists, 1939)
Midnight (with Edith Head, Paramount, 1939)
That Uncertain Feeling (Sol Lesser/United Artists, 1941)
The Palm Beach Story (with Edith Head, Paramount, 1942)
Take a Letter, Darling (Paramount, 1942)
Mr. and Mrs. Smith (1942)

ROBERT KALLOCH
(Columbia)
It Happened One Night (1934)
Twentieth Century (1934)
The Awful Truth (1937)
Holiday (with Howard Greer, 1938)
Joy of Living (with Edward Stevenson, RKO, 1938)
The Amazing Mr. Williams (1939)
His Girl Friday (1940)
Mr. and Mrs. North (1941)

ORRY-KELLY
(Warner Brothers)
Jimmy the Gent (1934)
Page Miss Glory (with Howard Greer, 1935)
It's Love I'm After (1937)
The Bride Came C.O.D. (1941)

OMAR KIAM
The Young in Heart (Selznick/United Artists, 1938)

BERNARD NEWMAN
(RKO)
The Bride Walks Out (1936)
The Ex-Mrs. Bradford (1936)

Theodora Goes Wild (Columbia, 1936)
Vivacious Lady (with Irene, 1939)

WALTER PLUNKETT
(RKO)
Down to Their Last Yacht (1934)
We're Rich Again (1934)
Nothing Sacred (with Travis Banton, Selznick/United Artists, 1937)

RENIÉ (Fox)
The Affairs of Annabel (1938)
Having Wonderful Time (with Edward Stevenson, RKO, 1938)
Tom, Dick and Harry (1941)

ROYER (Twentieth Century-Fox)
Day-Time Wife (1939)
Turnabout (Hal Roach/United Artists, 1940)

EDWARD STEVENSON
(RKO)
There Goes My Girl (1937)
There Goes the Groom (1937)
Breakfast for Two (1937)
Having Wonderful Time (with Renié, 1938)
Joy of Living (with Robert Kalloch, 1938)
The Mad Miss Manton (1938)
A Girl, a Guy, and a Gob (1941)

HELEN TAYLOR
The Moon's Our Home (Paramount, 1936)

TRAVILLA
Monkey Business (with Charles LeMaire, 1952)

DOLLY TREE (MGM)
The Thin Man (1934)
After the Thin Man (1936)
Libeled Lady (1936)
Fast Company (1938)
Fast and Loose (1939)

GWEN WAKELING
(Twentieth Century-Fox)
Danger—Love at Work (1937)
Second Honeymoon (1937)
Three Blind Mice (1938)
He Married His Wife (1940)

CLOCKWISE FROM BOTTOM LEFT: Edith Head's wedding gown for Barbara Stanwyck in *The Lady Eve* was a fashion sensation; groom Henry Fonda doesn't look too shabby either. Adrian's bohemian look for William Powell in *Double Wedding*. Katharine Hepburn in *Holiday*, for which Howard Greer and Robert Kalloch teamed up as designers. Howard Greer gave Hepburn a weird, otherwordly quality with this getup in *Bringing Up Baby*.

152

Bernard Newman's designs for *Theodora Goes Wild* greatly enhanced the sense of excess suggested by the title. Irene Dunne, pictured here in Newman's black feathered number, had originally recommended him to RKO for the 1935 *Roberta*. But Newman wasn't suited to the workaday studio routine and left after a few years.

Robert Kalloch's striped excess, said to have been inspired by Adela Rogers St. John, worn by Rosalind Russell in *His Girl Friday*.

CHAPTER 7

Caught in the Press: The Newspaper Screwball

*T*HE NEWSPAPER OFFICE, A TIGHT LITTLE WORLD OF COMPLACENCY and skepticism, mechanization and human error, routine and scandal, is one of the thirties' most persistent settings. In thirties films, even newsroom monotony comes across as fascinating. Like a debutante who gets no kick from champagne, all those cynical reporters are surrounded by so much excitement that they cease to feel much of anything, a luxury audiences of the period may well have craved.

Cultural historians have pointed out that America became obsessed with its own culture during the thirties. This burgeoning self-awareness can be seen in the way Hollywood depicted journalism as an essentially American phenomenon. Screwball comedies tell stories about newspapers that are somehow both plausible and outlandish, but they invariably depict news reporting as an indigenous activity conducted by a precisely American character type. (Try picturing Charles Boyer as a crack reporter.) In a self-fulfilling sort of way, Hollywood was right: like the film studios themselves, the global communications networks created by publishing conglomerates were giving the United States an unassailable monopoly on information and its spread. No wonder scrappy, unstoppable *American* types like Clark Gable, Pat O'Brien, or Spencer Tracy seemed so right as newspapermen.

OPPOSITE: The boys of *His Girl Friday*'s press room (*left to right*): Frank Jenks, Regis Toomey, Porter Hall, Cliff Edwards, and Roscoe Karns.

Myrna Loy

In newspaper comedies, the success or failure of a paper's business tends to be more important than the truth of what the paper reports. In MGM's *Libeled Lady* (1936), a miserably inaccurate story about an heiress, written by a notorious drunk of a reporter, winds up in print in a major New York newspaper, and although the editor stops the presses and recalls nearly all the papers, the heiress launches a $5 million libel suit. Morality is squarely on the heiress's side, but the plot depends on audiences hating to see the newspaper go out of business for lack of funds to pay her. These films take any doubts one harbors about the ethics of the newspaper business and magnify them. When the newspaper is threatened—or even when it's just a slow day and there's no news—morality be damned.

For younger viewers who assume that their TV-wise perceptions of the media are more skeptical than those of earlier generations, screwball comedy's representation of journalism may open a few eyes. For anyone wary of the power and influence of the press, the way screwball editors and reporters are presumed to think and act—always as cads—provides a ghastly confirmation. *Libeled Lady,* for example, tells us that newspapermen hire their old enemies to entrap their victims by marrying their fiancées, and they don't care because they only love themselves. In countless other films like *Cafe Society;* or the all-but-forgotten *Wedding Present* (1936), with Cary Grant and Joan Bennett; or *Love Is News* (1937), with Loretta Young and Tyrone Power, journalists are presumed to be craven, manipulative, and fantastically venal. They may be wise guys, but they're ethically irredeemable, and we usually get the impression that not even love will cure them.

Screwball newspaper comedies are morality tales in which the morals are notably absent. They show us how to behave in order to become a scoundrel (like Walter Connolly in *Nothing Sacred*) or a suave creep (like Cary Grant in *His Girl Friday*). They provide object lessons in how to make money by telling massive lies. And they teach us that given the right circumstances, cheaters always win.

"THAT'S ARSON"

By 1936, Mayer's MGM was Hollywood's great star stable, and overabundance was the studio's hallmark. Because of MGM's talent for grand-scale entertainment, *Libeled Lady* (like most other MGM screwballs, with the notable exception of *Love Crazy*) is wrapped in a lugubrious classiness that dampens its spirit. Even the credits sequence is ostentatious, since not two but *four* stars—Jean Harlow, Spencer Tracy, Myrna Loy, and William Powell, each dressed in a gorgeous wedding outfit—are introduced striding triumphantly toward the camera to the tune of Mendelssohn's Wedding March.

With two central love relationships, *Libeled Lady* more than doubles the screwball quotient by encouraging potential conflicts not only within the couples but also between them, the result being crossover complications and intragender battles as well. Notice that these mushrooming tensions occur between four *very* big stars. At the end, when William Powell punches Spencer Tracy in the nose and Jean Harlow follows through by punching Powell in the nose, the fighting achieves near epic status simply because of the noses involved. Only MGM could have flaunted itself in such a manner. Myrna Loy seems to have been exempted from the brawl for typological reasons, nose punching apparently being too un-Loy. Even in *Double Wedding* (1937), where she is required to bang Powell over the head with a frying pan, she performs the act accidentally. There, weirdly, the final knockout blow to Powell's head is delivered not by Loy but by a falling Oscar statuette.

After its star-studded credits sequence, the first shots of *Libeled Lady* show printing presses spewing out newspapers. It's the morning of a catastrophe—not in the news, but *of* the news, for the

paper has libeled an heiress. In 1936 nothing could be more awful, except perhaps for marriage. The editor, Warren Haggerty (Spencer Tracy), is burdened with both. Having stopped the presses and issued a series of commands in what turns out to be a vain attempt at disaster control, Haggerty proceeds to become frenetic over the prospect of his noon wedding. "And there'll be no reprieve from the governor this time," he says with morbid resignation. This isn't the first time a date has been set. His fiancée, Gladys (Jean Harlow), has been put off

countless times before, a fact Gladys herself reveals when she makes a spectacular entrance dressed in a sumptuous satin wedding gown complete with elaborate veil and massive white bouquet. Gladys clomps through the newspaper office, charging straight toward the camera on her way, and into Haggerty's inner sanctum, where she rages bitterly against her fate—she's always a bride but never a wife. Alas, the wedding is postponed once again.

For all their bluster and brass, Haggerty and Gladys are two fairly needy individuals. Con-

This is journalism? Reporter Clark Gable (why is he dressed like a musketeer?) romances heiress Joan Crawford as Donald Meek plays with a revolver in MGM's 1936 *Love on the Run*. Adrian, who once called Crawford "a female Johnny Weissmuller," designed the costumes.

really did libel Connie Allenbury, he seeks the help of his old nemesis Bill Chandler (William Powell), whose reputation rests on his sneaky ability to fight libel suits. Prompted by Haggerty, Chandler marries poor Gladys, who is apparently so desperate to be married to *anyone* that she agrees to wed a man she doesn't know. Now married, Chandler aims to pursue Connie, proving her to be the "husband stealer" the paper has falsely labeled her.

Chandler hastens away to worm himself into Connie's life, leaving hapless Gladys stuck in a hotel room alone. Having no success with Connie, who finds him suspiciously middle class, Chandler goes after her father (Walter Connolly); knowing that the old man takes a keen interest in fishing, Chandler hires a prissy fishing coach (E. E. Clive) to teach him all he needs to know. This leads to a forced gag in which the effeminate coach tries to create "atmosphere" by convincing Gladys to bend over and act like a boulder, with himself posing as a nearby tree. (You got it—Chandler hooks Gladys by the rump.) What's notable about the scene is not its humor, or lack of it, but the extent to which it punishes Gladys and the coach for their improper sexuality. You shouldn't act like that, MGM's lion seems to murmur. If you're a woman, tone it down; if you're a man, don't act like *that*.

Chandler gets his own reward later when he hooks an enormous fish and gets dragged downstream, landing momentarily—and painfully—with his legs straddling a big rock. Shaking Powell's character loose from his self-assurance, the scenes at the fishing lodge also shift Loy's character away from the cold aristocrat to potential wife. From here on, *Libeled Lady* races to get Connie married to Chandler and further reduces Gladys to idiocy. Haggerty cruelly convinces Gladys that Chandler has already married Connie. And Gladys, who has by now fallen in love with Chandler (who has shown her a bare amount of respect and affection, in marked contrast with Haggerty), quickly goes insane. "My dear, she's a case! A psychopathic case!

trast appears in the form of another loving couple, though they too are introduced as adversaries. The heiress Connie Allenbury (Myrna Loy) is first seen perched on her father's desk, casually pulling off a sweater, her back to the camera. Connie's introduction might be called a clean strip, for it's a way of getting a female character to remove her clothes and yet remain fully dressed. Connie can't be a seductress, like Gladys; she's too aristocratic. Connie's clean strip—contrasted with Gladys's skintight wedding gown—captures in an instant the essence of screwball's suppressed sexuality. Gladys is clearly aware of her physicality, yet in the screwball world, predicated as it is on the Production Code, such awareness is a sign of vulgarity. In Harlow's precode films, her body was an alluring threat, whether she played an aristocrat (*Platinum Blonde,* 1931), a working-class delinquent (*Hold Your Man,* 1933), or a gold digger (*Red Headed Woman,* 1932). But by the time of *Libeled Lady,* Harlow's body had become comic relief, a subtle put-down.

Because Haggerty knows that his paper

She was in a booth screaming, 'Get me out of here! Get me out of here!' " says the obnoxious Mrs. Burns-Norvell after Gladys causes a scene in a beauty parlor. But the biggest joke is on Haggerty, for Chandler *does* marry Connie, thereby abandoning his allegiance to the newspaper and ruining Haggerty's scheme.

The principals all meet in a suite at the Grand Plaza Hotel. Gladys sees Connie and Chandler's marriage certificate, and because she's a character in a thirties comedy, she can't help but remark that her husband is already married to another woman. "That's arson!" she declares. "You mean bigamy," Haggerty gently corrects. The already complicated story line then spins out of control. In brief: Gladys has been married before. Chandler has discovered that she got an illegal divorce in Yucatán, thus nullifying her marriage to Chandler, a fact that enables him to marry Connie. But no—Gladys announces that she also got a second divorce in Reno, and everybody becomes upset. Gladys seizes the upper hand and tells everyone off; it's one of the film's highlights, since the character finally rallies from several reels' worth of abuse. Connie takes Gladys into the next room and lectures her about men while the men dive into a fistfight.

"She'll feel sorrier for you if I punch you in the nose," Chandler announces, giving him a good excuse to inflict pain on Haggerty, only to have Gladys storm in and sock Chandler in the nose for revenge. Everyone ends up screaming at Mr. Allenbury, who has the misfortune to arrive for the final shot. The camera tracks forward on the hysterical and nauseatingly interrelated group as the desperate father cries, "Quiet! Will you all be quiet!" Unfortunately, the noise is for naught, for this is an unsatisfactory screwball ending. Naturally the genre demands disarray, but here it's stiffly predetermined and unimaginative. Then again, what do we expect? How chaotic can a film be when it conforms so predictably to L. B. Mayer's idea of high class? Even Haggerty, the crummy newspaperman whose profession is responsible for the whole mess, remains too pleasant in the brawl; he's supposed to be a cheat and a liar, but the film's polish forces him to maintain respectability even in a scene of physical violence. (Compare Tracy's polite performance in *Libeled Lady* to the caustic precision of his character in that great MGM anomaly, Fritz Lang's *Fury,* also 1936.) Unfortunately, MGM took the generic sleaze of newspapermen only so far. It was up to other studios to show the corrosion.

It's all in the wrist: an effeminate fishing coach (E. E. Clive, *center*) demonstrates the proper technique to Bill Chandler (William Powell) and Gladys Benton (Jean Harlow) in *Libeled Lady.*

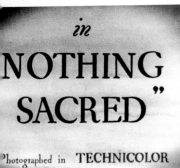

The clever credits sequence of *Nothing Sacred* is all of a piece with the film's corrosive point of view—the actors are shown as puppets.

THE BLESSINGS OF CULTURE

William Wellman's *Nothing Sacred* (1937), made by Selznick International, and Howard Hawks's *His Girl Friday* (1940), made by Columbia, both escape the gooey gentility that keeps *Libeled Lady* from getting off the ground. Wellman earned the nickname "Screwball Bill" in the early thirties because of his penchant for practical jokes; *Nothing Sacred* was his first and only screwball comedy. (Wellman's 1942 *Lady of Burlesque* is too much of a screwball-mystery hybrid.) The fact that both *Nothing Sacred* and *His Girl Friday* were directed by men who had prior experience with gritty crime dramas (Wellman with *The Public Enemy,* 1931, and Hawks with *Scarface,* 1932) may have something to do with the films' accurate appreciation of corruption. Even more important, however, is the guiding sensibility of the writer Ben Hecht, who loved and hated the newspaper business for all the right reasons.

Nothing Sacred is the story of a hard-nosed reporter (Fredric March) who capitalizes on the terminal illness of a young woman (Carole Lombard) by pumping up her impending death into a sob-story craze for his readers, only to discover that the "dying" heroine has been faking it all along. Oddly, this macabre portrait of a world saturated by cheats and liars is one of the very few screwball comedies made in Technicolor. The addition of color into the screwball world makes it clear by contrast how stark and sleek the rest of the genre looks; the grays, blacks, and whites of the other screwball classics seem much more appropriate to a world of moral tension than the bright blue skies and pink, fleshy skin tones of *Nothing Sacred.*

Producer David Selznick hired Hecht to write the screenplay for *Nothing Sacred* over the objections of financier John Hay "Jock" Whitney, who had become chairman of the board of Selznick International. According to film historian Ronald

Haver, Whitney, who had been pressing Selznick to do a comedy after becoming enamored with *My Man Godfrey,* told Selznick, "If you're absolutely convinced that there is no one else who can do the job, then go ahead and hire him." But even Selznick was disturbed by what he read in Hecht's first draft, and in an effort to get rid of at least some of the acid, he demanded various changes. Supposedly, Selznick was upset by Hecht's unsparing depiction of journalism out of personal embarrassment on behalf of his friends in the publishing industry, particularly Henry Luce. Whatever originally prompted Selznick's dissatisfaction, however, Hecht returned with an exceedingly nasty and obviously unfilmable rewrite, after which Hecht and Selznick parted company and the screenplay was turned over to others—Dorothy Parker, Robert Carson, Ring Lardner, Jr., and Budd Schulberg.

Hecht later wrote that "*Nothing Sacred,* done for Selznick in two weeks, had to be written on trains between New York and Los Angeles," and such haste may have been responsible for part of the screenplay's flippant tone. But there's a deeper biliousness to *Nothing Sacred,* a belly-clenching sense of amused disgust that cannot be attributed solely to train whistles and the speed of the rails. Not only does the story focus on the love between a cynical New York reporter and an opportunistic liar from the hinterlands—with an utterly craven and morally bankrupt publisher (Walter Connolly) thrown in on the side—but it features a knock-down brawl between the two stars. Such abrasiveness caught on. *Nothing Sacred* was a big hit, especially in New York, where it equaled the all-time long-run record of four weeks at Radio City Music Hall. (Nevertheless, because of the film's high distribution and advertising costs, it didn't quite make its money back during its first year of release.)

For Hecht, all newspapermen are invidious liars. Star reporters crank out stories simply to make a buck, and publishers print them simply to make millions. And because *Nothing Sacred* is set in New

Carole Lombard and Fredric March in an inappropriately romantic publicity shot for *Nothing Sacred*. Even when screwball comedies were unremittingly nasty, the studios felt compelled to include pictures like this as part of the ad package.

Black and white and read all over: After his farcical "Sultan of Mazipan" stunt fails, *Nothing Sacred*'s Wally Cook (Fredric March) is demoted to the obituary page while the "Sultan" (Troy Brown) has to clean up after him.

A slice of Americana: New York reporter Fredric March can't get much out of hatchet-faced Yankee shopkeeper Margaret Hamilton.

the head table. He is applauded by his publisher, Oliver Stone (Connolly), for having made possible the lavish event to which all of New York society has been invited—a tribute to an immense black potentate, the Sultan of Mazipan (Troy Brown), who has graciously agreed to finance some sort of bizarre cultural museum to be built under the auspices of Stone's newspaper, the *Morning Star*. "Peace be with you, my friends," the Sultan beatifies, "peace and the blessings of culture," at which point he is interrupted by the arrival of an outraged black woman (Hattie McDaniel) with several children in tow, pointing at the Sultan and yelling, "That's him! That's my husband!"

It might be too kind to call the scene's conclusion racist, because this familiar charge would enable Hollywood's apologists to respond that racism was endemic during the period and that *Nothing Sacred* is no worse than anything else. But it *is* worse than most, for it goes beyond the usual stereotyping of blacks as servants—not to mention the much more common Hollywood habit of simply segregating them off screen—to create a grotesque black clown. In this asinine "Sultan," who turns out to be a Harlem shoe shiner named Ernest (and who is subsequently hired as a janitor by Stone and forced by both type and circumstance to cower and beg for mercy), Hecht and Wellman construct a figure of more unsparing derision than any other character in this already derisive film. The level of contempt hurled at Ernest is especially galling given the general sleaziness of the other characters.

In his final draft of the script, Hecht actually refers to the Sultan as "the bogie" and one of the children as "a pickaninny," but it's his *image* of blacks more than the crude names he used to dismiss them that makes the film's racial angle hard to take. Unfortunately, subsequent rewriting eliminated a scene in which Ernest, in a rare glimmer of humanity, figures out that Hazel might be as big a fraud as he had been, and this leaves Hecht's most bigoted impulses without a positive counterbalance.

York, the level of fearless self-interest is even higher than usual. This is a world oversaturated by false claims, cheap scoops, and fraud—a place where, as the prologue claims, "Truth, crushed to earth, rises again more phony than a glass eye."

The film opens in a banquet hall, where reporter Wallace Cook (March) is seated, drunk, at

Ernest may be forced to work as a janitor, but for Hecht and Wellman, Wally's fate is far worse: he's banished to the obituary page. Desperately humiliated, he convinces Stone to let him milk a story the *Star* has thus far buried: a young woman from Warsaw, Vermont, is dying of radium poisoning. Stone agrees, and Wally departs for the north country to revitalize his career with the poor soul's death. One mark of the film's accuracy in this regard can be seen in the unintended similarity between the film's own cynicism and the ad campaign used to sell it. In a virtual replay of the movie's most bitter moments, United Artists actually suggested that theater owners mount a "30 Days to Live" letter-writing contest, noting soulfully that "it's an idea that touches the deepest, most personal feelings of every man and woman—which makes it a natural for a broad-appeal letter competition."

Wally Cook may be an ace reporter, but he can't get much out of the crusty Vermont townsfolk, all of whom speak in monosyllables. Seasoned scare-puss Margaret Hamilton appears as the proprietor of the general store, telling Cook that Warsaw is a company town, bought and paid for by the Paragon Watch Company, and since the company doesn't like either nosy reporters or scandals, he'd better just beat it. (Hecht's script was much harsher on capitalism than the finished film, for Hecht linked Hazel Flagg's radium poisoning directly to her job, which was to paint radioactive watch faces for the company; the precise cause of her purported illness is much more vague on screen.) Outside, a group of hostile children pelt Wally with stones and tell him to scram. Then, in a lovely shot of a quiet Vermont street, a toddler darts out from behind a classic white picket fence and bites Wally on the leg. Moments of gratuitous nastiness like this make *Nothing Sacred* special—they're invigorating antidotes to the corny Americana that Hollywood is so often accused of dispensing.

Unknown to Wally, Hazel's doctor, Enoch (Charles Winninger), has made a mistaken diagnosis, and she's actually healthy as sin. As relieved as Hazel is, however, she's distressed to learn that her planned out-with-a-bang trip to New York must now be canceled. Although she gets to live longer than six months, she's forced to live in Warsaw, an idea that drives her to tears. Wally's offer of a trip to New York at the *Morning Star*'s expense, then, is a godsend. No matter that she'll have to play dying, lie incessantly, and take mercenary advantage of her hosts. These are merely the moral risks she accepts in order to escape from the heartland and go where her unspoiled heart commands—to that Babylon on the Hudson, New York City, the screwball capital of the world.

Carole Lombard is exquisite as the swindling innocent, Hazel, one of several characters—Lily Garland in *Twentieth Century,* Irene Bullock in *My Man Godfrey,* and Maria Tura in *To Be or Not To Be*—who are impossible to imagine with another actress in the role. Lombard plays Hazel as calculating without being offputting, corrupt but not villainous, breezy but steady, and her dexterity with screwball's more or less indelicate balance between reason and insanity gives the character a sense of overjoyed precariousness that in the hands of a lesser actress could have been deadly. The deficiencies of *Nothing Sacred,* I think, are largely due to Fredric March, who seems unable to rise above the most meager attempts at lightness. Something stalls in his performance, but it may be a matter of miscasting. Although March can be a good romantic lead, he simply can't project the constrained anarchy of, say, Cary Grant or even Fred MacMurray. As a disreputable reporter, March is workmanlike; as a central screwball love interest, he's a washout.

In the big fight scene, which occurs after Cook discovers that Hazel is perfectly healthy, March seems especially ill suited to his task. He has to punch Lombard repeatedly as a way of making Hazel look sweaty and truly sick, but March's grim determination only serves to rid the scene of the romantic subtext his character's actions ought to

Fredric March

suggest. He slugs, shoves, and kicks the woman like a real Hollywood professional, but it's never clear that he both adores and hates her at the same time. Lombard, on the other hand, understands the scene perfectly, and while it's true that her tightly stretched emotions are built into her lines—"I'll never forgive you as long as I live! I won't! I hate you! I just hate you!"—their depth is the result of the actress's full-throttle performance. Cook may tell Hazel (while holding her at arm's length to fend off her fists), "I'm going to flirt and lie and cheat and swindle—right through to our golden wedding," but there's no honesty in the way March says it. It is quite simply a way of egging Hazel on, of methodically intensifying her fury so as to get the job done.

The fight is also infuriatingly one-sided, with Hazel bearing the entire weight (and pain and humiliation) of the violence. She's never allowed to connect on a single punch, though Cook is every bit as deserving of moral comeuppance as she is. In the boxing-match scene in *Breakfast for Two,* there's an explosive sense that rules are being abandoned, that limits are being trashed. Here, however, it's sheer punishment, with Hazel getting what she deserves for being a cheat. And it makes no sense, for whom has she harmed? The newspaper? Certainly not. The gullible, scandal-hungry people of New York? Hardly; we see plainly that emotions run shallow in the big city. Wally Cook himself, the self-interested reporter whose career she has revived? Not at all. The worst thing she's done to him is inspire his love, and that's the only element of positive humanity in his character. He should be grateful, not angry.

Profoundly frustrated—beaten, in fact—Hazel gasps, "Lemme sock you just once—just once on the jaw—and I won't care what happens." It's a most reasonable request, but Cook (not to mention Hecht and Wellman) doesn't grant it. He quickly creams her with a solid right to the head and knocks her cold.

Rolling with the Punches

Most contemporary reviewers picked up on the unusual harshness of *Nothing Sacred.* One writer noted that "not since Mr. Edison invented a little gadget that projected moving shadows on a stretched cloth has such clean-cut, vicious, inclusive meanness been made accessible to the great American public." United Artists, which released the film for Selznick, actually made the idea of bellicose romance into a central selling point in posters featuring March and Lombard posed as if for a boxing match, coupled with the tag line "See the big fight!" One ad even quoted prizefighter Jack Dempsey saying, "Carole Lombard swings the wickedest right I ever saw. . . ." To cap this carnival of abrasiveness, UA's publicity department went so far as to suggest this novel idea to theater owners:

"Suspend two overhead punching bags in your lobby, paste a cutout head of March on one and of Lombard on the other. Invite the customers to work off their grouches against the opposite sex with a placard reading: 'Lombard larrups March—March manhandles Lombard . . . step up and take a sock!' You can also offer them wallops at life-size compo board cutouts of the two battling stars, hingeing the cutouts to a floorboard so they'll rock back with the punch and come up again for the next sock."

Rosalind Russell

Nothing Sacred ends with a predicament. Its celebration of public fraud is so extreme that the two wily protagonists cannot be rehabilitated in a believable way. The ending supplied by Hecht himself, impossibly nasty and overtly racist, was almost certainly designed more to infuriate David Selznick than to serve as a reasonable conclusion, and although it was never filmed, it's worth describing for the sake of its sheer outrageousness. In Hecht's script, the film ends in a hospital. Ernest has donned his sultan's outfit because his wife is delivering quadruplets. Hazel is seen walking through various hospital rooms, including a psychiatric ward in which four men wildly shoot fire hoses at a naked man with a large cigar in his mouth. (Ahem.) Hazel then steals two more "nigger babies" from yet another extremely stupid black man and adds them to the quadruplets to create "sextuplets," the next big scoop for the *Morning Star*. Headlines about the fabulous babies appear, and on the bottom of the page is a hasty wrap-up of the Hazel Flagg story: "Hazel Flagg, radium victim, cured by fever, goes on vacation." There's a wedding scene between Hazel and Wally, and the film concludes—incredibly—with a shot of the six infants lying in their crib singing, "I wish I was in Dixie. . . ."

Faced with this mess, rewriters Ring Lardner, Jr., and Budd Schulberg simply dispatch Hazel and Wally away to the South Seas to be married, and the radium story dies on its own.

In the final analysis, it's the invigorating meanness of spirit in *Nothing Sacred,* not its artistic quality, that one remembers most fondly. Rarely does a Hollywood comedy attack American values in such a point-blank manner. It's racist and misogynistic. The color is offputting and the cutting is often splicy. Fredric March isn't the best screwball hero, and the ending doesn't entirely work. But its vision is so consistently bitter, so relentlessly discontented, that its artistic sins can be forgiven. How could anyone dislike a film in which a character (Enoch) matter-of-factly tells the hero (Wally):

"You're a newspaperman. I can smell 'em. I've always been able to smell 'em. Excuse me while I open the window?"

WALTER AND HILDY

*N*othing Sacred respects venality, but only to a point. Howard Hawks's *His Girl Friday* goes further. A dark-humored and hysterically speedy screwball comedy, *His Girl Friday* gender-switches Ben Hecht and Charles MacArthur's classic 1928 play *The Front Page*. Born out of the "jazz journalism" era of the twenties, *The Front Page* is the story of an editor, Walter Burns, who stops at nothing to keep his star reporter on the job, even though the reporter, Hildy Johnson, has had enough and wants to get married and settle down—as far from Walter as possible. Hugely successful on Broadway, *The Front Page,* with its brutally funny dialogue as well as its vast money-making ability, was a natural choice for the silver screen as Hollywood hit its stride in the sound era. When it appeared in 1931, the film, too, was a hit. Adolphe Menjou was charmingly detestable as Walter Burns, and Pat O'Brien made a fine Hildy. They were snide, scheming, irresponsible, and altogether marvelous. Still, there was something missing, and it had to do with love.

In *The Front Page,* the relationship between Walter and Hildy, as several critics have already noted, is really a love story, though neither the sexual mores of the era nor the sensibilities of the playwright/screenwriters would have allowed anything more than the faintest suggestion of homosexuality to appear. (Toward the end of the play, Hildy responds to Walter's seemingly sincere gesture of affection by saying, "Aw, Jesus, no, Walter! You make me feel like a fairy or something.") In the late thirties, as screwball comedy was reaching its zenith, Howard Hawks perceived this multitoned but suppressed passion while hearing a woman read Hildy's part in an after-dinner play-reading session, and he decided to film the story with a female Hildy, thereby allowing the deep-seated mistrust that rages between the two leads to find counterpoint in overt sexual attraction and, it might even be said, love.

To say that *His Girl Friday* is played quickly doesn't begin to describe the film's breakneck speed, an effect Hawks achieved by encouraging his actors to step on each other's lines. Movies had raced before. The quickest may have been William K. Howard's *The Trial of Vivienne Ware* (1932), a feature-length crime drama that ran less than an hour because of its fast-talking actors and attention-grabbing swish pans used as transitions between unrelated scenes. Pauline Kael, deriding critics who credit Hawks with having "invented overlapping dialogue," claims reductively that these supposedly overeager hero-worshipers "have never bothered to look at the text of the original Hecht and MacArthur play," but her defensive antiauteurism begs the issue. Reciting snappy dialogue on stage is one thing; recording it on film is another. In what contemporary accounts treat as an exciting innovation, Hawks dispensed with the usual boom and filmed many scenes in *His Girl Friday* with multiple microphones in order to achieve greater audio clarity. For technical reasons, the mikes couldn't operate simultaneously, so a sound engineer frantically switched from one to another on cue. That's the creative, technical triumph of *His Girl Friday,* and Hecht and MacArthur necessarily had little to do with it.

What the playwrights did invent, or at least perfect, was a particular vision of blithe corruption. In their depiction of what constitutes news, *The Front Page* and *His Girl Friday* are ruthless in their disregard of ordinary standards of behavior, not to mention truth. But since such cynicism appears in the form of fiction, we tend to call it satire rather than history. Indeed, *His Girl Friday* is one of the very few screwball comedies that actually merits the label "satire," for unlike most others, this satire has an *object*—journalism as practiced in the United

In *His Girl Friday*, Cary Grant and Rosalind Russell meet for the first time after their divorce. She tells him she's getting married and moving to Albany. She shows him her engagement ring. Then, reliving old times, she hurls her pocketbook at his head *(overleaf)*.

States—and its tone is openly derisive. Film critic and Columbia University professor Andrew Sarris once declared that no satire set in the world of academia could ever be too broad or too crass. The

169

Everyday News

Ben Hecht and Charles MacArthur wrote from experience about newspapers and the awesome, rancid way they operate. Before becoming playwrights, both had been ambitious young reporters in Chicago. Hecht, who worked uncredited on the script of *His Girl Friday,* later wrote that they had based Walter Burns on Walter Howey, the colorful editor who served as MacArthur's boss at the *Examiner.* In one incident, Howey assigned MacArthur to cover the story of a little girl locked in a safe. But, after witnessing the drama firsthand, MacArthur told Howey that the child had simply been hiding in the attic. Howey, a man of classical journalistic principles, told MacArthur to write it up as the magnificent human story of the valor and unshakable faith of the rescuers who could see in the pathetic antics of a frightened little girl a glimpse of the childlike frailty in us all. MacArthur cranked it out, and everyone loved it.

There seems to have been a real Hildy Johnson, too; according to one source, the *Examiner* had employed a journalist named Hilding Johnson, who, as legend has it, once

pieced together the torn scraps of a jury's ballots to get the verdict before it was announced. The industrious and conniving Johnson then made a bunch of phony scraps, scattered them in an obvious place, and let the other reporters puzzle together the wrong verdict.

The authenticity of the Howey-Johnson anecdotes isn't as important as the times they evoke. In 1928, the year *The Front Page* hit Broadway, the ghastly frenzy of reporting reached its nadir with the trial and execution of husband-killer Ruth Snyder in New York. In a tactic worthy of Walter Burns in any incarnation, the *Daily Graphic* advertised the paper's fabulous attraction: "A woman's final thoughts just before she is clutched in the deadly snare that sears and burns and FRIES AND KILLS! Her very last words! Exclusively in tomorrow's *Graphic.*" Unfortunately, another Walter Burns down the street at the *New York Daily News* beat the *Graphic* to the punch by running—in giant size on the front page—a suitably blurry picture of Mrs. Snyder caught in the act of frying, thereby scooping the *Graphic,* thrilling its readers, and appalling most of the more dignified arbiters of journalistic taste. Thus, when movie audiences saw *The Front Page,* they were watching something all too close to real life.

same can be said for journalism, especially given the wider social implications of an information industry governed by abject greed, meanness, egomania, and desexualized passion—lust that is reserved to a chilling degree for calamitous current events. (In *His Girl Friday,* Walter is said to have left Hildy on their wedding night in order to cover a fire.) It's frightening to see the extent to which *His Girl Friday* simply assumes the rottenness of its milieu, a point of view Hawks both inherited from *The Front Page* and enhanced on his own.

"Oh, Walter, you're wonderful—in a loathsome sort of way," Hildy tells Walter with unmistakable admiration. *The Front Page* is about two people with an unyielding contempt for the world and an equally unyielding respect for each other. The fact that the story of their perverse friendship is set against a prison backdrop only intensifies the bleakness of the moral universe they inhabit. In *His Girl Friday,* as in *The Front Page,* the story Walter Burns uses to lure Hildy Johnson away from her/his imminent marriage to a bland and unsatisfactory mate (Ralph Bellamy in *Friday,* Mary Brian in *Page*) is the violent end of the life of Earl Williams (John Qualen in *Friday,* George E. Stone in *Page*), a downtrodden schnook of a worker convicted of shooting a policeman and scheduled to be hanged the next morning. It is a story neither Hildy nor Walter can resist—not that a man's life means anything to them, for we're certain from the way they talk that Walter and Hildy have watched far too many people's necks snap for the tragedy of the pathetic Earl Williams to make emotional news. Walter and Hildy are two people with a deathless need to turn dreadful events to their own advantage, to use them for pleasure—their own as well as that of the eager reading public. It's the sport, the hunt for news, they crave.

The second scene in the film, in which Walter deftly humiliates Hildy's fiancé, Bruce, without Bruce's becoming aware of it, demonstrates Walter and Hildy's compulsion to be jour-nalists; it's the scene during which he convinces her to cover Earl Williams's final hours. Walter helpfully tells Bruce that if Hildy doesn't interview Williams and, through the interview, convince the governor to grant Williams a reprieve, he'll be "going on a honeymoon with blood on your hands!" But the scene also shows the romantic equivalent of Walter and Hildy's news vampirism, since we can see the palpable, irresistible irritation their love generates. These people cannot get along together; no matter. They're divorced for reasons we're sure are valid, but like Jerry and Lucy Warriner in *The Awful Truth,* Walter and Hildy nevertheless communicate in a cozy if hardhearted ironic language only they can understand. When she hurls her pocketbook at his head and misses, he calmly responds, "You're losing your arm—you used to be able to pitch much better than that."

Hildy is scheduled to marry Bruce the following day in Albany, the quiet city on the upper Hudson River where they will live—as Bruce puts it, "just for the first year"—with his mother. Walter is amused but appalled, and he's already trying to figure out ways to prevent the marriage and keep Hildy in his life, whatever the cost (to her). But as the following exchange reveals, Grant's Walter Burns is more than just a charming louse. He's *the* charming louse, the only one for Hildy:

WALTER: Bruce, I, uh . . . let me get this straight. I must have misunderstood you. You mean you're taking the sleeper today and then getting married tomorrow?
BRUCE: Oh, well, it's not like that.
WALTER: Well, what's it like?
HILDY: Poor Walter. He'll toss and turn all night. Perhaps we better tell him Mother's coming along, too.
WALTER: *(to Hildy)* Mother? Why, your mother kicked the bucket!
BRUCE: No, *my* mother, *my* mother.
WALTER: Oh, *your* mother. Oh, well, that relieves my mind.
HILDY: *(to Walter)* It was cruel of us to let

you suffer that way. *(to Bruce)* Isn't Walter sweet? Always wanting to protect me.

First there's Walter's smutty question, "What's it like?" but naturally the smut escapes Bruce completely. Then there's the stilted, sarcastic "that relieves my mind," which Bruce takes purely at face value. Hildy, however, picks up both of Walter's ironies, and she can't stop herself from getting sucked in. A few moments later, after Walter briefly exits (to receive a prearranged fake phone call, supposedly alerting him to another reporter's sudden inability to cover the Earl Williams story), Bruce discusses his newfound friend with Hildy, who finds herself amused by Walter despite her better judgment:

> BRUCE: You know, Hildy, he's not such a bad fellow.
> HILDY: No, he should make some girl real happy.
> BRUCE: Uh-huh.
> HILDY: *(to herself)* Slaphappy.
> BRUCE: He's not the man for you. I can see that. But I sort of like him. He's got a lot of charm.
> HILDY: Well, he comes by it naturally. His grandfather was a snake.

Once again, the presence of two bickering stars was highlighted in the film's ad campaign. "They're at each other's throats—when they're not in each other's arms!" one ad declared. "*The Awful Truth* didn't tell the half of what you gals can do to a guy!" another winked, as if the film offered handy torture tips for the romantically inclined. For all the film's adherence to the plot of *The Front Page,* for all its appropriation of dialogue and attitude, *His Girl Friday* is quintessentially screwball; what one remembers finally are the sparks generated between a man who's just a little smarter, just a little better-looking, than he should be, and a woman who equals him on every score.

In the face of such a rich, suggestive, and infinitely entertaining film, there's no chance of covering every detail. We'll leave aside, then, the whole issue of Earl Williams—the social vision his character helps to create, the morbid comedy he generates, and even the way his famous seclusion in the newsroom's roll-top desk becomes for Hildy and Walter a refracted symbol of the deep romantic feelings they dare not expose for fear of destroying their own emotional safety. It's all taken directly from *The Front Page,* but it means something very different in the context of screwball love. And we'll also simply note in passing another instance of Hecht's racism: Earl Williams is to be killed because the man he shot "happened to be a colored policeman" and "the colored vote's very important in this town." Finally, a number of perceptive critics—Molly Haskell, Tom Powers, and others—have noted the film's ambivalence toward Hildy's sexual and professional equality, especially the way she's driven to tears at the end as a way of reasserting her traditional femininity. Like nearly every screwball comedy, *His Girl Friday* is much better at exposing social and sexual tensions than at resolving them, a quality that says as much about the nature of comedy as it does about Hollywood's inability to solve the world's problems.

Ultimately, what we remember best about *His Girl Friday* is the way Russell and Grant make their characters delight in nailing each other, together with the means by which they sustain, in such rarefied air, their exhausting and impossible relationship. Earl Williams is saved, Bruce is dispatched home to Albany with his mother, and in the final scene Walter and Hildy make plans for a two-week honeymoon in Niagara Falls. Walter is on the phone with Duffy, the managing editor, who tells him that a strike has broken out in Albany and they need a reporter to cover it. Lo and behold—Albany is on the way to Niagara Falls. "Ha ha ha!" Walter cries none too convincingly as he and Hildy head for the train. "What a coincidence!" It is nothing less than utopian to see such falseness reveal such truth.

Oscar: I could cut
my throat!
Lily: If you did, grease-
paint would run out of it.

John Barrymore and
Carole Lombard in
Twentieth Century

CHAPTER 8

Acting Up and Acting Out: Screwball Role Playing

EARNEST EXPERTS ON SOCIAL INTERACTION TEND TO ADVISE THE socially maladept simply to be themselves, as if unsatisfying realities are somehow enhanced and rectified by making them more real. Certain screwball comedies preach a different moral lesson: pretense can be a means of personal liberation.

Despite the seamless vision of reality Hollywood often tries to create, everyone knows that one of the movies' great pleasures lies in their obvious theatricality—the hyperrealism of Technicolor or the starkness of black and white, the startling perfection of stars' skin tones and the beautifully unnatural way they talk and move. Screwball comedies aren't alone in this. But in a way that remains peculiar to the genre, they heighten our awareness of style by wrapping themselves in a comically artificial atmosphere, with "artificial" used in the best sense of the word. It's the glorious, put-on spirit that enables Walter Burns in *His Girl Friday* to describe the Ralph Bellamy character as looking like "that fellow in the movies, you know—Ralph Bellamy."

Artifice is as basic to screwball comedies as blood is to slasher movies, but some films make this essential theatricality more apparent than others by having characters engage in role playing, acting, telling stories (or lies), and performing for the amusement (or horror) of their

OPPOSITE: John Barrymore as Oscar Jaffe in *Twentieth Century*. As director Howard Hawks described it, "I went up there and told him the story, and he said, 'Mr. Hawks, just why do you think I would be any good in this picture?' I said, 'It's the story of the greatest ham in the world, and God knows you fit that.' "

174

RIGHT: So much in love. Lily Garland (Carole Lombard) and Oscar Jaffe (John Barrymore) in Howard Hawks's *Twentieth Century*.

INSET: Lily keeps "cheap ham" Oscar from committing suicide and thus depriving the world of a genius.

it into her rear end. She screams, after which Hawks cuts elliptically to Lily accepting flowers from her many applauding fans.

Backstage, Lily, now a glamorous star, recalls the pin. "The sorrows of life are the joys of art," Oscar declaims, whereupon the two radically egocentric individuals descend into a highly hammy love scene.

Hawks cuts again to the future: it's suddenly three years later, and we're probably better off not having witnessed the acute self-absorption of the intervening years. The duo of Oscar Jaffe and Lily Garland is now an entrenched smash hit, and the mature Lily matches Oscar perfectly in ego,

"Repent, for the time is at hand": Etienne Girardot, who plays a chaotic little man who pastes threatening religious stickers all over the train, is accused by impresario/egomaniac John Barrymore in *Twentieth Century*.

temper, and sensibility. These are traits we see in displaced form when Lily reclines on her grandiose bed—a big, gaudy, tublike thing fashioned in the shape of a boat, with a cupid plunked felicitously on the bow.

Grounded on self-interest and propelled by greed, this relationship has reached an impasse: Lily wants to go to the Mayfair Club, and Oscar doesn't. "That's not love," Lily states, "it's pure tyranny!" Oscar concludes in an appropriately theatrical vein: "Our little comedy has ended, just as I knew it would," he announces, and begins playing a suicide scene at the window:

> LILY: *(alarmed)* What are you going to do?!
> OSCAR: Nothing . . . while you're here. New York. Ha! It received me once, when I came here as a little farmboy.

It will receive me again! . . . *(Lily is seen heading to the door on tiptoes.)* I remember many a winter's eve . . . Lily Garland! *(He whirls around, pointing.)* I haven't finished yet!

Psychologists might say that suicides—some of them, at any rate—are essentially self-centered acts, but Oscar's egomania is such that he cannot imagine the world carrying on without him and hence could never leave it of his own volition. As a result, his so-called suicide attempt, which wouldn't even work in a road-show production of Sardou, is directed not toward death but toward the curtain call he plans to take afterward. "You horrible fake . . . you cheap ham!" Lily cries, after which she slugs him.

Hitting Oscar, though a positive step, is

not enough to counter the maestro's emotional onslaught. Lily ends up in tears on the floor. She does make up with Oscar, but it's a short-lived reconciliation, for when we see her again, she's on her way —alone—to Hollywood. Upon hearing the news of her departure, Oscar, aware that an audience is present, reels backward, his eyes rolling up into his head, and gasps, "She's left me!" His associate, Oliver Webb (Walter Connolly), who has seen this sort of thing before, matter-of-factly says, "Say the word, O. J., and I'll kill myself." But Oscar has something else on his mind, namely an elaborate mad scene played for the assembled crowd. "Gone! Lily! Lily!" he cries. "How could you do it?!" He laughs maniacally, spewing hyperbole and suicidal threats, reeling into the backstage area where he dramatically confronts a huge poster for *Bride of Bagdad,* their upcoming production. "Mockery!

Mockery!" he yells, and proceeds to hurl cans of black paint at it. "Anathema!" Oscar roars, nodding to the classics and pointing at Lily's name. "No more Lily Garland! Wipe her off the face of the earth!"

It doesn't work. When we see him next, he's in despair, for his Lily-free production of *Joan of Arc* has bombed badly in Chicago. (It's at this point that the original Hecht-MacArthur play begins.) Oscar's assistant O'Malley (Roscoe Karns) puts their lack of success in stark historical terms: "The sheriff's been playing a very large part in our last four productions." Oscar, sunk low in Illinois, is forced to skip town disguised as a southern gentleman, and he embarks on the Twentieth Century Ltd. bound for New York. When he's finally safe in his compartment, he begins removing his elaborate makeup—including a fake nose, which

John Barrymore

John Barrymore, Walter Connolly, and Roscoe Karns make sure Barrymore's not dying in *Twentieth Century*.

183

Barrymore, the famous "Great Profile" (seen in profile), stretches to Pinocchian length just at the moment when Oscar announces that *Joan of Arc* had been the most artistic show of his career. "If I am a genius, Oliver, it's because of my failure," he declares grandly, sticking his finger firmly up his nostril. "Just remember that."

It's been said that because *Twentieth Century* takes place on a locomotive, the bulletlike speed of the film's narrative mirrors the train's action, but in fact the film is half-over before anyone gets on board the train. The first part of the movie can scarcely be said to meander, but the pace does pick up considerably once Oscar and Lily find themselves trapped on board the speeding Twentieth Century. This sense of terrible romantic confinement, more than the simple velocity of the comedy, is what *Twentieth Century* is ultimately about.

Oscar and Lily's eventual reconciliation (to use the word loosely) is mandated by Hollywood. Even today it's rare to see romantic leads break up permanently. We know they'll get back together, especially since they're stuck on the same train, so the question is *how*. Hawks, Hecht, and MacArthur provide several wild-card answers in the form of farcical characters who by their simple presence throw the story into chaos. First, there's a strange little man, Mr. Clark (Etienne Girardot, who originated the role on stage), who darts in and out of scenes plastering signs that read "Repent, for the time is at hand" on all the windows. Second, there's a troupe of actors from the Oberammergau passion play, actors who, like Oscar, are addicted to high spiritual drama. This abundance of religion suggests to Oscar not a spiritual reawakening, but a practical solution to his problems, a grand coming together of his emotional and artistic lives: he vows to produce the story of Jesus Christ dying on the cross for man's sins and rising on the third day into heaven. "At last," Oscar declares, comparing himself favorably with the King of the Universe, "I've found something worthy of me."

It's at this point that Hawks really pushes *Twentieth Century* into high cynical gear, with the actors ripping through dialogue so fiercely and plot developments coming so furiously that the comedy becomes dizzying. For reasons of romantic complication, Lily is given a new beau, a good-looking but bland type named George (Ralph Forbes). George doesn't know about Oscar, who has feigned a broken arm in a cheap play for sympathy, and when he finds out that Lily's ex-Svengali is the man consorting with Lily in her compartment, George goes berserk and rushes screaming out the door. "What an exit!" Oscar remarks approvingly, snapping the fingers of his "broken" arm. "Not a word! That's what we should have had in *The Heart of Kentucky,* when Michael leaves Mary Jo in the first act."

Later, there's an elaborate fake death scene —Oscar's, of course—which convinces Lily that she and Oscar still share the same big, vacant heart. And Oscar and Lily finally end up together again on the stage. "Now don't be nervous, child," Oscar says patronizingly. "You are Betty Ann, this ragged little thing they found wandering in the cotton fields. . . ." Oscar draws Lily a chalk line, and *Twentieth Century* ends to the tune of Lily's uncontrollable screaming. Superimpose this film's abrasive conclusion over the more benign ending of *It Happened One Night,* and you have a purely visual statement of the eternal romantic conflicts out of which screwball comedy was born.

TRAPPED WOMEN

*I*n looking back on the screwball era, we often remember seeing a certain type of independent, stylish, superbly self-possessed woman on screen. Some of the credit goes to the stars— women like Irene Dunne or Rosalind Russell, whose images reflect not just an individual personality, but a whole range of popular dreams. But our sense of female independence also stems from the nature of the stories these talented, carefully ac-

Carole Lombard

coutred women helped to tell. The screwball era was devoted primarily to battling couples, but there was a not-so-subtle thematic undercurrent that pinned their frustration on the smothering environment in which women found themselves. Trapped by sexual and social conventions that hadn't officially been labeled out of date, a number of female characters in the middle and late thirties were forced to pit their own nascent self-esteem against an entire way of life. When they won, they won big. One woman's liberation, seen on a movie screen, could be universal.

In two of Irene Dunne's screwball comedies, *Theodora Goes Wild* (1936) and *Joy of Living* (1938), the ability to *pretend* gives the heroines an added measure of courage; in each film, a woman is drawn to freedom by way of a strong creative sensibility. Few actresses were better suited to an image of personal liberation than Irene Dunne. Look at her Dixie Bell routine in *The Awful Truth*. Dunne's character, Lucy, comes totally alive when she performs the broad pastiche, and even though it wrecks her estranged husband's plans, he loves it. There's also a serenity to Dunne's face that supersedes the most unflattering comic situations in which she finds herself, a graciousness and warmth that helps her look composed even when her characters aren't. When she's trapped, as she is in the beginnings of both *Theodora Goes Wild* and *Joy of Living,* Dunne holds out the promise of hope. When she finally sets herself free, she's the essence of emotional peace.

Theodora Goes Wild, directed by Richard Boleslawski, is the story of a repressed New Englander named Theodora Lynn who writes a racy best-seller, *The Sinner,* under the pseudonym Caroline Adams. Jed Waterbury (Thomas Mitchell), publisher of the *Lynnefield Bugle* ("the pulse of Lynnefield") has serialized the novel, much to the dismay and outrage of the local literary society—of which Theodora herself is a member—and the group meets to plan a course of action. Rebecca Perry (Spring Byington), the town gossip, offers a

Theodora Lynn (Irene Dunne, *left*), author of a racy pot-boiler called *The Sinner*, is in reality a repressed New England church organist in Columbia's *Theodora Goes Wild.*

dramatic reading of what amounts to a titillating rape scene: *The Sinner*'s protagonist, Pamela (evidently the descendant of the long-suffering heroine of *Pamela,* Samuel Richardson's 1740 novel), tries to escape a man's advances, "but her brain was reeling with drink!" Rebecca's performance is hilariously enthusiastic, and the society votes overwhelmingly to condemn the book. "If civilization is like what Caroline Adams writes about," says Theodora's prim aunt, "it's best that our children do *without* civilization."

Boleslawski and screenwriter Sidney Buchman have not yet revealed that Theodora is in fact Caroline Adams, although the question is answered by several close-ups and medium shots of Irene Dunne looking nervous and uncomfortable at the literary society. The actual revelation occurs a little later in the New York offices of Theodora's publisher, Arthur Stevenson (Thurston Hall), when a secretary announces the arrival of Caroline Adams and the camera pans from Stevenson to Theodora standing in the doorway. Theodora, caught between her career and her way of life, bitterly regrets the career. "I thought it was just romantic," she says of *The Sinner*. "I must have been out of my

In *Theodora Goes Wild*, Irene Dunne attempts to escape from Melvyn Douglas's chic New York apartment. Note the snazzy built-in radio in the banquette.

Irene Dunne (wearing yet another in a series of extravagant Bernard Newman gowns) and Robert Greig in *Theodora Goes Wild*.

Ages" on the church organ in Lynnefield.

In pursuit of Theodora, the free-spirited Michael arrives in Lynnefield and causes several public scenes, the best of which occurs when he hitches his little dog Jake to a lawnmower in the Lynns' front yard and makes the dog pull the mower like a mule. But the real shock is Theodora's discovery that Michael is married; it seems that Michael, like Theodora, is held at bay by misplaced propriety—in this case, his politician-father's demand that Michael not get divorced until the end of his term as lieutenant governor.

Having been freed by love, Theodora takes it upon herself to force a similar liberation upon Michael by going on a scandalous rampage. She moves into Michael's apartment. She reveals that she is Caroline Adams. She holds a press conference and tells "the modern girl to break out, be free, be independent" (although she herself repeatedly ignores the lone female reporter in the group). She is named as corespondent in Michael's wife's divorce suit. Michael is outraged: "I could kill that woman with my two bare hands!"

The Lynnefield ladies are aghast—Boleslawski goes so far as to intercut close-ups of cats with shots of the women gossiping—but as one might suspect, it all works out for the best. *Theodora Goes Wild* gets somewhat out of hand by the end, because of a subplot about Rebecca Perry's pregnant daughter, Adelaide, whom Theodora has been secretly protecting in New York. When Theodora steps triumphantly off the train in Lynnefield in the final scene, she's carrying a baby. Everyone's quite shocked and confused by the infant's existence—even Michael, whose credulity is so great that he suddenly believes Theodora has been pregnant all through the last few reels. "It isn't mine, stupid—it's Adelaide Perry's!" Theodora informs him, whereupon gossipy grandma Rebecca gets her comeuppance and faints.

After *Theodora*, *Joy of Living* is a letdown. As a matter of fact, it's a letdown all by itself. It's

mind." Given the torrid passages we've heard, she's right, though it's worth noting that the film pins the insanity directly on the everyday repression of small-town American life.

Screwball relief comes in the form of Theodora's love interest, Michael (Melvyn Douglas), *The Sinner*'s jacket designer, whom she dislikes immediately. When Stevenson invites her out to a Swedish restaurant, Michael crashes the dinner and makes an obnoxious nuisance of himself. It's a beautiful Depression-era scene: in tracking shots, Boleslawski films Theodora and Michael walking along the multitiered smorgasbord, the camera on one side of the food, the characters on the other. As if the potential romance of Irene Dunne and Melvyn Douglas weren't enough of a come-on, the audience's desire is pumped up to the drooling point by the abundant display of food in the foreground.

Michael convinces Theodora to have a drink. She has many, and they end up in Michael's high-style apartment where a wall of glass bricks, a circular window, and a built-in banquette with zebra-skin pillows tell us that Theodora isn't in Lynnefield anymore. Unfortunately, they (and Michael's romantic advances) have the same effect on Theodora, who panics and rushes out, after which Boleslawski cuts to Theodora playing "Rock of

not Dunne's fault that *Joy of Living* is actually pretty joyless. Lacking *Theodora*'s clever story line, *Joy of Living* goes through the motions of screwball comedy without ever engaging its spirit. In *Joy of Living,* which was directed by Tay Garnett for RKO, Dunne plays a successful Broadway actress, Margaret Garrett, whose prosperity is tempered by the grasping, dull-minded, and above all abundant family with whom she lives. Mom (Alice Brady), Dad (Guy Kibbee), sister Salina (Lucille Ball), Salina's husband (Warren Hymer), and their two daughters and newborn infant make Maggie pay dearly for her success. Not only do they share her living quarters in grand style, but they're also adept at hurling a lot of guilt Maggie's way. As they're the first to tell

her, Maggie's parents gave up their own acting careers to focus on Maggie's. And poor Salina can't develop her own talents because she's always in her famous sister's shadow. This is a group of deadbeats, all of them, a fact of which Maggie seems vaguely aware, yet she remains bound to them in a drab reverie of self-abnegation until the devil-may-care Dan (Douglas Fairbanks, Jr.) pops uninvited into her car one night after a performance.

Joy of Living embraces the idea of utopian escape popular in the late thirties, the pleasant notion that the best way to deal with an overcomplicated life is to run swiftly away from it. In *You Can't Take It With You,* resolving dissatisfaction means casting off such burdens as jobs and taxes and be-

Theodora (Irene Dunne), holding a baby (someone else's), makes her triumphant return to Lynnefield at the end of *Theodora Goes Wild*.

coming a dilettante. In *Joy of Living,* it means running off to a dreamboat's yacht. But while the pure escapism of *You Can't Take It With You* is tempered by the creation of a minicounterculture in the Vanderhof household, happiness in *Joy of Living* simply means getting the hell out. Maggie is given no choice other than vanishing; the film ends with Maggie abandoning her own career and completely accepting Dan's do-nothing-but-be-happy idyll. Theodora embarks on a journey of self-discovery; Maggie, on the other hand, takes so long to figure out what's wrong with her life that by the time she finally gets what she wants, she's lost her audience.

SOMBER SCREWBALLS

As *Joy of Living* goes to prove, theater people are able to symbolize the benefits of deceit only in certain contexts; there must be an underlying comic sensibility beneath the greasepaint—one that appreciates the essential comedy of playing roles. Without this skewed core of irony, the liberating value of performing is lost, and theatrical comedy slips into theatrical melodrama.

By the end of the thirties, screwball attitudes had thoroughly saturated screen comedy, and the assumptions about love that had originally spawned a genre full of maladjusted couples had begun to inflect films that might otherwise have been made as melodramas. In S. N. Behrman's original stage play *No Time for Comedy,* the marriage of a playwright to an actress is rarely played for laughs. Individual lines are funny, but the situation is treated with too much inherent reason to be screwball. But by the time the property was filtered through Warner Brothers to the big screen, *No Time for Comedy* (1940) chronicled the turmoils of a standard, though dampened, screwball couple—a gawky, naive playwright named Gaylord Esterbrook (James Stewart) paired with a Broadway star, Linda Paige (Rosalind Russell).

Beyond being a matter of style, the split between lighthearted comedy and supposedly weightier drama supplies the plot of both the play and the film. Gaylord, convinced that his talents as a comedy writer are superficial and out of place in an era of widespread poverty and impending global war, embarks on a neurotic odyssey to become a serious dramatist. In the play, he's a sophisticated, brooding genius; the role was originated by Laurence Olivier, with Katherine Cornell starring as Linda. The film, by contrast, begins solidly in screwball comedy, turning later into a hybrid of comic scuffles and tortured histrionics. In the film, Gaylord is a hick from the Midwest, a change prompted not only by the casting of James Stewart in the role, but also by the generic imperatives of screwball comedy, rules that dictate the couple shouldn't be suited to each other in an obvious way.

As he evolves from gangling innocent to adulterous martinet, Stewart's Gaylord makes an unusually vicious husband. In the second half of the film, Stewart tears into his role the way his character tears into his wife, rollicking in the zealous abuse that other actors, given the chance, might have been likely to mute with touches of easy charm. With such explicit nastiness, *No Time for Comedy* might have worked as a means of exposing some of screw-

OPPOSITE: In *Joy of Living,* Maggie (Irene Dunne) can't get rid of Dan (Douglas Fairbanks, Jr.), who follows her by riding on the back bumper of her limousine.

Nervous playwright Gaylord Esterbrook (James Stewart) prepares for opening night in *No Time for Comedy,* a stage drama that turned half-screwball when it was adapted for the screen.

Vivacious Lady: James Stewart, heir-apparent to a college presidency, has the bad taste to fall in love with vulgar showgirl Ginger Rogers. Everybody at the college treats Ginger with condescension and contempt —until she proves she's better than they are.

ball comedy's most bitter foundations, but it succeeds only halfway, since the sexual antagonism between Gaylord and Linda is actually much richer when conveyed through screwball's language and conventions. In terms of justifying comedy in a dark world, Preston Sturges achieved greater depth working along similar sociological lines the following year in *Sullivan's Travels* (1941). Still, *No Time for Comedy* has flashes of insight into the future of romance in an increasingly discouraging age. In one memorable scene, financier Philo Swift (Charles Ruggles), whose bombshell wife (Genevieve Tobin) is having an affair with Gaylord, sits staring at six glasses of straight Scotch as Linda approaches seeking help. "Don't bother me," he snaps. "I'm praying."

Barely comical and even more remotely funny is *Eternally Yours* (1939), a tale of marital turmoil directed by Tay Garnett. *Eternally Yours* has one bizarre distinction: this is a film in which ultra-religious Loretta Young plays a bigamist. Although its story line might have worked as a blueprint for screwball comedy, *Eternally Yours* is played as melodrama. Anita (Young), the granddaughter of a bishop (C. Aubrey Smith), marries "the Great Arturo," a magician/escape artist whose real name is Tony (David Niven). She builds a house in Connecticut, but he refuses to move in, so she gets a quickie Reno divorce and immediately marries a dull businessman named Tom (Broderick Crawford). Proving his superior wit and charm, Tony wins back Anita, and their unlikely marriage is restored, but not before the bishop—quaintly called "Gramps"—discovers that Anita's divorce "is not worth the paper it's written on." "But you wouldn't dare tell anyone! It's bigamy for Anita!" squeals Aunt Abbey (Billie Burke). "It's a pity you're not too old to spank, Abbey, or are you?" the bishop replies broad-mindedly.

In terms of love and frustration, *Eternally Yours* is like a number of screwball films, particularly those involving performers. Nevertheless, the film provides a great example of how a screwball-like story can wind up as melodrama. First, neither Garnett nor screenwriters Gene Towne and Graham Baker concern themselves with irony. They reveal nothing about the characters' emotional states that Tony and Anita don't already perceive themselves. The couple remains solidly in love until the very moment she leaves him, a departure occasioned by a single pointless argument rather than by an ongoing battle of wills and wits. Garnett does comment on the relationship at one significant moment—he dissolves from a shot of Tony's wrists struggling with a pair of handcuffs to a shot of Anita fidgeting with her wedding ring. The same device could have been used in a screwball film, except of course that the expressive point would be exactly the opposite. In screwball comedies, discomfiting bondage occurs between people who are in love, whereas in this case Anita is married *to the wrong man* at the time, thus making Garnett's equation of handcuffs and wedding rings the stuff of melodrama, not screwball comedy.

DRUM BOOGIE

Performing means having enough fluidity of character to change—to adopt another persona for the duration of a play or nightclub act, or else just to reveal an aspect of your personality that hadn't had the chance to show off before. A naturally resilient character like Theodora Lynn is able to cast off social constraints and personal inhibitions with relative ease, but more typical are those tense, unsupple types—David Huxley in *Bringing Up Baby,* Hopsie Pike in *The Lady Eve*—whose metamorphoses need to be forced.

In screwball comedies, as in life, it has often been fun to ridicule academics as stuffy, to depict their research as the thick and impenetrable product of repression and their solitude as a terrified refuge against sex—as if, say, businessmen and machinists were well-adjusted libertines by contrast.

Academics can be grateful, at least, that screwball comedy grants these crusty young scholars an opportunity to transmute and grow by forcing them to gravitate (often unwittingly) toward a beautiful performer, an image of liberation and sexual release.

George Stevens's *Vivacious Lady* (1938) and Howard Hawks's *Ball of Fire* (1941) are two such comedies in which freewheeling nightclub singers are pitted against men who are frozen in place by book learning. Stevens, a more leisurely comedy director than Hawks, takes pains to keep his film from becoming frenzied, but that's not always such a good idea in a screwball comedy. Maybe it's more accurate to say that *Vivacious Lady*—like George Cukor's *Holiday* (1938) and *The Philadelphia Story* (1940)—is really a straight romantic comedy enhanced by a few screwball situations. The film begins—after a lovely credits sequence in which all the names are etched onto a revolving glass hat rack—

in a New York nightclub, where Professor Peter Morgan (James Stewart) is enjoying the show. After the flashy Francey LaRoche (Ginger Rogers) finishes her song (which ends with the subtly brutal line "you'll be reminded of me—and I'll be laughin'!— you'll be reminded of me"), Peter explains his fascination with Francey in simple academic terms. "It's just a matter of chemistry, see? Anodes attract cathodes."

Given the straightforward differences between them, Francey and Peter might make a good screwball couple. The only trouble is that Peter falls totally, gushily in love with her on first sight and thus ruins the requisite hostility and distress in which they ought to founder. What saves him—and the comedy—is that he's already engaged to the dull, respectable Helen (Frances Mercer). Moreover, his parents are predestined by social as well as artistic conventions to hate the idea of a showgirl

Prof. Bertram Potts (Gary Cooper) examines Sugarpuss O'Shea (Barbara Stanwyck) in *Ball of Fire*, as Profs. Jerome (Henry Travers), Peagram (Aubrey Mather), Gurkakoff (Oscar Homolka), Quintana (Leonid Kinsky), Magenbruch (S. Z. Sakall), Robinson (Tully Marshall), and Oddly (Richard Haydn) look on.

FEATURE PRODUCTION

Snow White and the Seven Encyclopedists: Seven of the eight eccentric professors who have set up house together in Howard Hawks's *Ball of Fire* (Gary Cooper is missing) pose under their inspirations. *From left to right:* S. Z. Sakall, Leonid Kinsky, Richard Haydn, Henry Travers, Aubrey Mather, Tully Marshall, and Oscar Homolka. Like the Vanderhofs in Frank Capra's *You Can't Take It With You*, this little "family" lives in a world of its own creation in the middle of Manhattan.

daughter-in-law, particularly since it's assumed that Peter will one day take over the college presidency from his portly, patrician father (Charles Coburn).

Apparently governed by dynastic rule, Old Sharon College is the essence of Hollywood's vision of higher education. It's where people go to learn good taste. The ongoing presence of Francey, supposedly the height of vulgarity, is the film's "problem." But since she's played by Ginger Rogers in the thick of her wholesome late-thirties code-embracing God-and-country period, Francey's not much of a problem at all. Her best comic scene occurs when she finally decides to slug it out with her rival, Helen. They slap, kick, and wrestle each other to exhaustion, in the process drawing poor President Morgan into the fray when Francey punches him in the jaw.

Aside from this refreshing melee, the best moment comes in the form of a tossaway comment delivered by a minor character—Hattie McDaniel as, of course, the maid. Responding to the gender battles being waged between President and Mrs.

Morgan (Beulah Bondi), a marital Hundred Years' War that centers all too simplistically upon the husband's ban on cigarettes, McDaniel flatly declares, "If my husband wouldn't let me smoke, I'd find me a way to get a husband that would!" We're lucky most screwball characters aren't as self-motivated. Had they been as direct in their desires as McDaniel, the whole genre would have gone down the drain.

Ball of Fire, made three years later, sticks closer to the generic convention of a hostile, mismatched central couple, and the result is a better, funnier film. Hawks and screenwriters Charles Brackett and Billy Wilder create a female nightclub singer who is (in Hollywood terms, at least) deeply, enthusiastically vulgar. Instead of dropping this slinky, bare-midriffed gangster's moll into an instant love affair, they hurl her into an absurd situation—a house full of fogies who are spending their lives writing an encyclopedia. Led by Professor Bertram Potts (Gary Cooper), these academics are a quaint, endearing group: Professors Gurkakoff, Jerome, Magenbruch, Robinson, Quintana, Peagram, and, wonderfully, Oddly (played by assorted characters from Oscar Homolka to Richard Haydn).

The film begins with a prologue: "Once upon a time—in 1941, to be exact—there lived in a great, tall forest—called New York—eight men who were writing an encyclopedia." When we see them trooping through Central Park on their daily constitutional, the inspiration for their characters becomes clear; these earnest little men look and act very much like Disney's seven dwarfs. When she careens into their lives and ruins their scholarly concentration, Sugarpuss O'Shea (Barbara Stanwyck) is their eye-popping Snow White.

The professors are working on the letter *S;* Potts has just finished the entry on slang. After a garbageman barges in asking for help on a "quizzola," Potts realizes that he's out of touch, that all of his examples are out of date, so he ventures out into the world in search of new words. Wisely, he chooses a jazz club where Gene Krupa and his band are playing. Sugarpuss is Krupa's singer, and she does a number called "Boogie." From Prof. Potts's perspective, the lyrics couldn't be more meaningful: "drum boogie, drum boogie, drum boogie-woogie." Potts has hit paydirt. The problem is that Sugarpuss has to go on the lam because her boyfriend Joe Lilac is being held for murder; as Lilac's henchman Pastrami (Dan Duryea) tells her, she'd better beat it "before they slap a 'supeeny' on ya!" Potts appears and tries to get her to agree to an interview, but she's got an impending supeeny on her mind. "Scrow, scram, scraw," Sugarpuss says as she shuts the door on him; "The complete conjugation!" cries Potts.

When Sugarpuss discovers that Pastrami's idea of a hideout is a rat-infested warehouse, she decides to take Potts up on his offer. "This is the first time anybody moved in on my brain," Sugarpuss explains as Potts shows her into the professors' musty-looking Victorian living room. "Say," she says, "who decorated this place—the mug that shot Lincoln?" Potts, thrilled as he may be at the discovery of such a linguistic specimen, is uncomfortable about the idea of Sugarpuss spending the night. She responds by asking him to examine her throat. "It's as red as the *Daily Worker* and just as sore," she notes. The professors allow her to stay. Next thing you know, she's calling Prof. Potts "Potsy" and trying to seduce him, mostly because she needs to stay a few more days than she originally planned.

By the end of the film, the house has been thrown into anarchy not only by the incursion of sexual passion, but also by crime—the professors have been subjected to the indignity of being held at gunpoint by Pastrami, and Sugarpuss has been whisked away to marry Joe Lilac to keep her from being able to testify against him. Sugarpuss and Potsy do wind up together, but Hawks, Brackett, and Wilder are too smart to reduce their relationship to a formulaic brainy-guy-awakened-by-sexy-girl explanation. Potts changes Sugarpuss as much as she changes him; by falling in love with the bumbling Potts, Sugarpuss comes to understand that men don't have to be as brutish and manipulative as the crooked Joe Lilac. Under the strain of love, Sugarpuss's tough-talking performance style is revealed to be just that—a defensive snow job designed to protect herself from men who take advantage of her. Potsy is different; as she puts it, "He looks like a giraffe, and I love him."

WALK LIKE A MAN, TALK LIKE A WOMAN

*W*ith women storming the workplace and old codes of sexual behavior collapsing, the time was ripe for comedies about conflicting sex roles. "Boss lady" comedies like *Third Finger, Left Hand* (1940) and *Take a Letter, Darling* (1942) made fun of women for acting too much like men. But the broadest, most tasteless treatment of this nervous sex-change humor came at the hands of producer Hal Roach in *Turnabout* (1940). Here,

Barbara Stanwyck

Carole Landis and John Hubbard beg forgiveness from the genie who gender-switches them in Hal Roach's bizarre marital farce *Turnabout*.

husband and wife turn biology itself on its head. A bizarre statue of a genie, from its position at the foot of their bed, has overheard one too many fights between ad executive Tim Willows (John Hubbard) and his wife, Sally (Carole Landis). So when he hears them arguing over who could do a better job in their respective roles as husband and wife, he switches them. They *become* each other, literally. Sally acquires Tim's deep, manly voice while Tim suddenly talks like Sally. Sally's dressed in Tim's pajamas; Tim ends up in Sally's negligee. Sally becomes butch; Tim swishes around with a flop-wristed hand attracted as if by magnetism to his hip. "If only we'd kept on fighting!" Tim moans breathily in Sally's voice.

Turnabout treats the issue of sex roles in a particularly panic-stricken manner, especially at the very end of the film. It might seem impossible for a comedy animated entirely by male-female voice dubbing to become even *more* anxious. But it isn't. After slogging through this whole warped story—

with digressions provided by Adolphe Menjou as Tim's boss, Donald Meek as the couple's butler, and Franklin Pangborn as "Mr. Pingboom," a hosiery manufacturer—we wind up with Sally revealing that she's pregnant. The genie abruptly awakens and tells Tim and Sally that he's "made a terrible mistake." Yes, you guessed it—Tim is pregnant and the film abruptly ends, leaving the man distraught and with child.

Cross-dressing, a less drastic measure than male pregnancy, crops up more often. Cary Grant goes from a chic dressing gown in Hawks's *Bringing Up Baby* to a shapely WAC uniform in Hawks's postwar screwball comedy *I Was a Male War Bride* (1949) and then to a ritzy Persian lamb jacket in Hawks's still-later fifties screwball *Monkey Business*. Grant wasn't alone. Melvyn Douglas gets himself into a Mother Hubbard and gray wig in *The Amazing Mr. Williams* (1939), and William Powell dolls himself up in makeup, wig, and a prissy lace-embroidered blouse in *Love Crazy*. But there seems to have been something particularly compelling about the image of Cary Grant in drag—especially for Howard Hawks, who uses cross-dressing both to humiliate and liberate his star.

Of all Hawks's comedies, *I Was a Male War Bride* is in many ways the most brutal. It was also one of his most commercially successful films—the third-biggest money-maker of 1949. *I Was a Male War Bride* is the tale of a French officer, Henri Rochard (Cary Grant), who marries Lt. Catherine Gates (Ann Sheridan), an American officer, in Germany after the war. Caught in military red tape, which is based on the premise that all soldiers are men and all foreign spouses are women, Rochard is repeatedly ridiculed as a sort of joke on nature. There are no provisions for those who don't conform to expectations, and simply getting by requires an extraordinary effort. Rochard has to be on his toes at all times; for instance, when he's sitting in an enormous hall surrounded by hundreds of other "war brides," he hears over the loudspeaker a short orientation speech wherein the ladies are informed of fashion's return to the "natural bustline." Although he's still dressed as a man at that point, he quickly moves his wallet from his jacket to his hip pocket, just to be on the safe side.

In the first half of *I Was a Male War Bride,* Rochard is dominated by Catherine, Hawks's vision of the aggressive postwar American woman. Unlike many comedies in which women are eventually paid back for their modernity, *I Was a Male War Bride* is happy to leave Catherine on top and to move on in the second half of the film to a new series of devastating assaults on masculinity, this time at the hands of the state. There is, for example, no place for Rochard to sleep. The women's quarters are off limits, he's not an American officer and therefore can't sleep with the Americans, there's no room anywhere else, and thus Rochard is driven to complete exhaustion and frustration. And the worst is yet to come: Henri Rochard cannot get aboard the ship that will take him to America unless he transforms himself into a WAC named "Florence," complete with a hairpiece made—hideously, with all the worst implications—out of a horse's tail.

Rochard is an anomaly to the American officers he comes up against, but he isn't one to Hawks. For Hawks, he represents modern masculinity. Like a number of other screwball comedies, the humor in this film has a disconcertingly inevitable flavor. It might be painful for Rochard to make himself up into a woman, but it's *necessary.* What makes it particularly funny is that while Grant's own physical beauty is maintained even while he's stuck in *Bringing Up Baby*'s dressing gown or *Monkey Business*'s fur jacket, in this case he makes an incredibly *ugly* woman. "Florence" is a hatchet face, pure and simple. For Grant, as it would be for any modern man, it's the final degradation.

Throughout the genre, the ability to perform leads to liberation as characters discover that pretense can be its own higher truth. Role-playing enables Theodora to go wild; it helps Bette Davis and Leslie Howard to rediscover their love for each other in *It's Love I'm After;* and it makes it possible for Cary Grant and Irene Dunne to fake their way back to two happy marriages. In Hawks's comedies, however, there's an overarching pessimism that qualifies whatever freedom performance can bring. *Twentieth Century,* after all, ends with Lily screaming. In a way, the final shot of *I Was a Male War Bride* spells out one of the genre's underlying ironies: as the boat enters New York Harbor, Rochard and Gates are seen embracing in their cabin with the Statue of Liberty out the porthole. The trouble is, the shot is cramped; they've been *confined* to this cabin for the whole voyage, and even the final image of America's great welcoming symbol is presented in the distance, circumscribed by the small round window frame. The image says volumes about Hawks's worldview, but for a genre characterized by pain and frustration, it's most appropriate.

ABOVE: *I Was a Male War Bride.* According to director Howard Hawks, Grant wanted to "be feminine," but Hawks told him, "We're not gonna do that. Just act like a man in woman's clothes."

Nick: I'm a hero.
I was shot twice
in the *Tribune*.

Nora: I read where you
were shot *five* times
in the tabloids.

Nick: It's not true. He
didn't come anywhere
near my tabloids.

William Powell and
Myrna Loy in
The Thin Man

CHAPTER 9

In the Dark: Screwball Mysteries

OPPOSITE: In *The Thin Man*,
Myrna Loy, wearing her mink
coat indoors because "it's so
pretty," regards William
Powell's entertainment—
shooting ornaments off a
Christmas tree—with mock
skepticism.

CREWBALL COMEDY'S SEMINAL YEAR, 1934, MARKED THE GENESIS OF one of the most peculiar but durable genre hybrids in cinema history—the screwball mystery, epitomized by *The Thin Man* and embodied by William Powell and Myrna Loy. Dashiell Hammett's novel was an immediate hit when it was published in January of that year. It was about murder, just as so many other detective novels had been about murder, but it featured a married detective who liked and loved his wife, who argued with her, made jokes with her, and drank (to excess) with her. Hammett's novel provoked controversy because of a certain risqué line of dialogue alluding to Nick's uncontrollable physical response to another woman, but the real draw of the *The Thin Man* was the sophisticated detective duo who figured out a crime and fought off modern angst as a team.

Still, no one suspected that the film adaptation, shot at MGM in eighteen days and released without unusual fanfare, would go on to spawn sequels, direct imitations, variations on similar themes, and even a kind of romantic ethos, a sensibility that would thrive wherever repertory theaters, late night television, or videotape stores kept *The Thin Man* alive. Sophisticated detective films had appeared before, and Powell himself had starred in a number of them (*The Kennel Murder Case,* 1933, being one of the best). But just as other heiress comedies

196

Detective-bibliophile Joel Sloane (Robert Montgomery) and his wife, Garda (Rosalind Russell), try to figure out who swiped the Shakespeare folio in MGM's *Fast and Loose*. Weirdly, as in the first Sloane screwball-mystery, *Fast Company* (in which Joel was played by Melvyn Douglas), sick laughs are generated when Joel gets shot in the seat of the pants and is forced to wear an inner tube.

Two more Sloanes: In the third and final Joel and Garda mystery, *Fast and Furious*, Ann Sothern and Franchot Tone were the wacky well-read detective team. Busby Berkeley directed the movie, which concerns a beauty contest sham and a number of assorted killings.

had paved the way for *It Happened One Night, The Thin Man*'s wit and charm both crystallized and revolutionized the concept, and screwball comedy and detective fiction suddenly found themselves speeding on the same track.

Although the title *The Thin Man* refers not to Nick Charles but to a wealthy inventor character named Claude Wynant (Edward Ellis), the film's vast commercial success led MGM to produce five subsequent Nick and Nora efforts, each with the words "Thin Man" in the title. Although reviewers were pointing it out as far back as 1936, it's still a little surprising to learn that the real "thin man," Wynant, necessarily has nothing to do with any of the sequels since he disappears in the first few minutes of *The Thin Man* and later turns up dead. In terms of the various sequels' titles and their meaning, the true "thin man" is at best a vague memory throughout the series. The title *After the Thin Man* (1936) is reasonable if obvious, but the bluntly named *Another Thin Man* (1939) marks a transition, with Nick officially beginning to take over the moniker himself. The shift continues with the ominous, inadvertently self-critical *Shadow of the Thin Man* (1941). And with *The Thin Man Goes Home* (1944), at last, the title actually pertains to the plot: Nick and Nora visit Nick's parents.

The series isn't over until the thin man

sings; the final entry, *Song of the Thin Man* (1947), concerns the murder of a musician.

Seeing the commercial potential of screwball mysteries, the other studios got into the act as well. Universal came up with *Remember Last Night?* (1935), with Robert Young and Constance Cummings; RKO matched Powell with Jean Arthur in *The Ex-Mrs. Bradford* (1936); Paramount did *True Confession* (1937) with Carole Lombard and Fred MacMurray; and MGM itself started a new series of its own in 1938 with *Fast Company* (followed by *Fast and Loose* and *Fast and Furious*, both in 1939).

Despite the obvious money-making attraction of *Thin Man* variations, the nearly inexhaustible volume of screwball mysteries produced in the period suggests a deeper, more essential meaning than simple studio copycatting. There were simply too many imitations to be considered mere imitations. In addition to the screwball mysteries already mentioned, there was *Star of Midnight* (1935), with William Powell as yet another suave alcoholic and Ginger Rogers as the girl who forces herself upon him. There was *Adventure in Manhattan* (1936), with Jean Arthur and Joel McCrea; *The Mad Miss Manton* (1938), with Barbara Stanwyck and Henry Fonda; and *There's Always a Woman* (1938), in which Melvyn Douglas and Joan Blondell star as detectives Bill and Sally Reardon. In 1939 there was *It's a Won-*

derful World, scripted by Ben Hecht and starring James Stewart and Claudette Colbert, and *There's That Woman Again,* with Melvyn Douglas reappearing as Bill Reardon—though "that woman" Sally wasn't played by Blondell anymore but rather by Virginia Bruce. Also in 1939 was *The Gracie Allen Murder Case,* with daffy Gracie paired with William Warren in a screwball mystery that was itself number eleven in a series of fifteen Philo Vance mysteries; four of the first five starred William Powell. The series had degenerated by the time Gracie entered the scene, though Gracie's *Murder Case* seems to have been the most broadly comedic; she's prone to calling the hero "Fido."

In addition, there was *The Amazing Mr. Williams* (1939), with Melvyn Douglas and Joan Blondell again—only this time they weren't reunited as Bill and Sally Reardon but as detective Kenny Williams and his girlfriend Maxine. One of the things that makes Kenny truly "amazing" is his captivating appearance dressed as a woman in order to catch "the Phantom Slugger," a violent masher. This film also features a nice parallel between courtship and incarceration when the unorthodox Kenny drags a tough-guy prisoner (Edward S. Brophy) along on a date, hoping to fix him up with Maxine's roommate. The mug knows he's getting out of jail for the occasion, but he rebels nevertheless. "Nothin' doin'!" he growls in protest. "I knows me rights! I don't have to take no blind dates!" There was *Mr. and Mrs. North* (1941), with Gracie Allen again, this time paired with William Post, Jr. Here, the mystery is set in motion by way of the genre's propensity for alcohol consumption: in the beginning of the film, Gracie goes to the liquor closet to fix her husband a drink, and a corpse tumbles out. Finally there was William Wellman's *Lady of Burlesque,* based on Gypsy Rose Lee's *The G-String Murders.* Barbara Stanwyck plays Dixie, a burlesque queen who solves the case of the strangled strippers; in this film Stanwyck sings the immortal "Take It Off the E-String, Play It on the G-String."

An unusually bug-eyed Joan Blondell examines some evidence with Melvyn Douglas in Columbia's screwball mystery *There's Always a Woman.*

Something evidently clicked between detective drama and screwball comedy. The studios couldn't make enough of them. Beyond money-making, the attraction of the two genres is indeed a mystery—the convoluted, intrigue-laden plots of detective dramas meshes well with the breezy irrationality of screwball heroes and heroines. In addition, murder-mystery tension undercuts the heroes' wealth while enabling them to solve the crime in luxury. In *The Ex-Mrs. Bradford,* for example, William Powell tells his loving ex-wife Jean Arthur why he has outfitted the apartment with his own private screening room. Tastefully hidden behind a painting is a projection booth operated by his droll butler, Stokes (Eric Blore), and it's been built because, as Bradford explains, "Stokes and I don't like to stand in line." Consider the effect of such a casual declaration of wealth on a film-loving Depression audience; consider also the fact that Bradford's ability to show himself movies is what ultimately enables him to solve the racetrack murders on which the story hinges.

But beyond money, style, and suspense, there lies a more fundamental connection between screwball comedy and detective dramas. To see it requires a double leap of faith. First, one must be able to assume that reading about detective films won't spoil the mysteries; readers can be assured

that no endings will be revealed in the following pages. Second, one must accept a grander, more fantastic premise—that the particular details of a seemingly obscure subgenre may reveal something universal, not only about the nature of all screwball comedies, but also about the irresistible sensation of love.

NICK, NORA, AND ASTA

One wonders that this young couple should bother about a baby when they have already such a pleasant dog." This was *New Yorker* critic John Mosher's contemporary response to *Another Thin Man,* the third film in the series. Mosher saw the trend. With each new *Thin Man,* MGM was progressively domesticating a couple whose popularity had originally been sparked by their clean disavowal of proper family values.

In *The Thin Man,* Nick and Nora Charles are introduced as two rich, well-dressed drunks who don't give a damn about much of anything—anything, that is, beyond their love for each other, for the high style in which they live, and for their clever dog, Asta. These are people who do what they want, no matter what the consequences. At one point, for instance, Nora is seen wearing a sumptuous full-length mink coat—indoors. "Aren't you hot in that?" Nick asks. "Yes," she answers, "I'm stifling. But it's *so* pretty." But as the series progresses, the double imperative of conventional marriage and childbearing increasingly blunts the Charleses' comic edge. It's one thing to marry Asta off in the first sequel, *After the Thin Man.* It's quite another to drag a human baby into the act in *Another Thin Man.* Although the scene in which a bunch of shady underworld goons arrive for Nick Jr.'s birthday party each equipped with a baby of his own is undoubtedly amusing—and it's especially funny if one recognizes Three Stooges luminary "Shemp" Howard in the crowd, baby in tow—the sophisticated bite of the comedy is lost in a wave of prescribed

domesticity. And it goes downhill from there.

The Thin Man begins with an admiring shot of Dashiell Hammett's book. The novel wasn't yet six months old when the film was made, but MGM's sense of literary merit demanded that the best-selling book, complete with the famous jacket photograph of Hammett leaning stylishly against a wall, be placed on a shelf next to those dim leather-bound volumes known collectively in Hollywood as "the classics." Director W. S. "Woody" Van Dyke, fortunately, was too smart to follow the credits' implicit call for literary pomposity. The movie's tone, while considerably softer than that of the book, is still light and spirited, and as far as the detective plot is concerned, Van Dyke, following

That screwball animal: Asta was perhaps the most prolific actor in the genre. In addition to his appearances as himself in the Thin Man series, he also played Mr. Smith in *The Awful Truth* and George in *Bringing Up Baby.*

OPPOSITE: Nick, Nora, and Asta, the essence of style.

ABOVE: William Powell and Asta attempt to revive Myrna Loy in *The Thin Man*, in which the stars reel through most of the film in either an alcoholic blur or a hangover.

Hammett's lead, doesn't really care who done it. Like Hammett's, Van Dyke's interest lies instead in elucidating a certain modern attitude, the sense of dizzy joy that smart people embrace in the face of despair.

The first shot of Nick Charles finds him at a bar mixing a drink, but here as elsewhere it's not what he's doing but *how*. The scene is a nightclub dance floor; the band is playing a jazzy tune. Van Dyke tracks his camera forward through the crowd of dancing couples until it reaches the bar, where we see Nick, his back to the camera, moving rhythmically to the music. He is not dancing. "In mixing," he notes to an assembled group of bartenders and waiters as he turns slightly to reveal a cocktail shaker, "the important thing is the rhythm. You should always have rhythm in your shaking. Now a manhattan you shake to a foxtrot; a bronx to two-step time. A dry martini you *always* shake to waltz time." Nick pours the drink out of the shaker and into a glass, which he places carefully on the waiter's tray. The waiter takes a step to the right and ceremoniously offers Nick the same drink. He accepts it with a slight bow and downs it quickly.

Later, when Nora has trouble falling asleep, Nick suggests that she take a drink. She declines, so he takes one himself. These are people who like to drink; indeed, what they like is to be drunk. But they're also people who *must* drink. For one thing, like screwball couples throughout the genre, Nick and Nora Charles are fundamentally different from everyone else on earth. Nora seems the happier of the two, Nick being much more overtly troubled, but neither of them is entirely able to relate fully to anyone else. For them, such alienation is best felt through a boozy haze.

Some screwball couples are made up of individuals who are themselves dissimilar, but Nick and Nora are meant for each other in a way generally reserved for star-crossed lovers or regular melodramatic fools. Theirs is an old-fashioned immutable romance, saved by a bracing dose of ideal-

At home with the Charleses: Asta plays hide-and-seek with some important evidence in _After the Thin Man._

an alcoholic blur—who is the series' archetypically clear-thinking crime solver.

There are some great dramatic moments in the series—especially James Stewart's performance as the Charleses' helpful friend in _After the Thin Man_ —but the secondary characters are more or less interchangeable. Who cares, for example, that veteran character actor Leon Ames plays two entirely different people in the course of the series—Edgar Draque in _The Thin Man Goes Home_ and Mitchell Talbin in _Song of the Thin Man?_ One barely remembers who Edgar Draque is during the course of his own plot. What's important instead is the Charleses' cool, gaily cynical behavior in the midst of rampant confusion and crime, an attitude that is repeatedly expressed through the series' main conventions: omnipresent liquor, Nick's lowlife friends, Nora's desire to help Nick solve the crime, and Asta.

In the first two films, Nick is drunk from beginning to end; the world would be intolerable for him otherwise. "Is he working on a case?" an acquaintance asks Nora. "Yes," she says. "What case?" "A case of Scotch." The Charleses are social people who know what to say and when, but look at their friends—shallow, rich partygoers on the one hand, and on the other the many disreputable former criminals Nick is constantly running into. Picture Nora graciously meeting somebody named "Creeps" in _Another Thin Man._ This one's been sent up the river by Nick; that one's a safecracker; so-and-so is a forger. The bellboy, casing the Charleses' room for an imminent theft, suddenly wheels around to face Nick, and the crook greets him as warmly as a fraternity brother.

Nora, meanwhile, because she seems Nick's equal in terms of both savvy and style, is invariably drawn to helping him solve the case at hand, a project Nick unsuccessfully tries to frustrate. In fact, the Charleses are such a great couple that one forgets sometimes just how unequal the relationship really is. In _After the Thin Man,_ Nick actually locks his wife in the closet to prevent her

ized normality: they _like_ each other. Rich and intelligent, fashionable and witty, Nick and Nora Charles don't have to play by anyone's rules but their own. In _The Thin Man,_ for example, it's Christmastime, and Nick happily engages himself in a game of shooting expensive ornaments off the tree. Nora scolds him, but we can tell by her expression that she enjoys the demolition as much as he does. In _After the Thin Man,_ Nora is at one point taken into police custody. Although she insists that she's Mrs. Nick Charles, the police don't believe her, and when they call Nick for verification, he tells them that she must be an imposter. With a look of great self-satisfaction and amusement, he slurs into the phone, "Better throw 'er in the fishtank 'til I get there." Nora is furious, but only to a point; the Charleses' marriage is a game freely played by both parties, and they both like the sport.

The detective stories at the heart of the _Thin Man_ series are almost entirely irrelevant. They're always confusing to follow, and some of them are downright strained, but that's the point. Strange as it may seem, what's happening simply doesn't matter in these stories, except insofar as it keeps us unsettled and perplexed. Ironically, it's Nick—who staggers through the first three plots in assistance. And finally, because they have their delightful dog, they have no need for a child—at least at first. Asta gives them all the companionship of a child with none of the fuss, and in his own doggy way, he's just as urbane as they are. These conventions are the basis of the series; without them *The Thin Man* and all five sequels would collapse under the weight of indecipherable plots.

Critics past and present almost always complain that the later *Thin Man* films suffer from artistic exhaustion. As long ago as the early forties, reviewers were declaring that these originally bright conventions had gotten "tired," that we'd seen the liquor and the lowlifes too often for them to be fresh. The same criticisms crop up today whenever the series is discussed, but the truth of the matter is precisely the opposite: beginning with *Another Thin Man,* the old conventions don't appear often enough, and in their absence the films lose their punch.

As a comic convention, Nick and Nora are too slick to have children; they have Asta instead. But following the old American cultural dictum that forces screen couples to bear children no matter who they are or what they desire from life, the Charleses get stuck with a little Hollywood baby in *Another Thin Man.* There, at least he's only a baby; by the time of *Shadow of the Thin Man,* some creative soul at MGM had unfortunately decided that Nick Jr. was old enough to be a little gentleman, the concept apparently being that two such sophisticated parents would produce a beaming, well-dressed child in the form of the intolerable child actor Dickie Hall. It wasn't a good idea. We first encounter Dickie walking through the park dressed in a little captain's suit complete with cap. It's the kind of outfit—and the kind of child—the earlier, truer Nick and Nora would have ridiculed, and their image suffers greatly because of it. To be fair to poor Dickie, this jarring lapse into insipid taste isn't all his fault; whenever we see him on screen, his squinty dimpled face bursting with baby fat and

Wit and Wisdom of <u>The Thin Man</u>

"*W*e had a *lovely* trip. Nick was sober in Kansas City."
Myrna Loy in *Another Thin Man*

NICK: You know that jockey Golez? The one that was caught throwing the fourth race? He was shot.
NORA: My, they're strict at this track.
William Powell and Myrna Loy
in *Shadow of the Thin Man*

NORA: Who is she?
NICK: Oh, darling, I was hoping I wouldn't have to answer that.
NORA: Go on.
NICK: Well, Dorothy is really my daughter. You see, it was spring in Venice, and I was so young I didn't know what I was doing! We're all like that on my father's side.
NORA: By the way, how *is* your father's side?
NICK: Oh, it's much better, thanks.
NORA: Say, how many drinks have you had?
NICK: This will make six martinis.
NORA: Alright, will you bring me five more martinis, Leo? Line them right up here.
William Powell and Myrna Loy in *The Thin Man*

innocence, we're certain that the tiny actor is doing precisely what he's been told. Come to think of it, Dickie's dull obedience only serves to further lower our estimation of his fictional parents. How could such fabulously unfettered people have borne *this?*

Strangely but mercifully, the writers of *The Thin Man Goes Home* did away with Nick Jr., though perhaps not in as happy and violent a way as they might have. Robert Riskin, Capra's frequent collaborator, co-wrote this one with Dwight Taylor, and he was far too skillful to permit an awful child to bring the film down. The Oscar-winning Riskin may or may not have had the clout to convince MGM that Nick Jr. was better off dead, but

we'll never know, for he chose an easier route. First, Riskin and Taylor retrieve some of the original spirit by having Nick and Nora wrap Asta in a baby blanket as a way of getting people in a crowded train corridor to move aside "for the mother." Later, Nora—finally acting like the kind of delightfully carefree mother she ought to have been all along—casually utters a single line of dialogue abut how they had left the kid at home because he so enjoys his school. That's the end of Nick Jr. for the duration of the film. The child does return for *Song of the Thin Man,* but his presence there isn't nearly as loathsome as it might have been, mostly because his final incarnation takes the form of Dean Stock-

The Thin Man Goes Home signaled a return to the original spirit of the series; the Charleses ditch their child at home and take a train trip—in the animal car—with Asta.

OPPOSITE: Nick, Nora, and Asta ponder the future, seen in insets. RIGHT: William Powell regresses to cope with baby William Anthony Poulson in *Another Thin Man*. LEFT: What a letdown to see Nick and Nora raise a child like Dickie Hall in *Shadow of the Thin Man*.

well, who—fortunately—actually could act.

Of all the problems that crop up in the *Thin Man*'s waning years, the most dreadful is the gratuitous temperance drive forced, one presumes, by MGM's morality monitors. Nick's incessant drinking keeps the first two films lightheaded in an appropriately disturbing way. He drinks because he's bored, because the world isn't a friendly place, because he's stuck with the nagging (if implicit) idea that he's been emasculated by his wife's enormous wealth, and because he doesn't know what else to do. Fictional alcoholism, in contrast with the genuine disease, can be great fun as a relief from anxiety, and indeed Nick's round-the-clock inebriation provides one of the series' best screwball themes. There's an element of madness and glee to it, and it's a constant source of unnerving humor. Evidently it was too unnerving for MGM's story department, which progressively downplayed both alcohol and glee and thus made Nick Charles, of all people, seem not only sober but *contented.*

Alcoholism, the central convention in the series, didn't get tired; it got cleaned up, watered down, and finally eliminated. It is impossible to believe until you see it on the screen, but Nick Charles, the greatest drunk in the history of the movies, drinks nothing but apple cider in *The Thin Man Goes Home.* In real life, the transformation of a drunken malcontent to a self-possessed man of the world is cause for celebration; in a series of dark detective comedies, it's deadening.

DYING LAUGHING

*M*ore bizarre than any of the screwball mysteries is Norman Z. McLeod's *Topper* (1937), in which the stylish and witty married couple at the film's center is not only screwy but dead. Screwball husbands and wives are always better-than-average mortals, but *Topper* takes this otherworldly quality and literalizes it midway through the film by killing

its fantastically wealthy protagonists and turning them into ghostly spirits. George Kerby (Cary Grant) is the largest stockholder in a bank; he and his wife, Marion (Constance Bennett), sail through life on a cloud of cocktails and irresponsibility until the day George drives his roadster over an embankment. It's a marvel of understated ghastliness when we see their contusion-free corpses lying next to the wrecked car. No slouches, the Kerbys then begin to float (thanks to process photography) in an even freer fashion than before.

"You know something, George?" Marion remarks just after they step out of their bodies. "I think we're dead." Like Nick and Nora Charles, the Kerbys aren't averse to new experiences, and they enter the afterlife without any of the fears that might trouble less sophisticated highway fatalities. At the same time, the Kerbys' death shocks them into a sudden awareness of morality. They realize that they haven't done any good deeds in their lives—

OPPOSITE: Bank president Roland Young receives a ghostly guest (much to his secretary's horror) in the supernatural comedy *Topper*, in which screwball couple Cary Grant and Constance Bennett return from the dead to do good deeds.

In *Topper Takes a Trip*, Roland Young confronts the spirit world in the form of Constance Bennett, courtesy of Roy Seawright's process photography.

and are therefore at risk of being barred from heaven—so they resolve to liberate their friend Cosmo Topper (Roland Young), the bank president, from his stuffy, overbearing wife (Billie Burke).

The Kerbys' plan might seem to work nicely as a screwball premise, for, after all, what could be more irrationally delightful than two style-conscious ghosts trying to right somebody else's ruined marriage? As it happens, though, this comedy makes sense only if one believes that the Ker-

bys' predeath existence is indeed empty and meaningless, and it's simply too much fun to be so. In other screwball comedies, the protagonists don't have to be paid back for their high living; their carelessness is itself redemptive. Here, however, they're *killed* because of it and forced to settle down and be good. It's sad to see such fine characters put to the service of a Sunday school lesson.

Topper was a most successful film commercially. Audiences loved seeing Cary Grant and Constance Bennett fading in and out of the image, automobile tires appearing to change themselves, and other spectacular instances of special effects cameraman Roy Seawright's handiwork. Two sequels soon followed, both sans Grant. In the first, *Topper Takes a Trip* (1938), Constance Bennett, Roland Young, and a ghostly dog named Mister Atlas cavort through Paris, where Topper has fled to obtain a divorce. By the time of *Topper Returns* (1941), Bennett, too, has departed, and a new ghost must be created; the lucky victim is Joan Blondell as a murdered woman who enlists Topper's help in finding her killer.

Neither of the *Topper* sequels has much to do with romance, and the screwball aspect of the original *Topper* disappears in a giddy stream of trick photography gags. Other comedies also skirted around the idea of love in death. If screwball comedy's premise is that people in love are essentially incompatible, these cross-mortality romances might have pushed it to a weird extreme. None of them did, probably because in this context the sexual sparks generated by screwball comedy would have played too close to necrophilia. In René Clair's *I Married a Witch,* Veronica Lake plays a ghost who first haunts then falls in love with Fredric March, a descendant of the Puritans who had burned her at the stake. In *Here Comes Mr. Jordan,* Robert Montgomery is killed because of the incompetence of angel Edward Everett Horton; since his own body has been destroyed, Montgomery is granted the chance to remain alive in someone else's. After one unsuccessful stint in the body of a man murdered by his wife, Montgomery takes over the form of a prizefighter and falls in love with Evelyn Keyes.

Ghosts, angels, and devils reappeared throughout the forties—*The Invisible Woman* (1941), *The Remarkable Andrew* (1942), *Heaven Can Wait* (1943), *The Canterville Ghost* (1944), *That's the Spirit* (1945), *The Time of Their Lives* (1946), *The Ghost and Mrs. Muir* (1947). . . . But their concerns were no longer screwball in nature. Like the second half of *Topper,* these were comedies about righting wrongs and earning places in paradise—the kind of bluntly moral issues that screwball characters blithely tend to put off for the rainy day that with any luck will never come.

CHAMPAGNE AND ASPIC

When we first meet Dr. Lawrence Bradford (William Powell) in *The Ex-Mrs. Bradford,* his butler, Stokes (Eric Blore), is offering a bottle of champagne for him to uncork. The sense of the scene is not one of celebration, but rather of routine —opening a bottle of champagne is obviously a daily ritual for Bradford, just as serving it is for Stokes, but this doesn't mean that it can't be done with style. Indeed, a crucial part of the ritual, as we quickly see, is for Bradford to fire the cork at a large Chinese gong, the sound of which signals, like bells in a Catholic mass, the presence of a felicitous governing spirit.

Bradford's divorced wife, Paula (Jean Arthur), interrupts the service; she glides in, kisses him warmly, introduces him to her nervous companion, and watches with great enjoyment as the little man serves Bradford with papers for nonpayment of alimony. Paula is a mystery writer—or so we're told, for we see no books and hear no titles or references to any previous publishing successes, though Bradford's proficiency as a doctor, in contrast, is altogether integral to the story. In any case, we're invited to see this couple as so complementary—he the rational thinker, she the intuitive imaginer— that they couldn't bear to live together and thus sought and obtained a divorce. And we know, as we know throughout the screwball genre, that for people such as the Bradfords, divorce is every bit as lousy as marriage.

The Ex-Mrs. Bradford goes through the motions of questioning the couple's eventual remarriage, with Bradford expressing some discomfort at Paula's conciliatory onslaught. But there's really no

Cary Grant

William Powell

doubt about the romance's conclusion, except for the fact that they're investigating the killing of a jockey and stand some chance of being killed themselves.

In the purest screwballs, the central narrative question is how, given the palpable irritation between the stars, the two lovers will finally get together, and the working-out of the story involves a certain anxiety: *maybe they won't.* Of course this is a more or less irrational fear, since genre convention is one of the few things on earth that adequately guarantees love. Yet the fear persists, perhaps because artistic conventions seem so fragile next to daily experience, and our ability to be sucked into the tenth, twentieth, or fiftieth movie plot is never really in jeopardy. In screwball mysteries like *The Ex-Mrs. Bradford,* some of this anxiety is displaced onto an apparently unrelated plot—who is the killer? what do the clues mean? who will die next? and will the heroes survive? Of these questions, the first three couldn't matter less. It's really the *sensation of doubt,* not the specific answers, that keeps our interest.

The primary mystery of *The Ex-Mrs. Bradford* involves a racetrack, some jockeys, some gelatin, and a black widow spider; the secondary mystery, the one found in nearly every screwball comedy, asks whether two people in love can endure each other. These two issues lock together in a marvelous scene in which Paula serves dinner. Ever inquisitive, Paula has analyzed the substance Bradford has found on the dead jockey's skin and discovered it to be gelatin. So as a way of experimenting to see whether gelatin really can kill, she fixes a meal for herself and her husband in which every dish is awash in aspic. The scene is quintessential Jean Arthur: there's no chance that simple gelatin could be dangerous, yet Arthur's gracious perseverance somehow convinces us—and Powell, judging by his expression—that it could be fatal.

As detective fiction, *The Ex-Mrs. Bradford* makes good enough sense and its action is ade-

quately paced, but one cannot look to it for coherent meaning—as with, say, *The Awful Truth*—as much as for the expression of a screwball sensibility, an airy charm maintained in the face of darkness and death. Films like *The Ex-Mrs. Bradford* don't have the strong, personal imprint of a talented director like Leo McCarey, and while we can see all kinds of cultural meanings in the frenetic behavior of men and women, these ideas never quite come together. Instead, what we see is the playing out of a certain mood that remains both comic and sad. We see two delightful, life-loving people struggling to maintain their balance together in a world of threats, violence, and unease. These are men and women who were made to live in a world far better than the one they're stuck in. It's a test of character, this endurance of reality, and only the good-natured survive.

Screwball codes of behavior stand on the idea that brutality should only be used sparingly and always in the service of a higher moral or emotional purpose. The killers and thieves who crowd the screwball-mysteries are craven; their goals—money, power, crude revenge—are crass. Screwball heroes and heroines are better; they know that the little cruelties they inflict upon one another are signs of love. All too often the pain is lopsided, with women getting more than their share. But if one is able to get beyond the standard sexism of the period, to imagine for a moment that the roles could be reversed, the dazzling style of the screwball way of life comes shining through. There's a moment in *The Ex-Mrs. Bradford* that says it all. Bradford, Paula, and Stokes, having adjourned to the morgue, are confronted with a cadaver on a slab. Paula immediately faints, and Bradford orders some assistants to haul her back to her hotel room. Later, he asks Stokes how Paula behaved once she regained consciousness and discovered she was no longer part of the action. Not well, Stokes answers. "Did you have to use force?" Bradford asks calmly, seeing it as a necessity. Stokes replies, "Only in a mild way, sir, and *always* with tact."

GETTING A LITTLE VIOLENT

*B*arbara Stanwyck, as the abominably named heiress Melsa Manton, is walking four tiny, pretentious dogs late at night on a New York City sidewalk. As if the toy pooches weren't bad enough, Melsa is wearing a capricious flowing cape that for some reason makes her look utterly contemptible in a winning sort of way. Suddenly, a man comes running out of a building. The intrepid Melsa investigates, venturing inside, but when she sees another man's corpse lying on the floor, she loses her cool and runs out onto the street shrieking at the top of her lungs, leaving her cape caught in the door.

This is the opening of *The Mad Miss Manton* (1938), a screwball mystery of the heiress-newspaperman school. Melsa, according to the cops, is "one of the bunch who held a treasure hunt last week and stole a traffic light." She's also been known to call a Bellevue ambulance upon the onset of a dog's illness. And now she's caught up in a murder. "Either your education or your spanking has been neglected," says the chief sternly. "Chief," says his underling, motioning with his gun, "why can't I use this, just this once?"

We then meet journalist Peter Ames, played as a perfect grouch by Henry Fonda. He's reading a newspaper account of Melsa's latest escapade, and he spells out the sociological irony behind those kooky "Park Avenue pranksters": "Wall Street has hit a new low, unemployment has hit a new high peak, an additional $4 million has been added to the budget. But Miss Manton and her ilk continue on their merry, million-dollar, ermine-lined way. Make a note—according to the police, Miss Manton's costume was fetching." Right on cue, Melsa rushes into the office, slaps Ames's assistant, and then defiantly slaps Ames himself. Ames slaps her on the back—"To complete the circle," he explains.

Madcap heiress Melsa Manton (Barbara Stanwyck) confronts newspaperman Peter Ames (Henry Fonda) with the morning paper in *The Mad Miss Manton*. Note the sensational and hilariously inappropriate headline.

Debutante detectives: Barbara Stanwyck surrounded by a gaggle of fur-draped fellow crime-solvers in *The Mad Miss Manton*.

Here we have them: heiress, dog(s), corpse, money, madcap attitude, newspaperman, irritation, and slaps—every critical element in a classical screwball mystery, briskly and, surprisingly, freshly introduced in the first few minutes of the film. It's 1938, the height of the screwball era. Everyone has seen this combination before, but it doesn't matter. *The Mad Miss Manton* is pure genre, and that's its strength. We later meet Melsa's ding-

James Stewart

bat friends. Swathed in furs and dripping in satin, they too are familiar, but instead of being tedious reiterations, they're strangely reassuring, seeing as we're now caught up in a world of sudden, violent death. Screwball style incarnate, these dizzy women are helping to investigate a killing, and they're doing it using the precepts of their class. "Look!" one cries. "I found a bloodstain!" "Oh, *how* can it be blood?" Melsa responds impatiently. "It's blue!"

Beyond the standard screwball conventions, *The Mad Miss Manton* has an underlying social awareness that sets it apart from many screwball comedies. There's a "forgotten man" character (John Qualen) who lives beneath the streets of New York in an abandoned subway tunnel, and at one point an angry fellow turns his ire on Melsa, barking, "I'm class conscious, see—I don't like society dames!" But the best lines of social awareness are delivered by two of the scatterbrained debs, who have the misfortune of walking into a standoff in which Melsa's life is hanging on a murderer's whim. "If you kill her," one of them declares bravely, "you'll have to kill all of us!" Her friend is terribly annoyed: "Oh, you're always talking communism!"

The tensions in this film aren't all so sociological. Henry Fonda, whose ability to suffer abuse at the hands of women was only equaled by that of Cary Grant, carries the brunt of the film's sexual jokes, and his precise expressions of male humiliation are both endearing and horrifying. At one point, Melsa and the other debutantes attack him physically; they wrestle him to the ground, tie him up, and gag him. Later in the film they repeat their victory, binding and gagging him once again. Even perennial maid Hattie McDaniel gets her licks in. At one point, Melsa's employee and ally hurls a pitcher of water in Ames's face, saying with peculiar logic, "It was orders—but I used distilled water."

Because Fonda is such a master of repressed fury, he makes an excellent screwball hero, bound up in a love relationship with a woman he despises. And because the sexual antagonism between Melsa and Peter is so intense, and because they play out their grating romance in the context of a murder mystery, *The Mad Miss Manton*'s anxiety level is abnormally high even for screwball comedy. There are times when one wishes they'd just get it over with and relax.

Having survived the literally deadly events of the film, the screwball couple is bound to each other like two disaster victims whose ordeal no one else has shared. And because it's a screwball comedy, of course, above and beyond the murder plot they are *themselves* the ordeal. Hear Fonda milk the following double-edged lines, leaning heavily, quirkily, on the word *insane:* "Listen, before I knew you I disliked you intensely. When I met you, I disliked you intensely. Even now I dislike you intensely. That was the sensible, sane portion of me. But there's an *insane* portion of me that gets a little violent every time I think of you!" The speech well describes both characters' reactions when Melsa, after pledging her undying love to Peter only to discover that he's deceived her, flies into a superb screwball rage and stabs him firmly in the rear with a fork—just to let him know that she cares.

SURVIVING

For the last eighty years, Hollywood has been reworking old scenarios, repeating stories with varying characters, telling the same stories over and over until the market is exhausted, at which point the stories reappear in new guises nobody recognizes. Reviewers bemoan it, as if they'd still have jobs in a world of pure originality, but repetition in the movies can be a pleasure in itself, especially when the ideas being repeated—love, hate, sex, death—are ones that can never be fully exhausted.

Seeing the 1939 *It's a Wonderful World* in the most ungenerous light, one could say that it's merely a detective-story remake of *It Happened One Night.* Written by Ben Hecht and directed by W. S.

Fugitive detective Guy Johnson (James Stewart) gets himself up as a myopic Boy Scout leader as he and poet Edwina Corday (Claudette Colbert) fitfully attempt to solve a murder in *It's a Wonderful World.*

Van Dyke, *It's a Wonderful World* stars Claudette Colbert as a runaway poet who gets caught up in the moral universe of a tough-talking man she initially fears and despises. The man, played by James Stewart, spirits her ungraciously away from the genteel life she has previously led, and he learns, after much hardship on the road, that she is his equal. They even play one scene Capra style atop a wooden fence.

It's a Wonderful World is a perfect genre piece. Every device has been seen somewhere else, every motivation is derived from past screwball history, and every attitude, far from being unique, comes across as shiningly typical. Hecht's appreciation of crime drama may be keener than that of other screwball screenwriters, and the cinematography is certainly darker than usual (especially for MGM), but what we see and hear beneath these tonal variations is pure generic compulsion, the repeated expression of romantic anger and ambiva-

lence. In all the great screwball classics, from *It Happened One Night* and *Twentieth Century* through *The Awful Truth* and *Bringing Up Baby* to *The Lady Eve* and *The Palm Beach Story,* comedy erupts out of the characters' ability to express love and anger simultaneously, to allow themselves to break through the codes of polite restraint and slug it out whenever their hearts grow too full of love. *It's a Wonderful World* isn't different in this regard, but like any good genre work, it's more than a simple restatement of what we already know. It's a *complex* restatement, an embellished working out of a timeless emotional problem, and it makes regular, recognizable sense of the contradictions of human experience in a way that only genre pieces can.

As a crime solver, Guy Johnson (James Stewart) has a problem: his former boss, the besotted tobacco heir Willie Heyward (Ernest Truex), has been framed for murder, convicted, and sentenced to die in the electric chair, all of which means

The owner of a summer theater is startled to find her new actor (James Stewart) with a knocked-out patron (Claudette Colbert) in *It's a Wonderful World.*

that Johnson will not collect the $100,000 that Heyward promised him if he nails the real killer. Moreover, Guy is himself on his way to prison, having been convicted of conspiracy after the police found him harboring the fugitive Heyward. Handcuffed to a guard and trapped on a train to Sing Sing, Guy notices a small personal ad in the newspaper that he recognizes as a major clue. The dead woman, a subdued floozy named Gonzalez, died clutching a half-a-dime charm that Guy is certain belonged to the real killer, Heyward's grasping bride. The personal, signed "Half-a-Dime," advises the reader to meet him at a summer-stock theater.

Movie buffs know—and screenwriting professors teach—that in the Hollywood cinema every protagonist has a clear and identifiable goal. Guy Johnson's is money. It's true that Heyward's life will be saved if he discovers the real murderer, but heroism is an afterthought. Guy wants cash, and he risks his own life to get it. Convincing the cop to whom he is handcuffed that it's time to stretch his legs, Guy leads the imbecilic symbol of social order to the door and hurls them both out the speeding train and into the river. He beats the cop to the point of unconsciousness, springs the handcuffs, and begins to make a getaway, but he is spotted—first by a yapping dog, and then by the talented poet Edwina Corday (Claudette Colbert), who instantly makes herself eligible for kidnapping.

This is what has long been known as meeting cute, but notice how screwball conventions toughen up the cuteness. Guy, disheveled and crazed looking, comes staggering out of the water like a homicidal maniac to meet the love of his life, who is terrorized. When Guy confronts Edwina, he immediately begins menacing her. Jimmy Stewart couldn't be better at conveying this sense of threat. His portrayal of reckless single-mindedness could work in any *film noir;* unlike other actors, he doesn't pull back simply because the film is a comedy. At this moment in the film, the impression Guy Johnson makes—on us as well as on Edwina—is that of

a scary, nasty psychopath, especially when he throws Edwina harshly into her own car and spirits her away to an unknown fate. "Are you 'taking me for a ride?!'" Edwina inquires in a panic as the car roars down the highway, and with this doubly funny and frightening line, their screwball love affair begins.

"I always thought criminals were gallant," Edwina shouts from the backseat, "but you've got a stupid, degenerate face!" Genre convention tells us that these two will eventually be locked together in love, so when Guy dumps Edwina in the middle of nowhere and speeds off alone, we know he'll be back. Soon enough, he hits a roadblock, returns, forcibly picks up Edwina, throws her even more violently into the car, and drives away, completely unaware that Edwina is about to set the car on fire. The car blows up, and Guy is enraged. "I never met a dame yet that wasn't a nitwit and a lunkhead," he yells. "Oh, *you're* bright," says Edwina, reacting badly to Guy's vocabulary. Guy then physically drags her through the woods in a scene of primordial conquest.

They reach an apple orchard. Since they've had nothing to eat for hours, Guy helps Edwina climb onto his shoulders to reach the apples, and Edwina, now in a position of authority, begins plunking Guy on the head with one apple after another. There is no chance of knocking him out, and Edwina knows it—the point is simply to torture him. Guy's limited patience quickly reaches its limit. *"I'm a detective!"* he barks, spitting a piece of half-chewed apple directly in her eye. "You're the most loathsome human being I ever met!" she says. "Same to you," he snarls.

In soft-headed romances, the principals are all too apt to believe that the purest expression of love is the coo. In screwball comedies, it's the shout and the slap, and while these romantic assaults are usually pumped up to comic proportions, they are evidence of great psychological health. Prevented by the Production Code from expressing human sexuality, screwball characters are in an unbearable emotional bind; if they were unable to express the rage they so abundantly feel, they'd go mad. They're teetering on the edge of sanity as it is— confronted by others they simply can't abide, gravitating toward these irritatingly attractive people against their will, finding their own individuality breaking down under the strain of someone else's. When we see and hear screwball characters berating, hitting, insulting, and denouncing one another, as we do in *It's a Wonderful World* and countless other comedies, we are witnessing personal liberation in its purest and most therapeutic form, the end of repression and the beginning of a healthy life. Their anger is real, and they express it *loudly*.

Screwball mysteries like *It's a Wonderful World* take bickering, distressed couples and pull them through a world of fear and death, darkness and confusion. But these mystery plots only literalize the sense of murky anxiety that permeates even the brightest screwball comedy. It's not just the comic abrasiveness of films like *Mr. and Mrs. Smith* or *His Girl Friday* that makes them seem tougher and sharper than other nonscrewball comedies. Men and women are literally killed in films like *It's a Wonderful World*. But in every screwball comedy, there's a deadness to the surrounding world against which the heroes and heroines raucously struggle. Throughout the genre, the world depicted isn't especially kind or generous. And we get the sense that people who can't allow themselves to experience the blasting emotional release that love offers are doomed to lives of tedium and premature death. The rage screwball characters feel for one another is the passion that keeps them alive.

Edwina Corday is not a great poet. Her most famous poem is just a few shaky steps up from doggerel, but what it says about screwball love is rather nice:

> The night will be here when we are gone.
> When we are gone, the stars will be here
> And other throats will sing in the dawn,
> It's a wonderful world, my dear.

Guy's response is quick and to the point: "I don't get it." Later in the film, she recites another poem about him, and he responds with greater enthusiasm—he punches her and knocks her out. Granted, Edwina's lyrics aren't very good, but what they lack in quality they more than make up for in truth. "It's a Wonderful World" is a poem about love and death. It's about a world of darkness made bright by men and women like Guy and Edwina. At the end, when the killer has been found and the many deceits Guy and Edwina have perpetrated against each other have served their purposes, Guy composes his own love poem. It's stupid but perfect:

> Roses are red
> Violets are blue
> I get a hundred grand for this
> But I want you.

They've done it. They've survived.

The Directors

RICHARD
BOLESLAWSKI
Theodora Goes Wild (1936)

EDWARD BUZZELL
Fast Company (1938)
Married Bachelor (1941)
Song of the Thin Man (1947)

FRANK CAPRA
It Happened One Night (1934)
Mr. Deeds Goes to Town (1936)
You Can't Take It With You (1938)
Mr. Smith Goes to Washington (1939)
Arsenic and Old Lace (1944)

JACK CONWAY
The Girl From Missouri (1934)
Libeled Lady (1936)
Love Crazy (1941)

GEORGE CUKOR
Holiday (1938)
The Philadelphia Story (1940)

MICHAEL CURTIZ
Jimmy the Gent (1934)

TAY GARNETT
Love Is News (1937)
Eternally Yours (1939)
Joy of Living (1938)

EDWARD GRIFFITH
Cafe Society (1939)
Honeymoon in Bali (1939)

ALEXANDER HALL
There's Always a Woman (1938)
There's That Woman Again (1938)
The Amazing Mr. Williams (1940)
Here Comes Mr. Jordan (1941)

HOWARD HAWKS
Twentieth Century (1934)
Bringing Up Baby (1938)
His Girl Friday (1940)
Ball of Fire (1941)
I Was a Male War Bride (1949)
Monkey Business (1952)

ALFRED HITCHCOCK
Mr. and Mrs. Smith (1941)

WILLIAM K. HOWARD
The Princess Comes Across (1936)

LEIGH JASON
The Bride Walks Out (1936)
The Mad Miss Manton (1938)
Model Wife (1941)

GARSON KANIN
Bachelor Mother (1939)
My Favorite Wife (1940)
Tom, Dick and Harry (1940)

WILLIAM KEIGHLEY
No Time for Comedy (1940)
The Man Who Came to Dinner (1942)
George Washington Slept Here (1942)

GREGORY LA CAVA
She Married Her Boss (1935)
My Man Godfrey (1936)
Fifth Avenue Girl (1939)

SIDNEY LANFIELD
Red Salute (1935)

WALTER LANG
Second Honeymoon (1937)

MITCHELL LEISEN
Hands Across the Table (1935)
Easy Living (1937)
Midnight (1939)
Take a Letter, Darling (1942)

ROBERT Z. LEONARD
After Office Hours (1935)
Third Finger, Left Hand (1940)

ERNST LUBITSCH
Design for Living (1932)
Bluebeard's Eighth Wife (1938)
That Uncertain Feeling (1942)

NORMAN Z. McLEOD
Topper (1937)
Merrily We Live (1938)
Topper Takes a Trip (1938)
There Goes My Heart (1938)

ARCHIE MAYO
It's Love I'm After (1937)

LEO McCAREY
Ruggles of Red Gap (1935)
The Awful Truth (1937)

ELLIOTT NUGENT
Three-Cornered Moon (1933)
It's All Yours (1938)
The Cat and the Canary (1939)

GREGORY RATOFF
Wife, Husband and Friend (1939)
Daytime Wife (1939)
Public Deb No. 1 (1940)

HAL ROACH
Turnabout (1940)

STEPHEN ROBERTS
Star of Midnight (1935)
The Ex-Mrs. Bradford (1936)

WESLEY RUGGLES
I Met Him in Paris (1937)
True Confession (1937)
Too Many Husbands (1940)

ALFRED SANTELL
Breakfast for Two (1937)
Having Wonderful Time (1938)

WILLIAM SEITER
The Richest Girl in the World (1934)
The Moon's Our Home (1936)
Three Blind Mice (1938)
Hired Wife (1940)

GEORGE STEVENS
Vivacious Lady (1938)
The More the Merrier (1943)

PRESTON STURGES
Christmas in July (1940)
The Lady Eve (1941)
The Palm Beach Story (1942)
The Miracle of Morgan's Creek (1942)
Hail the Conquering Hero (1944)
Unfaithfully Yours (1948)

RICHARD THORPE
Double Wedding (1937)
The Thin Man Goes Home (1944)

W. S. VAN DYKE
The Thin Man (1934)
After the Thin Man (1936)
Love on the Run (1936)
Another Thin Man (1939)
It's a Wonderful World (1939)
I Love You Again (1940)
Shadow of the Thin Man (1941)

RICHARD WALLACE
Wedding Present (1936)
The Young In Heart (1938)

WILLIAM WELLMAN
Nothing Sacred (1937)
Lady of Burlesque (1943)

WILLIAM WYLER
The Good Fairy (1935)

The Writers

GRAHAM BAKER
Stand-In (with Gene Towne, 1937)
Joy of Living (with Gene Towne and Allen Scott, 1938)
Eternally Yours (with Gene Towne, 1939)

CLAUDE BINYON
The Bride Comes Home (1935)
I Met Him in Paris (1937)
True Confession (1937)
Too Many Husbands (1940)
Take a Letter, Darling (1942)

CHARLES BRACKETT
Bluebeard's Eighth Wife (with Billy Wilder, 1938)
Midnight (with Billy Wilder, 1939)
Ninotchka (with Billy Wilder and Walter Reisch, 1939)
Ball of Fire (with Billy Wilder, 1941)
The Major and the Minor (with Billy Wilder, 1942)

SIDNEY BUCHMAN
Theodora Goes Wild (1936)
Holiday (with Donald Ogden Stewart, 1938)
Mr. Smith Goes to Washington (1939)
Here Comes Mr. Jordan (with Seton I. Miller, 1942)

ISABEL DAWN AND BOYCE DEGAW
The Moon's Our Home (1936)

VINA DELMAR
The Awful Truth (1937)

PHILIP G. EPSTEIN
The Bride Walks Out (with P. J. Wolfson, 1936)
The Mad Miss Manton (1938)
There's That Woman Again (1939)
No Time for Comedy (with Julius J. Epstein, 1940)
Arsenic and Old Lace (with Julius J. Epstein, 1944)

FRANCES GOODRICH AND ALBERT HACKETT
The Thin Man (1934)
After the Thin Man (1936)
Another Thin Man (1939)

BERT GRANET
The Affairs of Annabel (with Paul Yawitz, 1938)
A Girl, a Guy, and a Gob (with Frank Ryan, 1941)

JAMES EDWARD GRANT
The Ex-Mrs. Bradford (with Anthony Veiller, 1936)
Danger—Love at Work (1937)

ERIC HATCH
My Man Godfrey (with Morrie Ryskind, 1936)
Topper (with Jack Jevne and Eddie Moran, 1937)

BEN HECHT
Design for Living (1932)
Twentieth Century (with Charles MacArthur, 1934)
Nothing Sacred (1937)
It's a Wonderful World (1939)
His Girl Friday (uncredited, with Charles Lederer, 1940)
Monkey Business (with Charles Lederer and I. A. L. Diamond, 1952)

PAUL JARRICO
Tom, Dick and Harry (1938)

JACK JEVNE AND EDDIE MORAN
Topper (with Eric Hatch, 1937)
Merrily We Live (1938)
There Goes My Heart (1938)
Topper Takes a Trip (1938)

NUNNALLY JOHNSON
Wife, Husband and Friend (1939)

GARSON KANIN
The More the Merrier (uncredited, 1943)

ARTHUR KOBER
Having Wonderful Time (1938)

NORMAN KRASNA
Hands Across the Table (with Vincent Lawrence and Herbert Fields, 1935)
Bachelor Mother (1939)
Mr. and Mrs. Smith (1941)

HARRY KURNITZ
Fast and Loose (1939)
Fast and Furious (1939)
I Love You Again (with Charles Lederer and George Oppenheimer, 1940)
Shadow of the Thin Man (with Irving Brecher, 1941)
The Thin Man Goes Home (1944)

CHARLES LEDERER
The Front Page (1931)
His Girl Friday (with Ben Hecht, uncredited, 1940)
I Love You Again (with George Oppenheimer and Harry Kurnitz, 1940)
Love Crazy (with William Ludwig and David Hirtz, 1941)
I Was a Male War Bride (with Leonard Spigelgass and Hagar Wilde, 1949)
Monkey Business (with Ben Hecht and I. A. L. Diamond, 1952)

GLADYS LEHMAN
There's Always a Woman (1938)
Good Girls Go to Paris (with Ken Englund, 1939)
Hired Wife (with Richard Connell, 1940)

CHARLES MacARTHUR
Twentieth Century (with Ben Hecht, 1934)

DUDLEY NICHOLS
Bringing Up Baby (with Hagar Wilde, 1938)

GEORGE OPPENHEIMER
Libeled Lady (with Maurine Watkins and Howard Emmett Rogers, 1936)
I Love You Again (with Charles Lederer and Harry Kurnitz, 1940)

DOROTHY PARKER AND ALAN CAMPBELL
The Moon's Our Home (credited only with additional dialogue, 1936)
Woman Chases Man (1937)
Weekend for Three (1941)

ROBERT RISKIN
It Happened One Night (1934)
Mr. Deeds Goes to Town (1936)
You Can't Take It With You (1938)
The Thin Man Goes Home (with Dwight Taylor, 1944)

CASEY ROBINSON
It's Love I'm After (1934)

MORRIE RYSKIND
My Man Godfrey (with Eric Hatch, 1936)

ALLAN SCOTT
Joy of Living (with Gene Towne and Graham Baker, 1938)
Fifth Avenue Girl (1939)

BELLA AND SAMUEL SPEWACK
My Favorite Wife (1940)

DONALD OGDEN STEWART
Holiday (with Sidney Buchman, 1938)
The Philadelphia Story (1940)
That Uncertain Feeling (1942)

PRESTON STURGES
The Good Fairy (1935)
Easy Living (1937)
Christmas in July (1940)
The Lady Eve (1941)
The Palm Beach Story (1942)
The Miracle of Morgan's Creek (1942)
Hail the Conquering Hero (1944)
Unfaithfully Yours (1948)

JO SWERLING
Double Wedding (1937)

GENE TOWNE
Joy of Living (with Graham Baker and Allen Scott, 1938)
Eternally Yours (with Graham Baker, 1939)

VIRGINIA VAN UPP
Cafe Society (1939)
Honeymoon in Bali (1939)

ANTHONY VEILLER
The Ex-Mrs. Bradford (with James Edward Grant, 1936)

DARRELL WARE
Wife, Doctor and Nurse (1937)
Second Honeymoon (with Kathryn Scola, 1937)
Public Deb No. 1 (with Karl Tunberg, 1940)
He Married His Wife (1940)

HAGAR WILDE
Bringing Up Baby (with Dudley Nichols, 1938)
I Was a Male War Bride (with Charles Lederer and Leonard Spigelgass, 1949)

BILLY WILDER
Bluebeard's Eighth Wife (with Charles Brackett, 1938)
Midnight (with Charles Brackett, 1939)
Ninotchka (with Charles Brackett and Walter Reisch, 1939)
Ball of Fire (with Charles Brackett, 1941)
The Major and the Minor (with Charles Brackett, 1942)

P. J. WOLFSON
The Bride Walks Out (with Philip G. Epstein, 1936)
Vivacious Lady (with Ernest Pagano, 1938)
He Stayed for Breakfast (with Michael Fessier and Ernest Vajda, 1940)
This Thing Called Love (with George Seaton and Ken Englund, 1941)

PAUL YAWITZ
Breakfast for Two (with Charles Kaufman and Viola Brothers Shore, 1938)
The Affairs of Annabel (with Bert Granet, 1938)

The Cinematographers

Cinematographers, or directors of photography, are the technicians whose understanding of film stock and lighting design gave screwball comedies their *look*. Generally, screwball comedies are characterized by high-key lighting that gives them a particularly glossy and elegant appearance. (Exceptions include James Wong Howe's moody *The Thin Man* and the exceptionally dark second half of Russell Metty's *Bringing Up Baby*.) All but one of these comedies are in black and white; *Nothing Sacred* was filmed in Technicolor. Of all the cinematographers listed here, Ted Tetzlaff is perhaps the most characteristic in terms of screwball style; his films are notable for their sparkling, somewhat brittle patina.

JOSEPH AUGUST
Twentieth Century (1934)

GEORGE BARNES
That Uncertain Feeling (1942)

NORBERT BRODINE
The Good Fairy (1935)
Libeled Lady (1936)
Topper (1937)
There Goes My Heart (1938)
Merrily We Live (1938)
Turnabout (1940)
I Was a Male War Bride (with O. H. Borradaile, 1949)

WILLIAM H. DANIELS
Double Wedding (1937)
Another Thin Man (with Oliver T. Marsh, 1939)
Ninotchka (1939)
Shadow of the Thin Man (1941)

ROBERT DE GRASSE
Vivacious Lady (1938)
Having Wonderful Time (1938)
Bachelor Mother (1939)
Fifth Avenue Girl (1939)
Lady of Burlesque (1943)

KARL FREUND
The Thin Man Goes Home (1944)

MERRIT GERSTAD
Eternally Yours (1939)
Tom, Dick and Harry (1940)

W. HOWARD GREENE
Nothing Sacred (1937)

ERNEST HALLER
No Time for Comedy (1940)

JAMES WONG HOWE
The Thin Man (1934)

J. ROY HUNT
The Bride Walks Out (1936)
The Ex-Mrs. Bradford (1936)
Breakfast for Two (1937)

RAY JUNE
The Girl from Missouri (1934)
Love Crazy (1941)

MILTON KRASNER
Hired Wife (1940)
Monkey Business (1952)

CHARLES LANG
Midnight (1939)

OLIVER T. MARSH
After the Thin Man (1936)
Love on the Run (1936)
Another Thin Man (with William Daniels, 1939)

It's a Wonderful World (1939)
I Love You Again (1940)

RUDOLPH MATÉ
My Favorite Wife (1940)

JOHN MESCALL
Take a Letter, Darling (1942)

RUSSELL METTY
The Affairs of Annabel (1938)
Bringing Up Baby (1938)
A Girl, a Guy, and a Gob (1941)

VICTOR MILNER
Design for Living (1933)
The Lady Eve (1941)
The Palm Beach Story (1942)
Unfaithfully Yours (1948)

NICHOLAS MUSURACA
The Richest Girl in the World (1934)
The Mad Miss Manton (1938)

ERNEST G. PALMER
Love Is News (1937)
Second Honeymoon (1937)
Three Blind Mice (1938)
Wife, Husband and Friend (1939)
Public Deb No. 1 (1940)

ROBERT PLANCK
Red Salute (1935)

FRANZ PLANER
Holiday (1938)

CHARLES ROSHER
Song of the Thin Man (1947)

JOSEPH RUTTENBERG
The Philadelphia Story (1940)

LEON SHAMROY
She Married Her Boss (1935)
Wedding Present (1936)
The Young in Heart (1938)

HARRY STRADLING
Mr. and Mrs. North (1940)
Mr. and Mrs. Smith (1941)

TED TETZLAFF
Hands Across the Table (1935)
The Princess Comes Across (1936)
My Man Godfrey (1936)
Easy Living (1937)
True Confession (1937)
Cafe Society (1939)
The More the Merrier (1943)

GREGG TOLAND
Ball of Fire (1941)

LEO TOVER
I Met Him in Paris (1937)
Bluebeard's Eighth Wife (1938)
The Major and the Minor (1942)

JOSEPH VALENTINE
The Moon's Our Home (1936)

JAMES VAN TREES
It's Love I'm After (1937)

JOSEPH WALKER
It Happened One Night (1934)
Theodora Goes Wild (1936)
Mr. Deeds Goes to Town (1936)
The Awful Truth (1937)
You Can't Take It With You (1938)
His Girl Friday (1940)
Too Many Husbands (1940)

★★★ Classic: don't miss it.

★★ Respectable: not first-rate, but not worth ignoring, either.

★ For Film Buffs Only: rough going for the average viewer.

V Available on videotape.

THE AFFAIRS OF ANNABEL
1938, RKO
A temperamental movie star is forced to become a maid (69 minutes). ★V

Director	BEN STOLOFF
Producer	LOU LUSTY
Screenplay	BERT GRANET and PAUL YAWITZ, based on a story by CHARLES HOFFMAN
Cinematographer	RUSSELL METTY
Music	ROY WEBB

Annabel Allison	LUCILLE BALL
Lanny Morgan	JACK OAKIE
Josephine	RUTH DONNELLY
Howard Webb	BRADLEY PAGE
Vladimir	FRITZ FELD
Major	THURSTON HALL
Mr. Fletcher	GRANVILLE BATES
Mrs. Fletcher	ELIZABETH RISDON
Bobby Fletcher	LEE VAN ATTA

AFTER THE THIN MAN
1936, MGM
Nick and Nora Charles drink their way through the investigation of a murder in Nora's family (113 minutes). ★★★V

Director	W. S. VAN DYKE
Producer	HUNT STROMBERG
Screenplay	FRANCES GOODRICH and ALBERT HACKETT, from the story by DASHIELL HAMMETT
Cinematographer	OLIVER T. MARSH
Art Director	CEDRIC GIBBONS
Music	HERBERT STROTHART and EDWARD WARD

Nick Charles	WILLIAM POWELL
Nora Charles	MYRNA LOY
David	JAMES STEWART
Selma	ELISSA LANDI
"Dancer"	JOSEPH CALLEIA
Aunt Katherine	JESSIE RALPH
Dr. Kammer	GEORGE ZUCCO
Robert	ALAN MARSHAL
Asta	HIMSELF
Mrs. Asta	HERSELF

THE AMAZING MR. WILLIAMS
1940, COLUMBIA
Melvyn Douglas is a detective, Joan Blondell is his screwball girlfriend, and together they solve various mysteries (86 minutes). ★★

Director	ALEXANDER HALL
Screenplay	DWIGHT TAYLOR, SY BARTLETT, and RICHARD MAIBAUM
Cinematographer	ARTHUR TODD

Kenny Williams	MELVYN DOUGLAS
Maxine Carroll	JOAN BLONDELL
Capt. McGovern	CLARENCE KOLB
Effie	RUTH DONNELLY
Buck Moseby	EDWARD S. BROPHY

ANOTHER THIN MAN
1939, MGM
Nick and Nora Charles solve the murder of a paranoid old gentleman on a Long Island estate (102 minutes). ★★V

Director	W. S. VAN DYKE
Producer	HUNT STROMBERG
Screenplay	FRANCES GOODRICH and ALBERT HACKETT, based on an original story by DASHIELL HAMMETT
Cinematographer	OLIVER T. MARSH and WILLIAM DANIELS
Art Director	CEDRIC GIBBONS
Music	EDWARD WARD

Nick Charles	WILLIAM POWELL
Nora Charles	MYRNA LOY
Col. Burr MacFay	C. AUBREY SMITH
Van Slack	OTTO KRUGER
Lt. Guild	NAT PENDLETON
Lois MacFay	VIRGINIA GREY
Landlady	MARJORIE MAIN
Asta	HIMSELF
Nick Jr.	WILLIAM ANTHONY POULSON

THE AWFUL TRUTH
1937, COLUMBIA
An extremely ironic husband and wife attempt to get a divorce, battle over custody of their dog, and irritate themselves back into a healthy relationship (89 minutes). ★★★V

Director	LEO McCAREY
Screenplay	VINA DELMAR, from a story by ARTHUR RICHMOND
Cinematographer	JOSEPH WALKER
Set Decoration	BABS JOHNSTONE
Costumes	ROBERT KALLOCH

Lucy Warriner	IRENE DUNNE
Jerry Warriner	CARY GRANT
Daniel Leeson	RALPH BELLAMY
Armand Duvalle	ALEXANDER D'ARCY
Aunt Patsy	CECIL CUNNINGHAM
Barbara Vance	MARGUERITE CHURCHILL
Mrs. Leeson	ESTHER DALE
Dixie Bell	JOYCE COMPTON
Mr. Smith	ASTA

BACHELOR MOTHER
1939, RKO
An unwed shopgirl finds a baby on her doorstep, gets fired for her supposed immorality, but ends up in love with her boss anyway (81 minutes). ★★V

Director	GARSON KANIN
Producer	B. G. DeSYLVA
Screenplay	NORMAN KRASNA, based on a story by FELIX JACKSON
Cinematographer	ROBERT DE GRASSE
Art Directors	VAN NEST POLGLASE and CARROLL CLARK
Set Decoration	DARRELL SILVERA
Music	ROY WEBB
Costumes	IRENE

Polly Parrish	GINGER ROGERS
David Merlin	DAVID NIVEN
J. B. Merlin	CHARLES COBURN
Freddie Miller	FRANK ALBERTSON
Butler	E. E. CLIVE
Johnnie	ELBERT COPLEN, JR.
Investigator	ERNEST TRUEX

BALL OF FIRE
1942, GOLDWYN
A gangster's moll named Sugarpuss moves into a house full of quaint professors (111 minutes). ★★★V

Director	HOWARD HAWKS
Producer	SAMUEL GOLDWYN
Screenplay	BILLY WILDER, CHARLES BRACKETT, from the story "From A to Z" by BILLY WILDER and THOMAS MONROE
Cinematographer	GREGG TOLAND

Art Director	PERRY FURGUSON
Music	ALFRED NEWMAN
Prof. Bertram Potts	GARY COOPER
Sugarpuss O'Shea	BARBARA STANWYCK
Prof. Gurkakoff	OSCAR HOMOLKA
Joe Lilac	DANA ANDREWS
Duke Pastrami	DAN DURYEA
Prof. Jerome	HENRY TRAVERS
Prof. Magenbruch	S. Z. SAKALL
Prof. Robinson	TULLY MARSHALL
Prof. Quintana	LEONID KINSKY
Prof. Oddly	RICHARD HAYDN
Prof. Peagram	AUBREY MATHER
Gene Krupa and His Band	THEMSELVES

BLUEBEARD'S EIGHTH WIFE
1938, PARAMOUNT
A much-married American millionaire meets his match in a stylish but impoverished French aristocrat (80 minutes). ★★★

Director	ERNST LUBITSCH
Producer	ERNST LUBITSCH
Screenplay	CHARLES BRACKETT and BILLY WILDER, from a play by ALFRED SAVOIR
Cinematographer	LEO TOVER
Set Decoration	HANS DREIER, ROBERT USHER
Music	FREDERICK HOLLANDER, WERNER R. HEYMANN
Costumes	TRAVIS BANTON

Nicole de Loiselle	CLAUDETTE COLBERT
Michael Brandon	GARY COOPER
Marquis de Loiselle	EDWARD EVERETT HORTON
Albert de Regnier	DAVID NIVEN
Aunt Hedwige	ELIZABETH PATTERSON
M. Pepinard	HERMAN BING
Kid Mulligan	WARREN HYMER
Asst. Hotel Mgr.	FRANKLIN PANGBORN

BREAKFAST FOR TWO
1937, RKO
A Texas heiress tortures a degenerate New Yorker into loving her by taking over his company (65 minutes). ★★

Director	ALFRED SANTELL
Producer	EDWARD KAUFMAN
Screenplay	CHARLES KAUFMAN, PAUL YAWITZ, and VIOLA BROTHERS SHORE
Cinematographer	J. ROY HUNT

Valentine Ransom	BARBARA STANWYCK
Jonathan Blair	HERBERT MARSHALL
Carol	GLENDA FARRELL

Butch	ERIC BLORE
Meggs	ETIENNE GIRARDOT
Justice of the Peace	DONALD MEEK

THE BRIDE WALKS OUT
1936, RADIO PICTURES
Working girl Barbara Stanwyck is torn between middle-class Gene Raymond and upper-crust Robert Young (81 minutes). ★V

Director	LEIGH JASON
Producer	EDWARD SMALL
Screenplay	P. J. WOLFSON and PHILIP G. EPSTEIN, original story by HOWARD EMMETT ROGERS
Cinematographer	J. ROY HUNT
Art Director	VAN NEST POLGLASE
Costumes	BERNARD NEWMAN

Caroline	BARBARA STANWYCK
Michael	GENE RAYMOND
Hugh	ROBERT YOUNG
Paul	NED SPARKS
Maddy	HELEN BRODERICK

BRINGING UP BABY
1938, RKO
An exceptionally irritating heiress forces a befuddled paleontologist to escort her aunt's pet leopard to Connecticut (102 minutes). ★★★V

Director	HOWARD HAWKS
Producer	HOWARD HAWKS
Screenplay	DUDLEY NICHOLS and HAGAR WILDE, from the story by HAGAR WILDE
Cinematographer	RUSSEL METTY
Art Directors	VAN NEST POLGLASE, PERRY FURGUSON
Set Decoration	DARRELL SILVERA
Music	ROY WEBB
Costumes	HOWARD GREER

David Huxley	CARY GRANT
Susan Vance	KATHARINE HEPBURN
Major Horace Applegate	CHARLES RUGGLES
Constable Slocum	WALTER CATLETT
Gogarty	BARRY FITZGERALD
Aunt Elizabeth	MAY ROBSON
Dr. Lehmann	FRITZ FELD
Alice Swallow	VIRGINIA WALKER
George	ASTA
Baby	NISSA

CAFE SOCIETY
1939, PARAMOUNT
A reporter finds a madcap heiress so deeply annoying that he falls in love with her—even after they get married (84 minutes). ★★

Director	EDWARD H. GRIFFITH
Producer	JEFF LAZARUS
Screenplay	VIRGINIA VAN UPP
Cinematographer	TED TETZLAFF
Art Directors	HANS DREIER and ERNST FEGTE
Music	BORIS MORROW; songs by BURTON LANE and FRANK LOESSER
Costumes	EDITH HEAD

Christopher West	MADELEINE CARROLL
Chick O'Bannon	FRED MACMURRAY
Bells Browne	SHIRLEY ROSS
Old Christopher West	CLAUDE GILLINGWATER
Mrs. DeWitt	JESSIE RALPH
Sonny DeWitt	ALLYN JOSLYN
Bartender	PAUL HURST

DESIGN FOR LIVING
1933, PARAMOUNT
An open-minded love triangle, from a bohemian garret to a London drawing room (90 minutes). ★★★

Director	ERNST LUBITSCH
Producer	ERNST LUBITSCH
Screenplay	BEN HECHT, based on the play by NOEL COWARD
Cinematographer	VICTOR MILNER
Art Director	HANS DREIER
Costumes	TRAVIS BANTON

Tom Chambers	FREDRIC MARCH
George Curtis	GARY COOPER
Gilda Farrell	MIRIAM HOPKINS
Max Plunkett	EDWARD EVERETT HORTON
Mr. Douglas	FRANKLIN PANGBORN

DOUBLE WEDDING
1937, MGM
Complications ensue when a successful businesswoman finds a bohemian artist to be a bad influence on her sister (87 minutes). ★★

Director	RICHARD THORPE
Producer	JOSEPH L. MANKIEWICZ
Screenplay	JO SWERLING, based on the play *Great Love* by FERENC MOLNAR
Cinematographer	WILLIAM DANIELS
Art Director	CEDRIC GIBBONS
Music	EDWARD WARD

Margit Agnew	MYRNA LOY
Charlie Lodge	WILLIAM POWELL
Waldo Beaver	JOHN BEAL
Irene Agnew	FLORENCE RICE
Mrs. Kensington Bly	JESSIE RALPH
Spike	EDGAR KENNEDY
Rev. Dr. Flynn	DONALD MEEK

EASY LIVING
1937, PARAMOUNT PICTURES
A working girl from Morningside Heights is inadvertently swept into a life of East Side luxury when an industrialist sets her up in a fancy hotel (88 minutes). ★★★

Director	MITCHELL LEISEN
Producer	ARTHUR HORNBLOW, JR.
Screenplay	PRESTON STURGES, based on a story by VERA CASPARY
Cinematographer	TED TETZLAFF
Art Directors	HANS DREIER and ERNST FEGTE

Mary Smith	JEAN ARTHUR
J. B. Ball	EDWARD ARNOLD
Johnny Ball	RAY MILLAND
Louis Louis	LUIS ALBERNI
Mrs. Ball	MARY NASH
Van Buren	FRANKLIN PANGBORN
Wallace Whistling	WILLIAM DEMAREST
E. F. Hulgar	ANDREW TOMBES
Lillian	ESTHER DALE
Office Manager	HARLAN BRIGGS

ETERNALLY YOURS
1939, WALTER WANGER
An heiress marries a professional magician, loves him, leaves him, and loves him again (95 minutes). ★V

Director	TAY GARNETT
Producer	WALTER WANGER
Screenplay	GENE TOWNE, GRAHAM BAKER
Cinematographer	MERRIT GERSTAD
Art Director	ALEXANDER GOLITZEN
Interior Decorations	JULIA HERON
Music	WERNER JANSSEN
Miss Young's gowns	IRENE
Other gowns	TRAVIS BANTON

Anita	LORETTA YOUNG
Tony	DAVID NIVEN
Benton	HUGH HERBERT
Aunt Abbey	BILLIE BURKE
Tom	BRODERICK CRAWFORD
Gramps	C. AUBREY SMITH
Mr. Bingham	RAYMOND WALBURN
Mrs. Bingham	ZASU PITTS
Lola de Vere	VIRGINIA FIELD
Gloria	EVE ARDEN

THE EX-MRS. BRADFORD
1936, RKO
A doctor and a mystery writer, who have been divorced, rediscover love while solving a bizarre racetrack murder case (80 minutes). ★★★V

Director	STEPHEN ROBERTS
Producer	EDWARD KAUFMAN
Screenplay	ANTHONY VEILLER and JAMES EDWARD GRANT
Cinematographer	J. ROY HUNT
Music	ROY WEBB

Dr. Lawrence Bradford	WILLIAM POWELL
Paula Bradford	JEAN ARTHUR
Inspector Corrigan	JAMES GLEASON
Stokes	ERIC BLORE
Mike	ROBERT ARMSTRONG
Miss Prentiss	LILA LEE

FIFTH AVENUE GIRL
1939, RKO
A sort of My Girl Godfrey, with Ginger Rogers being taken into a Fifth Avenue mansion to teach the rich how to be human (83 minutes). ★★V

Director	GREGORY LA CAVA
Producer	GREGORY LA CAVA
Screenplay	ALLAN SCOTT
Cinematographer	ROBERT DE GRASSE
Art Director	VAN NEST POLGLASE
Set Decoration	DARRELL SILVERA
Music	RUSSELL BENNETT

Mary Grey	GINGER ROGERS
Mr. Borden	WALTER CONNOLLY
Mrs. Borden	VERREE TEASDALE
Michael	JAMES ELLISON
Tim Borden	TIM HOLT
Katherine Borden	KATHRYN ADAMS
Higgins	FRANKLIN PANGBORN
Dr. Kessler	LOUIS CALHERN

THE FRONT PAGE
1931, HOWARD HUGHES
The granddaddy of cynical newspaper movies—with Adolphe Menjou and Pat O'Brien caught in a love-hate relationship on the job (101 minutes). ★★★V

Director	LEWIS MILESTONE
Producer	HOWARD HUGHES
Screenplay	BARLETT CORMACK and CHARLES LEDERER, from the play by BEN HECHT and CHARLES MACARTHUR
Cinematographer	GLEN MACWILLIAMS

Walter Burns	ADOLPHE MENJOU
Hildy Johnson	PAT O'BRIEN
Peggy	MARY BRIAN
Bensinger	EDWARD EVERETT HORTON
Murphy	WALTER CATLETT
Earl Williams	GEORGE E. STONE
Molly	MAE CLARKE
Pincus	SLIM SUMMERVILLE

THE GIRL FROM MISSOURI
1934, MGM
A blond bombshell from the Midwest turns her charms into a lucrative career (75 minutes). ★★

Director	JACK CONWAY
Producer	BERNARD H. HYMAN
Screenplay	ANITA LOOS and JOHN EMERSON
Cinematographer	RAY JUNE
Music	WILLIAM AXT

Eadie	JEAN HARLOW
Tom Paige	LIONEL BARRYMORE
Tom Paige, Jr.	FRANCHOT TONE
Frank Cousins	LEWIS STONE
Kitty Lennihan	PATSY KELLY
Lord Douglas	ALAN MOWBRAY

A GIRL, A GUY, AND A GOB
1941, HAROLD LLOYD
A love triangle in which two of the corners are middle-class and the third is rich (91 minutes). ★V

Director	RICHARD WALLACE
Producer	HAROLD LLOYD
Screenplay	FRANK RYAN and BERT GRANET, from a story by GROVER JONES
Cinematographer	RUSSELL METTY
Art Director	VAN NEST POLGLASE
Set Decoration	DARRELL SILVERA
Music	ROY WEBB
Costumes	EDWARD STEVENSON
Special Effects	VERNON L. WALKER

Coffee Cup	GEORGE MURPHY
Dorothy Duncan	LUCILLE BALL
Steven Herrick	EDMOND O'BRIEN
Abel Martin	HENRY TRAVERS
Pet Shop Owner	FRANKLIN PANGBORN

THE GOOD FAIRY
1935, UNIVERSAL
Ferenc Molnar's fable about a girl who can't help but get involved in men's lives (90 minutes). ★★★

Director	WILLIAM WYLER
Producer	HENRY HENIGSON
Screenplay	PRESTON STURGES, based on the play by FERENC MOLNAR
Cinematographer	NORBERT BRODINE

Luisa Ginglebusher	MARGARET SULLAVAN
Max Sporum	HERBERT MARSHALL
Konrad	FRANK MORGAN
Detlaff	REGINALD OWEN
Schlapkohl	ALAN HALE
Dr. Schultz	BEULAH BONDI
Joe	CESAR ROMERO
Dr. Betz	ERIC BLORE

HANDS ACROSS THE TABLE
1935, PARAMOUNT PICTURES
A gold-digging manicurist makes the mistake of falling in love with a man with no money (88 minutes). ★★★

Director	MITCHELL LEISEN
Producer	E. LLOYD SHELDON
Screenplay	NORMAN KRASNA, VINCENT LAWRENCE, HERBERT FIELDS, based on the story "Bracelets" by VINA DELMAR
Cinematographer	TED TETZLAFF
Music	SAM COSLOW, FREDERICK HOLLANDER
Costumes	TRAVIS BANTON

Regi Allen	CAROLE LOMBARD
Theodore Drew III	FRED MACMURRAY
Allen Macklyn	RALPH BELLAMY
Vivian Snowden	ASTRID ALLWYN
Laura	RUTH DONNELLY
Nona	MARIE PREVOST
Peter	JOSEPH TOZER
Natty	WILLIAM DEMAREST

HAVING WONDERFUL TIME
1938, RKO
Fun and romance at a Catskills summer camp (70 minutes). ★★V

Director	ALFRED SANTELL
Producer	PANDRO S. BERMAN
Screenplay	ARTHUR KOBER, adapted from his play
Cinematographer	ROBERT DE GRASSE
Art Director	VAN NEST POLGLASE
Music	ROY WEBB
Costumes	EDWARD STEVENSON and RENIÉ
Special Effects	VERNON L. WALKER

Teddy Shaw	GINGER ROGERS
Chick Kirkland	DOUGLAS FAIRBANKS, JR.
Fay	PEGGY CONKLIN
Miriam	LUCILLE BALL
Buzzy	LEE BOWMAN
Henrietta	EVE ARDEN
Maxine	DOROTHEA KENT
Itchy	RICHARD (RED) SKELTON
P. U. Rogers	DONALD MEEK
Gus	GRADY SUTTON

HIRED WIFE
1940, UNIVERSAL
A no-nonsense secretary marries her boss on a purely business level (96 minutes). ★★

Director	WILLIAM A. SEITER
Producer	WILLIAM A. SEITER
Screenplay	RICHARD CONNELL and GLADYS LEHMAN, based on a story by GEORGE BECK

Kendal Browning	ROSALIND RUSSELL
Stephen Dexter	BRIAN AHERNE

Phyllis Walden	VIRGINIA BRUCE
Van Horn	ROBERT BENCHLEY
José	JOHN CARROLL

HIS GIRL FRIDAY
1940, COLUMBIA
The Front Page transformed by Howard Hawks into an essential screwball romance (92 minutes). ★★★V

Director	HOWARD HAWKS
Producer	HOWARD HAWKS
Screenplay	CHARLES LEDERER (and BEN HECHT, uncredited), from the play *The Front Page,* by BEN HECHT and CHARLES MACARTHUR
Cinematographer	JOSEPH WALKER
Art Director	LIONEL BANKS
Music	MORRIS W. STOLOFF
Costumes	ROBERT KALLOCH

Walter Burns	CARY GRANT
Hildy Johnson	ROSALIND RUSSELL
Bruce Baldwin	RALPH BELLAMY
Earl Williams	JOHN QUALEN
Mollie Malloy	HELEN MACK
Sheriff Hartwell	GENE LOCKHART
Murphy	PORTER HALL
Bensinger	ERNEST TRUEX
Duffy	FRANK ORTH
Endicott	CLIFF EDWARDS
Mayor	CLARENCE KOLB
McCue	ROSCOE KARNS
Dr. Egelhoffer	EDWIN MAXWELL
Mrs. Baldwin	ALMA KRUEGER

HOLIDAY
1938, COLUMBIA
A middle-class guy thinks he's in love with an heiress but falls for her eccentric sister instead (93 minutes). ★★★

Director	GEORGE CUKOR
Producer	EVERETT RISKIN
Screenplay	DONALD OGDEN STEWART and SIDNEY BUCHMAN, based on the play by PHILIP BARRY
Cinematographer	FRANZ PLANER
Art Directors	STEPHEN GOOSSON and LIONEL BANKS
Music	MORRIS STOLOFF
Costumes	ROBERT KALLOCH

Linda Seton	KATHARINE HEPBURN
Johnny Case	CARY GRANT
Nick Potter	EDWARD EVERETT HORTON
Ned Seton	LEW AYRES
Edward Seton	HENRY KOLKER
Julia Seton	DORIS NOLAN
Laura Cram	BINNIE BARNES
Susan Potter	JEAN DIXON

I LOVE YOU AGAIN
1940, MGM
Fuddy-duddy husband William Powell gets bonked on the head and turns back into his real self—a conniving crook (99 minutes). ★★

Director	W. S. VAN DYKE
Producer	LAWRENCE WEINGARTEN
Screenplay	CHARLES LEDERER, GEORGE OPPENHEIMER, and HARRY KURNITZ
Cinematographer	OLIVER T. MARSH
Music	FRANZ WAXMAN

Larry Wilson/ George Carey	WILLIAM POWELL
Kay Wilson	MYRNA LOY
Doc Ryan	FRANK MCHUGH
Duke Sheldon	EDMUND LOWE
Herbert	DONALD DOUGLAS
Kay's mother	NELLA WALKER
Harkspur, Jr.	CARL "ALFALFA" SWITZER

I MET HIM IN PARIS
1937, PARAMOUNT PICTURES
A European love triangle with an American shopgirl at the center (85 minutes). ★★

Director	WESLEY RUGGLES
Producer	WESLEY RUGGLES
Screenplay	CLAUDE BINYON, from a story by HELEN MEINARDI
Cinematographer	LEO TOVER

Kay Denham	CLAUDETTE COLBERT
George Potter	MELVYN DOUGLAS
Gene Anders	ROBERT YOUNG
Helen Anders	MONA BARRIE
Cutter Driver	GEORGE DAVIS
Hadley	ALEXANDER CROSS
Berk Sutter	LEE BOWMAN
Desk Clerk	FRITZ FELD

IT HAPPENED ONE NIGHT
1934, COLUMBIA
A flighty heiress runs off to marry a notorious playboy but falls in love with a reporter on the way (105 minutes). ★★★V

Director	FRANK CAPRA
Producer	HARRY COHN, FRANK CAPRA
Screenplay	ROBERT RISKIN, from the story "Night Bus" by SAMUEL HOPKINS ADAMS
Cinematographer	JOSEPH WALKER
Art Director	STEPHEN GOOSSON
Costumes	ROBERT KALLOCH

Peter Warne	CLARK GABLE
Ellie Andrews	CLAUDETTE COLBERT
Alexander Andrews	WALTER CONNOLLY
Oscar Shapely	ROSCOE KARNS
Danker	ALAN HALE
Bus Driver	WARD BOND
King Westley	JAMESON THOMAS

IT'S LOVE I'M AFTER
1937, WARNER BROTHERS
Two battling theater people find themselves on the same side when an heiress tries to come between them (90 minutes). ★★★

Director	ARCHIE MAYO
Producer	HAL B. WALLIS
Screenplay	CASEY ROBINSON, based on a story by MAURINE HANLINE
Cinematographer	JAMES VAN TREES
Music	HEINZ ROEMHELD
Art Director	CARL JULES WEYL
Costumes	ORRY-KELLY

Basil Underwood	LESLIE HOWARD
Joyce Arden	BETTE DAVIS
Marcia West	OLIVIA DE HAVILLAND
William West	GEORGE BARBIER
Digges	ERIC BLORE

IT'S A WONDERFUL WORLD
1939, MGM
A detective on the lam from the law meets a poet who helps him solve a murder (84 minutes). ★★★

Director	W. S. VAN DYKE
Producer	FRANK DAVIS
Screenplay	BEN HECHT, from a story by BEN HECHT and HERMAN J. MANKIEWICZ
Cinematographer	OLIVER T. MARSH

Edwina Corday	CLAUDETTE COLBERT
Guy Johnson	JAMES STEWART
"Cap" Streeter	GUY KIBBEE
Sgt. Koretz	NAT PENDLETON
Vivian Tarbel	FRANCES DRAKE
Lt. Miller	EDGAR KENNEDY
Willie Heyward	ERNEST TRUEX
Herman Plotka	LEONARD KIBRICK
Lupton Peabody	GRADY SUTTON

I WAS A MALE WAR BRIDE
1949, TWENTIETH CENTURY-FOX
A Frenchman marries an American officer, with endlessly degrading results (105 minutes). ★★★

Director	HOWARD HAWKS
Producer	SOL C. SIEGEL
Screenplay	CHARLES LEDERER, LEONARD SPIGELGASS, HAGAR WILDE, from a story by HENRI ROCHARD
Cinematographer	NORBERT BRODINE and O. H. BORRADAILE
Art Directors	LYLE WHEELER and ALBERT HOGSETT
Set Decoration	THOMAS LITTLE, WALTER M. SCOTT
Music	CYRIL MOCKRIDGE

Henri Rochard	CARY GRANT
Lt. Catherine Gates	ANN SHERIDAN

Capt. Jack Rumsey	WILLIAM NEFF
Tony Jewitt	EUGENE GERICKE
Kitty	MARION MARSHALL

JIMMY THE GENT
1934, WARNER BROTHERS
Two rival genealogists, one a bit more crooked than the other, fight and fall in love (67 minutes). ★★★

Director	MICHAEL CURTIZ
Screenplay	LAIRD DOYLE and RAY NAZARRO, from a story by BERTRAM MILHAUSER
Cinematographer	IRA MORGAN
Art Director	ESDRAS HARTLEY
Costumes	ORRY-KELLY

Jimmy Corrigan	JAMES CAGNEY
Joan Martin	BETTE DAVIS
Mabel	ALICE WHITE
Louie	ALLEN JENKINS
Joe	ARTHUR HOHL
James J. Wallingham	ALAN DINEHART

JOY OF LIVING
1938, RKO
An actress finds reason to escape from her grasping family in the form of a wealthy fan (90 minutes). ★

Director	TAY GARNETT
Screenplay	GENE TOWNE, GRAHAM BAKER, and ALLAN SCOTT, based on a story by DOROTHY and HERBERT FIELDS
Music	JEROME KERN
Lyrics	DOROTHY FIELDS

Maggie	IRENE DUNNE
Dan	DOUGLAS FAIRBANKS, JR.
Minerva	ALICE BRADY
Dennis	GUY KIBBEE
Harrison	JEAN DIXON
Potter	ERIC BLORE
Salina	LUCILLE BALL
Mike	WARREN HYMER
Band Leader	FRANKLIN PANGBORN
Oswego	JOHN QUALEN

THE LADY EVE
1941, PARAMOUNT PICTURES
An experienced con-lady tortures a millionaire snake expert to the point of marriage, forces him to hate her, then refuses to divorce him (97 minutes). ★★★V

Director	PRESTON STURGES
Producer	PAUL JONES
Screenplay	PRESTON STURGES, based on a story by MONCKTON HOFFE
Cinematographer	VICTOR MILNER
Art Directors	HANS DREIER and ERNEST FEGTE

Editor	STUART GILMORE
Music	SIGMUND KRUMGOLD
Costumes	EDITH HEAD

Jean/Eve	BARBARA STANWYCK
Charles "Hopsie" Pike	HENRY FONDA
Col. Harrington	CHARLES COBURN
Mr. Pike	EUGENE PALLETTE
Mugsy	WILLIAM DEMAREST
Curly	ERIC BLORE
Gerald	MELVILLE COOPER
Martha	MARTHA O'DRISCOLL
Mrs. Pike	JANET BEECHER

LIBELED LADY
1936, MGM
A newspaper is accused of libeling an heiress, and the editor responds by trying to entrap her (98 minutes). ★★

Director	JACK CONWAY
Producer	LAWRENCE WEINGARTEN
Screenplay	MAURINE WATKINS, HOWARD EMMETT ROGERS, and GEORGE OPPENHEIMER, based on an original story by WALLACE SULLIVAN
Cinematographer	NORBERT BRODINE
Music	WILLIAM AXT

Gladys Benton	JEAN HARLOW
Bill Chandler	WILLIAM POWELL
Connie Allenbury	MYRNA LOY
Warren Haggerty	SPENCER TRACY
James Allenbury	WALTER CONNOLLY
Hollis Bane	CHARLEY GRAPEWIN
Mrs. Burns-Norvell	CORA WITHERSPOON
Babs	LAURIE BEATTY
Maid	HATTIE McDANIEL
Fishing Instructor	E. E. CLIVE

LOVE CRAZY
1941, MGM
A husband is forced to act insane in order to keep his wife from divorcing him (100 minutes). ★★★

Director	JACK CONWAY
Producer	PANDRO S. BERMAN
Screenplay	WILLIAM LUDWIG, CHARLES LEDERER, DAVID HIRTZ
Cinematographer	RAY JUNE
Art Director	CEDRIC GIBBONS
Music	DAVID SNELL

Susan Ireland	MYRNA LOY
Stephen Ireland	WILLIAM POWELL
Isobel Grayson Ward	GAIL PATRICK
Willoughby	JACK CARSON
Mrs. Cooper	FLORENCE BATES
George Hennie	SIDNEY BLACKMER

Dr. Kugle VLADIMIR SOKOLOFF
Mrs. Bristol KATHLEEN LOCKHART
Dr. Wuthering SIG RUMANN

LOVE IS NEWS
1937, TWENTIETH CENTURY-FOX
An heiress despises newspapers so much that she marries a reporter (78 minutes). ★

Director	TAY GARNETT
Screenplay	HARRY TUGEND and JACK YELLEN, from a story by WILLIAM R. LIPMAN and FREDERICK STEPHANI
Cinematographer	ERNEST PALMER
Steve Layton	TYRONE POWER
Tony Gateson	LORETTA YOUNG
Martin J. Canavan	DON AMECHE
Judge Hart	SLIM SUMMERVILLE
Cyrus Jeffrey	DUDLEY DIGGES
Eddie Johnson	WALTER CATLETT
Penrod	STEPIN FETCHIT
Mrs. Flaherty	JANE DARWELL

LOVE ON THE RUN
1936, MGM
A foreign correspondent keeps an heiress from marrying a prince, with a spy plot thrown in for good measure (80 minutes). ★

Director	W. S. VAN DYKE
Producer	JOSEPH L. MANKIEWICZ
Screenplay	JOHN LEE MALIN, MANUEL SEFF, and GLADYS HURLBUT, from a story by ALAN GREEN and JULIAN BRODIE
Cinematographer	OLIVER T. MARSH
Art Director	CEDRIC GIBBONS
Music	FRANZ WAXMAN
Costumes	ADRIAN
Sally Parker	JOAN CRAWFORD
Michael Anthony	CLARK GABLE
Barnebas Pells	FRANCHOT TONE
Baron	REGINALD OWEN
Baroness	MONA BARRIE
Igor	IVAN LEBEDEFF
Editor	WILLIAM DEMAREST

THE MAD MISS MANTON
1938, RKO
An obnoxious heiress and her dizzy friends stumble into a murder (80 minutes). ★★★V

Director	LEIGH JASON
Producer	PANDRO S. BERMAN
Associate Producer	P. J. WOLFSON
Screenplay	PHILIP G. EPSTEIN, from a story by WILSON COLLISON
Cinematographer	NICHOLAS MUSURACA

Art Director	VAN NEST POLGLASE
Music	ROY WEBB
Costumes	EDWARD STEVENSON
Melsa Manton	BARBARA STANWYCK
Peter Ames	HENRY FONDA
Lt. Brent	SAM LEVENE
Helen Frayne	FRANCES MERCER
Edward Norris	STANLEY RIDGES
Pat James	WHITNEY BOURNE
Maid	HATTIE MCDANIEL

THE MAJOR AND THE MINOR
1942, PARAMOUNT
A woman poses as a child in order to ride half-fare on the train, then gets caught up in a questionable relationship with an army major (100 minutes). ★★★

Director	BILLY WILDER
Producer	ARTHUR HORNBLOW, JR.
Screenplay	CHARLES BRACKETT and BILLY WILDER, based on the story "Sunny Goes Home" by FANNIE KILBOURNE and the play *Connie Goes Home* by EDWARD CHILDS CARPENTER
Cinematographer	LEO TOVER
Art Directors	ROLAND ANDERSON and HANS DREIER
Music	ROBERT EMMETT DOLAN
Susan Applegate	GINGER ROGERS
Major Philip Kirby	RAY MILLAND
Pamela	RITA JOHNSON
Mr. Osborne	ROBERT BENCHLEY
Lucy	DIANA LYNN

MIDNIGHT
1939, PARAMOUNT PICTURES
A down-and-out gold digger is recruited by a multimillionaire to make his adulterous wife jealous (95 minutes). ★★★

Director	MITCHELL LEISEN
Producer	ARTHUR HORNBLOW, JR.
Screenplay	CHARLES BRACKETT and BILLY WILDER, based on a story by EDWIN JUSTUS MAYER and FRANZ SCHULZ
Cinematographer	CHARLES LANG
Art Directors	HANS DREIER and ROBERT USHER
Costumes	IRENE
Eve Peabody	CLAUDETTE COLBERT
Tibor Czerny	DON AMECHE
Georges Flammarion	JOHN BARRYMORE
Jacques Picot	FRANCIS LEDERER
Helene Flammarion	MARY ASTOR
Simone	BLAINE BARRIE

Stephanie	HEDDA HOPPER
Judge	MONTY WOOLLEY
Marcel	REX O'MALLEY

MONKEY BUSINESS
1952, TWENTIETH CENTURY-FOX
A middle-aged couple's marriage is reduced to chaos when they take a fountain-of-youth drug invented by a chimp (97 minutes). ★★★V

Director	HOWARD HAWKS
Producer	SOL C. SIEGEL
Screenplay	BEN HECHT, I. A. L. DIAMOND, and CHARLES LEDERER, from a story by HARRY SEGALL
Cinematographer	MILTON KRASNER
Art Directors	LYLE WHEELER and GEORGE PATRICK
Music	LEIGH HARLINE
Costumes	CHARLES LE MAIRE, TRAVILLA
Barnaby Fulton	CARY GRANT
Edwina Fulton	GINGER ROGERS
Oliver Oxly	CHARLES COBURN
Miss Laurel	MARILYN MONROE
Hank Entwhistle	HUGH MARLOWE
Gravel-voiced boy	GEORGE WINSLOW

THE MOON'S OUR HOME
1936, PARAMOUNT
An heiress who's also a movie star falls in love with a famous travel writer; they marry, fight, and split up, until he finally gets her in a straitjacket (83 minutes). ★★★V

Director	WILLIAM A. SEITER
Producer	WALTER WANGER
Screenplay	ISABEL DAWN and BOYCE DEGAW, adapted from the *Cosmopolitan* serial "The Moon's Our Home," by FAITH BALDWIN
Additional Dialogue	DOROTHY PARKER and ALAN CAMPBELL
Cinematographer	JOSEPH A. VALENTINE
Art Director	ALEXANDER TOLUBOFF
Music	BORIS MORROS
Costumes	HELEN TAYLOR
Cherry Chester	MARGARET SULLAVAN
Anthony Amberton	HENRY FONDA
Horace	CHARLES BUTTERWORTH
Boyce Medford	BEULAH BONDI
Lucy (Grandmother)	HENRIETTA CROSMAN
Lem	WALTER BRENNAN
Mrs. Simpson	MARGARET HAMILTON
Mr. Simpson	SPENCER CHARTERS

THE MORE THE MERRIER
1943, COLUMBIA
Washington's wartime housing shortage leads to romance in an overcrowded building, particularly on the front stoop (104 minutes). ★★★

Director	GEORGE STEVENS
Producer	GEORGE STEVENS
Screenplay	RICHARD FLOURNOY, LEWIS R. FOSTER, ROBERT RUSSELL, and FRANK ROSS (and GARSON KANIN, uncredited)
Cinematographer	TED TETZLAFF
Music	LEIGH HARLINE

Connie Milligan	JEAN ARTHUR
Joe Carter	JOEL MCCREA
Benjamin Dingle	CHARLES COBURN
Charles J. Pendergast	RICHARD GAINES
Evans	BRUCE BENNETT
Pike	FRANK SULLY
Senator Noonan	CLYDE FILLMORE

MR. AND MRS. NORTH
1940, MGM
Dizzy Gracie Allen tries to figure out a murder (67 minutes). ★

Director	ROBERT B. SINCLAIR
Producer	IRVING ASHER
Screenplay	S. K. LAUREN, from the play by OWEN DAVIS, based on stories by RICHARD and FRANCES LOCKRIDGE
Cinematographer	HARRY STRADLING

Pamela North	GRACIE ALLEN
Gerald P. North	WILLIAM POST, JR.
Lt. Weigand	PAUL KELLY
Carol Brent	ROSE HOBART
Jane Wilson	VIRGINIA GREY
Arthur Talbot	FELIX BRESSART

MR. AND MRS. SMITH
1941, RKO
Alfred Hitchcock's underrated comedy about a squabbling Park Avenue couple who discover they're not legally married (95 minutes). ★★★V

Director	ALFRED HITCHCOCK
Producer	HARRY E. EDINGTON
Screenplay	NORMAN KRASNA
Cinematographer	HARRY STRADLING
Art Directors	VAN NEST POLGLASE AND L. P. WILLIAMS
Music	ROY WEBB

Ann Krausheimer Smith	CAROLE LOMBARD
David Smith	ROBERT MONTGOMERY
Jeff Custer	GENE RAYMOND
Mr. Custer	PHILIP MERIVALE
Mrs. Custer	LUCILE WATSON
Chuck Benson	JACK CARSON
"Mama Lucy"	WILLIAM EDMUNDS

MR. DEEDS GOES TO TOWN
1936, COLUMBIA
A tuba-playing volunteer fireman inherits $20 million and proceeds to be viciously exploited by everyone he meets (115 minutes). ★★★V

Director	FRANK CAPRA
Producer	FRANK CAPRA
Screenplay	ROBERT RISKIN, based on the story "Opera Hat" by CLARENCE BUDINGTON KELLAND
Cinematographer	JOSEPH WALKER
Art Director	STEPHEN GOOSSON

Longfellow Deeds	GARY COOPER
Babe Bennett	JEAN ARTHUR
Mr. Woods	GEORGE BANCROFT
Cornelius Cobb	LIONEL STANDER
Cedar	DOUGLAS DUMBRILLE
Psychiatrist	WYRLIE BIRCH

MY FAVORITE WIFE
1940, RKO
A gender-switched screwball retelling of the Enoch Arden story, in which a wife returns from a deserted island to find her husband remarried (88 minutes). ★★★V

Director	GARSON KANIN
Producer	LEO MCCAREY
Screenplay	BELLA and SAMUEL SPEWACK, from a story by the SPEWACKS and LEO MCCAREY
Cinematographer	RUDOLPH MATÉ
Art Director	VAN NEST POLGLASE
Set Decoration	DARRELL SILVERA
Music	ROY WEBB
Costumes	HOWARD GREER

Ellen Arden	IRENE DUNNE
Nick Arden	CARY GRANT
Stephen Burkett	RANDOLPH SCOTT
Bianca	GAIL PATRICK
Ma	ANN SHOEMAKER
Tim	SCOTTY BECKETT
Chinch	MARY LOU HARRINGTON
Hotel Clerk	DONALD MCBRIDE
Johnson	HUGH O'CONNELL
Judge	GRANVILLE BATES
Dr. Kohlmar	PEDRO DE CORDOBA

MY MAN GODFREY
1936, UNIVERSAL
An heiress picks up a bum at the town dump for use in a scavenger hunt, then hires him to be her family's butler (95 minutes). ★★★V

Director	GREGORY LA CAVA
Executive Producer	CHARLES P. ROGERS
Screenplay	MORRIE RYSKIND and ERIC HATCH, based on the novel *1011 Fifth Avenue* by ERIC HATCH
Cinematographer	TED TETZLAFF
Art Director	CHARLES D. HALL
Music	CHARLES PREVIN
Costumes	TRAVIS BANTON

Godfrey	WILLIAM POWELL
Irene Bullock	CAROLE LOMBARD
Angelica Bullock	ALICE BRADY
Cornelia Bullock	GAIL PATRICK
Alexander Bullock	EUGENE PALLETTE
Molly	JEAN DIXON
Carlo	MISCHA AUER
Tommy Gray	ALAN MOWBRAY
Mike	PAT FLAHERTY

NOTHING SACRED
1937, SELZNICK INTERNATIONAL
To escape her stifling hometown, a young woman pretends to be dying of radium poisoning in order to win an all-expenses-paid trip to New York, courtesy of a cynical newspaper (75 minutes; in Technicolor). ★★★V

Director	WILLIAM WELLMAN
Producer	DAVID O. SELZNICK
Screenplay	BEN HECHT, from the story "Letter to the Editor" by JAMES STREET
Cinematographer	W. HOWARD GREENE
Art Director	LYLE WHEELER
Set Decoration	EDWARD G. BOYLE
Music	OSCAR LEVANT
Costumes	TRAVIS BANTON and WALTER PLUNKETT

Hazel Flagg	CAROLE LOMBARD
Wally Cook	FREDRIC MARCH
Oliver Stone	WALTER CONNOLLY
Dr. Enoch Downer	CHARLES WINNINGER
Dr. Eggelhoffer	SIG RUMANN
M. C.	FRANK RAY
Sultan/Ernest	TROY BROWN
Mrs. Walker	HATTIE MCDANIEL
Fireman	JOHN QUALEN
Drug Store Lady	MARGARET HAMILTON
Max	MAXIE ROSENBLOOM

NO TIME FOR COMEDY
1940, WARNER BROTHERS
A hick from the Midwest becomes a successful Broadway playwright who marries the star of his plays, only to become intolerable (98 minutes). ★★

Director	WILLIAM KEIGHLEY
Producer	HAL WALLIS

Screenplay	JULIUS J. and PHILIP G. EPSTEIN, based on the play by S. N. BEHRMAN
Cinematographer	ERNEST HALLER
Music	HEINZ ROEMHELD
Gaylord Esterbrook	JAMES STEWART
Linda Paige	ROSALIND RUSSELL
Amanda Swift	GENEVIEVE TOBIN
Philo Swift	CHARLIE RUGGLES
Morgan Carrel	ALLYN JOSLYN
Clementine	LOUISE BEAVERS

THE PALM BEACH STORY
1942, PARAMOUNT
A Park Avenue couple splits up when the wife decides the husband can't afford her, after which she has an affair with the richest man on earth (90 minutes). ★★★V

Director	PRESTON STURGES
Producer	PAUL JONES
Screenplay	PRESTON STURGES
Cinematographer	VICTOR MILNER
Art Directors	HANS DREIER and ERNST FEGTE
Costumes	IRENE
Geraldine Jeffers	CLAUDETTE COLBERT
Tom Jeffers	JOEL MCCREA
Princess Centimillia	MARY ASTOR
J. D. Hackensacker III	RUDY VALLEE
Apartment Manager	FRANKLIN PANGBORN
The Wienie King	ROBERT DUDLEY
Toto	SIG ARNO

THE PHILADELPHIA STORY
1940, MGM
A Main Line heiress tries to come to terms with her first husband before marrying someone else. Not really screwball comedy, but great nonetheless (112 minutes). ★★★V

Director	GEORGE CUKOR
Producer	JOSEPH L. MANKIEWICZ
Screenplay	DONALD OGDEN STEWART, based on the play by PHILIP BARRY
Cinematographer	JOSEPH RUTTENBERG
Art Director	CEDRIC GIBBONS
Set Decoration	EDWIN B. WILLIS
Music	FRANZ WAXMAN
Costumes	ADRIAN
C. K. Dexter Haven	CARY GRANT
Tracy Lord Macaulay	KATHARINE HEPBURN
Connor	JAMES STEWART
Elizabeth Imbrie	RUTH HUSSEY

George Kittredge	JOHN HOWARD
Uncle Willie	ROLAND YOUNG
Seth Lord	JOHN HALLIDAY
Margaret Lord	MARY NASH
Dinah Lord	VIRGINIA WEIDLER
Sidney Kidd	HENRY DANIELL
Edward	LIONEL PAPE
Thomas	REX EVANS

THE PRINCESS COMES ACROSS
1936, PARAMOUNT
A shipboard romance between a bandleader and a Swedish princess who's really from Brooklyn (76 minutes). ★★

Director	WILLIAM K. HOWARD
Producer	ARTHUR HORNBLOW, JR.
Screenplay	WALTER DE LEON, FRANCES MARTIN, FRANK BUTLER, and DON HARTMAN, based on a story by PHILIP MACDONALD, as adapted from a novel by LOUIS LUCIEN ROGGER
Cinematographer	TED TETZLAFF
Music	PHIL BOUTELJE
Princess Olga/ Wanda Nash	CAROLE LOMBARD
King Mantell	FRED MACMURRAY
Lorel	DOUGLAS DUMBRILLE
Lady Gertrude Allwyn	ALISON SKIPWORTH
Benton	WILLIAM FRAWLEY
Darcy	PORTER HALL
Steindorf	SIG RUMANN
Morevitsch	MISCHA AUER

PUBLIC DEB NO. 1
1940, TWENTIETH CENTURY-FOX
A frenzied anticommunist tale of a debutante who's so dizzy that she falls for red propaganda until a greedy waiter beats some sense into her (80 minutes). ★

Director	GREGORY RATOFF
Producer	DARRYL F. ZANUCK
Screenplay	KARL TUNBERG and DARRELL WARE
Cinematographer	ERNEST PALMER
Music	ALFRED NEWMAN
Alan Blake	GEORGE MURPHY
Penny Cooper	BRENDA JOYCE
Bruce	RALPH BELLAMY
Elsa Maxwell	HERSELF
Grisha	MISCHA AUER
Uncle Milburn	CHARLIE RUGGLES
Bartender	FRANKLIN PANGBORN

RED SALUTE
1935, EDWARD SMALL/UNITED ARTISTS
The spoiled daughter of an army general runs off to marry a communist but falls in love with a working-class patriot on the way (80 minutes). ★

Director	SIDNEY LANFIELD
Producer	EDWARD SMALL
Screenplay	HUMPHREY PEARSON, MANUEL SEFF, and ELMER HARRIS
Cinematographer	ROBERT PLANCK
Art Director	JOHN DUCASSE SCHULZE
Drue Van Allen	BARBARA STANWYCK
Jeff	ROBERT YOUNG
Arner	HARDIE ALBRIGHT
Rooney	CLIFF EDWARDS
Mrs. Rooney	RUTH DONNELLY
Lefty	GORDON JONES
Major General Van Allen	PURNELL PRATT

THE RICHEST GIRL IN THE WORLD
1934, RKO
A protoscrewball comedy about how difficult it is to be rich (76 minutes). ★★

Director	WILLIAM SEITER
Producer	PANDRO S. BERMAN
Screenplay	NORMAN KRASNA
Cinematographer	NICHOLAS MUSURACA
Art Director	VAN NEST POLGLASE
Music	MAX STEINER
Dorothy Hunter	MIRIAM HOPKINS
Anthony Travis	JOEL MCCREA
Sylvia Hernon	FAY WRAY
Jonathan Connors	HARRY STEPHENSON
Philip Vernon	REGINALD DENNY

SECOND HONEYMOON
1937, TWENTIETH CENTURY-FOX
Loretta Young and Tyrone Power: they're divorced but still not happy (79 minutes). ★

Director	WALTER LANG
Producer	RAYMOND GRIFFITH
Screenplay	KATHRYN SCOLA and DARRELL WARE, from a story by PHILIP WYLIE
Cinematographer	ERNEST PALMER
Music	DAVID BUTTOLPH
Raoul McLeish	TYRONE POWER
Vicky	LORETTA YOUNG
Leo MacTavish	STUART ERWIN
Marcia	CLAIRE TREVOR
Joy	MARJORIE WEAVER

SHADOW OF THE THIN MAN
1941, MGM
Nick and Nora Charles solve a racetrack murder (97 minutes). ★★V

Director	W. S. VAN DYKE
Producer	HUNT STROMBERG

Screenplay	IRVING BRECHER and HARRY KURNITZ, based on a story by HARRY KURNITZ
Cinematographer	WILLIAM DANIELS
Nick Charles	WILLIAM POWELL
Nora Charles	MYRNA LOY
Paul Clarke	BARRY NELSON
Molly Ford	DONNA REED
Lt. Abrams	SAM LEVENE
Whitey Barrow	ALAN BAXTER
Major Jason Sculley	HENRY O'NEILL
Claire Porter	STELLA ADLER
Stella	LOUISE BEAVERS
Nick, Jr.	DICKIE HALL

SONG OF THE THIN MAN
1947, MGM
The final Nick and Nora effort, with the Charleses trying to make sense of a musician's death (86 minutes). ★★V

Director	EDWARD BUZZELL
Producer	NAT PERRIN
Screenplay	NAT PERRIN and STEVE FISHER, based on a story by STANLEY ROBERTS
Cinematographer	CHARLES ROSHER
Art Directors	CEDRIC GIBBONS and RANDALL DUELL
Nick Charles	WILLIAM POWELL
Nora Charles	MYRNA LOY
Nick, Jr.	DEAN STOCKWELL
Clarence Krause	KEENAN WYNN
Tommy Drake	PHILIP REED
Phyllis Talbin	PATRICIA MORRISON
Fran Page	GLORIA GRAHAME
Janet Thayer	JAYNE MEADOWS
Buddy Hollis	DON TAYLOR
Mitchell Talbin	LEON AMES
Asta, Jr.	HIMSELF

TAKE A LETTER, DARLING
1942, PARAMOUNT
An advertising executive falls in love with her secretary (93 minutes). ★★

Director	MITCHELL LEISEN
Producer	FRED KOHLMAR
Screenplay	CLAUDE BINYON, based on a story by GEORGE BECK
Cinematographer	JOHN MESCALL
Art Directors	HANS DREIER and ROLAND ANDERSON
Music	VICTOR YOUNG
Costumes	MITCHELL LEISEN and IRENE
A. M. MacGregor	ROSALIND RUSSELL
Tom Verney	FRED MACMURRAY

Jonathan Caldwell	MACDONALD CAREY
Ethel Caldwell	CONSTANCE MOORE
G. B. Atwater	ROBERT BENCHLEY

THAT UNCERTAIN FEELING
1942, UNITED ARTISTS
A Park Avenue socialite seeks psychiatric help for a bad case of hiccups that erupt whenever she thinks about her marriage (84 minutes). ★★★V

Director	ERNST LUBITSCH
Producer	ERNST LUBITSCH
Screenplay	DONALD OGDEN STEWART
Adaptation	WALTER REISCH, from a play by VICTORIEN SARDOU and EMILE DE NAJAC
Cinematographer	GEORGE BARNES
Art Director	ALEXANDER GOLITZEN
Music	WERNER R. HEYMANN
Costumes	IRENE
Jill Baker	MERLE OBERON
Larry Baker	MELVYN DOUGLAS
Sebastian Alexander	BURGESS MEREDITH
Dr. Vengard	ALAN MOWBRAY
Margie	OLIVE BLAKENEY
Attorney Jones	HARRY DAVENPORT
Mr. Kofka	SIG RUMANN
Sally	EVE ARDEN

THEODORA GOES WILD
1936, COLUMBIA PICTURES
A prim New Englander turns out to be the author of a racy best-seller (94 minutes). ★★★

Director	RICHARD BOLESLAWSKI
Producer	EVERETT RISKIN
Screenplay	SIDNEY BUCHMAN, from a story by MARY McCARTHY
Cinematographer	JOSEPH WALKER
Art Director	STEPHEN GOOSSON
Music	MORRIS STOLOFF
Costumes	BERNARD NEWMAN
Theodora Lynn	IRENE DUNNE
Michael Grant	MELVYN DOUGLAS
Jed Waterbury	THOMAS MITCHELL
Arthur Stevenson	THURSTON HALL
Adelaide Perry	ROSALIND KEITH
Rebecca Perry	SPRING BYINGTON
Aunt Mary	ELISABETH RISDON
Aunt Elsie	MARGARET McWADE
Ethel Stephenson	NANA BRYANT
Jonathan Grant	HENRY KOLKER
Agnes Grant	LEONA MARICLE
Uncle John	ROBERT GREIG
Governor Wyatt	FREDERICK BURTON

THE THIN MAN
1934, MGM
The first appearance of detectives Nick and Nora Charles, who try to find out who killed the title character (93 minutes). ★★★V

Director	W. S. VAN DYKE
Producer	HUNT STROMBERG
Screenplay	ALBERT HACKETT and FRANCES GOODRICH, from a novel by DASHIELL HAMMETT
Cinematographer	JAMES WONG HOWE
Art Director	CEDRIC GIBBONS
Music	WILLIAM AXT
Costumes	DOLLY TREE
Nick Charles	WILLIAM POWELL
Nora Charles	MYRNA LOY
Dorothy	MAUREEN O'SULLIVAN
Guild	NAT PENDLETON
Mimi	MINNA GOMBELL
McCaulay	PORTER HALL
Tommy	HENRY WADSWORTH
Claude Wynant	EDWARD ELLIS
Asta	HIMSELF

THE THIN MAN GOES HOME
1944, MGM
Nick and Nora Charles visit Nick's parents; their trip is made tolerable by a convenient murder in Nick's dull hometown (100 minutes). ★★V

Director	RICHARD THORPE
Producer	EVERETT RISKIN
Screenplay	ROBERT RISKIN and DWIGHT TAYLOR, from a story by HARRY KURNITZ and ROBERT RISKIN
Cinematographer	KARL FREUND
Art Directors	CEDRIC GIBBONS and EDWARD CARFAGNO
Nick Charles	WILLIAM POWELL
Nora Charles	MYRNA LOY
Mrs. Charles	LUCILE WATSON
Dr. Charles	HARRY DAVENPORT
Laura Ronson	GLORIA DeHAVEN
Crazy Mary	ANNE REVERE
Edgar Draque	LEON AMES
Helena Draque	HELEN VINSON
Bruce Clayworth	LLOYD CORRIGAN
Brogan	EDWARD BROPHY
Willie Crump	DONALD MEEK

THREE BLIND MICE
1938, TWENTIETH CENTURY-FOX
A gold-digging trio of sisters descend upon Santa Barbara and try to hook that perfect millionaire (75 minutes). ★★

Director	WILLIAM SEITER
Producers	DARRYL F. ZANUCK and RAYMOND GRIFFITH
Screenplay	BROWN HOLMES and LYNN STARLING, based on the play by STEPHEN POWYS
Cinematographer	ERNEST PALMER
Pamela Charters	LORETTA YOUNG
Van Smith	JOEL McCREA

Steve Harrington	DAVID NIVEN
Mike Brophy	STUART ERWIN
Moira Charters	MARJORIE WEAVER
Elizabeth Charters	PAULINE MOORE
Miriam	BINNIE BARNES
Mrs. Killian	JANE DARWELL
Clerk	FRANKLIN PANGBORN

TOM, DICK AND HARRY
1940, RKO
Poor Janie just can't decide whom to marry. She has three choices (86 minutes). ★★V

Director	GARSON KANIN
Producer	ROBERT SISK
Screenplay	PAUL JARRICO
Cinematographer	MERRITT GERSTAD
Art Director	VAN NEST POLGLASE
Set Decoration	DARRELL SILVERA
Music	ROY WEBB
Costumes	RENIÉ

Janie	GINGER ROGERS
Tom	GEORGE MURPHY
Dick	ALAN MARSHAL
Harry	BURGESS MEREDITH
Pop	JOE CUNNINGHAM
Ma	JANE SEYMOUR
Babs	LENORE LONERGAN
Paula	VICKI LESTER
Ice Cream Man	PHIL SILVERS

TOO MANY HUSBANDS
1940, COLUMBIA
A man becomes alarmed when he returns from being shipwrecked and finds his wife married to someone else (84 minutes). ★★

Director	WESLEY RUGGLES
Producer	WESLEY RUGGLES
Screenplay	CLAUDE BINYON, based on the play *Home and Beauty* by W. SOMERSET MAUGHAM
Cinematographer	JOSEPH WALKER
Music	FREDERICK HOLLANDER

Vicky Lowndes	JEAN ARTHUR
Bill Cardew	FRED MACMURRAY
Henry Lowndes	MELVYN DOUGLAS
George	HARRY DAVENPORT
Gertrude Houlihan	DOROTHY PETERSON
Peter	MELVILLE COOPER
McDermott	EDGAR BUCHANAN
Sullivan	TOM DUGAN

TOPPER
1937, HAL ROACH/MGM
Two witty, sophisticated drunks die in a car crash and return as screwball ghosts to help liberate a henpecked banker (98 minutes). ★★★V

Director	NORMAN Z. MCLEOD
Producer	HAL ROACH
Screenplay	JACK JEVNE, ERIC HATCH, and EDDIE MORAN, from a story by THORNE SMITH
Cinematographer	NORBERT BRODINE
Art Director	ARTHUR I. ROYCE
Special Effects	ROY SEAWRIGHT
Marion Kerby	CONSTANCE BENNETT
George Kerby	CARY GRANT
Cosmo Topper	ROLAND YOUNG
Mrs. Topper	BILLIE BURKE
Wilkins	ALAN MOWBRAY
Casey	EUGENE PALLETTE
Mrs. Stuyvesant	HEDDA HOPPER
Hoagy Carmichael	HIMSELF

TRUE CONFESSION
1937, PARAMOUNT
A lawyer's wife can't stop telling fibs, even when she's on trial for murder (85 minutes). ★★

Director	WESLEY RUGGLES
Producer	ALBERT LEWIN
Screenplay	CLAUDE BINYON, based on the play *My Crime* by LOUIS VERNEUIL and GEORGES BERR
Cinematographer	TED TETZLAFF
Music	FREDERICK HOLLANDER

Helen Bartlett	CAROLE LOMBARD
Kenneth Bartlett	FRED MACMURRAY
Charley	JOHN BARRYMORE
Daisy McClure	UNA MERKEL
Prosecutor	PORTER HALL
Darsey	EDGAR KENNEDY

TURNABOUT
1940, UNITED ARTISTS/HAL ROACH
Sick of hearing a couple's constant arguments, a genie switches their identities (83 minutes). ★

Director	HAL ROACH
Producer	HAL ROACH
Screenplay	MICKELL NOVAK, BERN GILER, and JOHN MCCLAIN, from a novel by THORNE SMITH
Additional Dialogue	RIAN JAMES
Cinematographer	NORBERT BRODINE
Art Director	W. L. STEVENS
Costumes	ROYER

Paul Manning	ADOLPHE MENJOU
Sally Willows	CAROLE LANDIS
Tim Willows	JOHN HUBBARD
Joel Clare	WILLIAM GARGAN
Laura Bannister	VERREE TEASDALE
Marion Manning	MARY ASTOR
Henry	DONALD MEEK
Mr. Pingboom	FRANKLIN PANGBORN
Nora	MARJORIE MAIN

TWENTIETH CENTURY
1934, COLUMBIA
The most raucous and hilarious backstage story ever: two egomaniacs, a producer and an actress, fall in love (91 minutes). ★★★V

Director	HOWARD HAWKS
Producer	HOWARD HAWKS
Screenplay	BEN HECHT and CHARLES MACARTHUR, based on their play, based on the play *Napoleon of Broadway* by CHARLES BRUCE MILLHOLLAND
Cinematographer	JOSEPH AUGUST

Oscar Jaffe	JOHN BARRYMORE
Mildred Plotka/ Lily Garland	CAROLE LOMBARD
Oliver Webb	WALTER CONNOLLY
Owen O'Malley	ROSCOE KARNS
George Smith	RALPH FORBES
Max Jacobs	CHARLES LEVISON
Matthew J. Clark	ETIENNE GIRARDOT
Sadie	DALE FULLER
McGonigle	EDGAR KENNEDY
Anita	BILLIE SEWARD
Porter	SNOWFLAKE

UNFAITHFULLY YOURS
1948, COLUMBIA
An orchestra conductor goes mad when he thinks his wife is having an affair with his secretary (105 minutes). ★★★V

Director	PRESTON STURGES
Producer	PRESTON STURGES
Screenplay	PRESTON STURGES
Cinematographer	VICTOR MILNER
Art Directors	LYLE WHEELER and JOSEPH C. WRIGHT
Set Decoration	THOMAS LITTLE and PAUL S. FOX
Costumes	BONNIE CASHIN

Sir Alfred de Carter	REX HARRISON
Daphne de Carter	LINDA DARNELL
August Heckscher	RUDY VALLEE
Barbara Heckscher	BARBARA LAWRENCE
Tony	KURT KREUGER
Hugo	LIONEL STANDER
Sweeney	EDGAR KENNEDY

VIVACIOUS LADY
1938, RKO
The heir apparent to a college presidency screws everything up by falling in love with a showgirl (90 minutes). ★★

Director	GEORGE STEVENS
Producer	GEORGE STEVENS

Screenplay — P. J. WOLFSON and ERNEST PAGANO, from a story by I. A. R. WYLIE
Cinematographer — ROBERT DE GRASSE
Art Director — VAN NEST POLGLASE
Costumes — IRENE and BERNARD NEWMAN

Francey LaRoche — GINGER ROGERS
Peter Morgan — JAMES STEWART
Keith — JAMES ELLISON
Mrs. Morgan — BEULAH BONDI
Pres. Morgan — CHARLES COBURN
Helen — FRANCES MERCER
Apt. Manager — FRANKLIN PANGBORN
Maid — HATTIE MCDANIEL
Culpepper — GRADY SUTTON

WEDDING PRESENT
1936, PARAMOUNT
Two reporters battle it out, especially after one of them gets a promotion (81 minutes). ★

Director — RICHARD WALLACE
Producer — B. P. SCHULBERG
Screenplay — JOSEPH ANTHONY, from a story by PAUL GALLICO
Cinematographer — LEON SHAMROY

Charlie — CARY GRANT
Rusty — JOAN BENNETT

"Slagg" — GEORGE BANCROFT
Dodacker — CONRAD NAGLE
Archduke — GENE LOCKHART
"Smiles" Benson — WILLIAM DEMAREST
Squinty — EDWARD BROPHY

YOU CAN'T TAKE IT WITH YOU
1938, COLUMBIA PICTURES
A family of eccentrics teaches a stuffy banker and his wife to understand the meaning of life (127 minutes). ★★★

Director — FRANK CAPRA
Producer — FRANK CAPRA
Screenplay — ROBERT RISKIN, based on the play by MOSS HART and GEORGE S. KAUFMAN
Cinematographer — JOSEPH WALKER
Music — DIMITRI TIOMKIN

Alice Sycamore Martin — JEAN ARTHUR
Vanderhof — LIONEL BARRYMORE
Tony Kirby — JAMES STEWART
Anthony P. Kirby — EDWARD ARNOLD
Kolenkhov — MISCHA AUER
Essie — ANN MILLER
Mrs. Sycamore — SPRING BYINGTON
Judge — HARRY DAVENPORT

Poppins — DONALD MEEK
Ramsey — H. B. WARNER
De Pinna — HALLIWELL HOBBES
Ed — DUB TAYLOR
Mrs. Kirby — MARY FORBES

THE YOUNG IN HEART
1938, SELZNICK INTERNATIONAL/UNITED ARTISTS
A kindly old lady succeeds in reforming the deadbeats who try to take advantage of her (91 minutes). ★★

Director — RICHARD WALLACE
Producer — DAVID O. SELZNICK
Screenplay — PAUL OSBORN and CHARLES BENNETT, based on the novella *The Gay Banditti* by I. A. R. WYLIE
Cinematographer — LEON SHAMROY
Art Director — LYLE WHEELER
Music — FRANZ WAXMAN
Costumes — OMAR KIAM

George-Anne Carleton — JANET GAYNOR
Richard Carleton — DOUGLAS FAIRBANKS, JR.
Leslie Saunders — PAULETTE GODDARD
Col. Anthony Carleton — ROLAND YOUNG
Marmy Carleton — BILLIE BURKE
Duncan MacCrae — RICHARD CARLSON
Ellen Fortune — MINNIE DUPREE

Screwball Comedy and the Oscars

The Academy Awards are certainly a measure of something, though nobody's ever quite sure what it is. They're hardly an accurate reflection of quality. (Carole Lombard never won one, though she was nominated for *My Man Godfrey;* Howard Hawks's only Oscar was an honorary one presented in 1974—forty years after he made *Twentieth Century,* which wasn't nominated for anything.) Maybe one could say that the Oscars reflect what the members of the Academy of Motion Picture Arts and Sciences *think* is quality, though the truth of the matter is that the Oscars simply reflect what the Academy thinks should win. In any case, seeing which films win Oscars is a good indication of Hollywood's sensibilities; seeing which films *don't* win is even better. What follows is a guide to screwball comedies and the Oscars, including films peripheral to screwball like *You Can't Take It With You, Mr. Deeds Goes to Town,* and *The Philadelphia Story.*

WINNERS

1934 *It Happened One Night*—Picture, Actor (Clark Gable), Actress (Claudette Colbert), Director (Frank Capra), Screenplay Adaptation (Robert Riskin)

1936 *Mr. Deeds Goes to Town*—Director (Frank Capra)

1937 *The Awful Truth*—Director (Leo McCarey)

1938 *You Can't Take It With You*—Picture, Director (Frank Capra)

1940 *The Philadelphia Story*—Actor (James Stewart), Screenplay (Donald Ogden Stewart)

1943 *The More the Merrier*—Supporting Actor (Charles Coburn)

NOMINEES *

1934 *Ruggles of Red Gap*—Picture

1936 *Libeled Lady*—Picture

Mr. Deeds Goes to Town—Picture, Actor (Gary Cooper), Screenplay (Robert Riskin), Sound Recording (John Livadary)

---

* Excluding winning nominees

My Man Godfrey—Actor (William Powell), Actress (Carole Lombard), Supporting Actor (Mischa Auer), Supporting Actress (Alice Brady), Director (Gregory La Cava), Screenplay (Eric Hatch and Morrie Ryskind)

After the Thin Man—Screenplay (Frances Goodrich and Albert Hackett)

Theodora Goes Wild—Film Editing (Otto Meyer)

1937 *The Awful Truth*—Picture, Actress (Irene Dunne), Supporting Actor (Ralph Bellamy), Screenplay (Vina Delmar), Film Editing (Al Clark)

Topper—Supporting Actor (Roland Young), Sound Recording (Elmer Raguse)

1938 *You Can't Take It With You*—Supporting Actress (Spring Byington), Screenplay (Robert Riskin), Cinematography (Joseph Walker), Sound Recording (John Livadary), Film Editing (Gene Havlick)

Vivacious Lady—Cinematography (Robert De Grasse), Sound Recording (James Wilkinson)

Merrily We Live—Supporting Actress (Billie Burke), Interior Decoration (Charles D. Hall), Sound Recording (Elmer Raguse), Song ("Merrily We Live," by Phil Craig and Arthur Quenzer)

Holiday—Interior Decoration (Stephen Goosson and Lionel Banks)

There Goes My Heart—Score (Marvin Hatley)

The Young in Heart—Cinematography (Leon Shamroy), Score (Franz Waxman)

1939 *Bachelor Mother*—Original Story (Felix Jackson)

Topper Takes a Trip—Special Effects (Roy Seawright)

1940 *The Philadelphia Story*—Picture, Director (George Cukor), Actress (Katharine Hepburn), Supporting Actress (Ruth Hussey)

My Favorite Wife—Original Story (Leo McCarey, Bella Spewack, and Samuel Spewack), Interior Decoration (Van Nest Polglase and Mark-Lee Kirk), Original Score (Roy Webb)

Too Many Husbands—Sound Recording (John Livadary)

1941 *Ball of Fire*—Actress (Barbara Stanwyck), Original Story (Thomas Monroe and Billy Wilder), Sound Recording (Thomas Moulton), Scoring of a Dramatic Picture (Alfred Newman)

The Lady Eve—Original Story (Monckton Hoffe)

Tom, Dick and Harry—Original Screenplay (Paul Jarrico)

Topper Returns—Sound Recording (Elmer Raguse), Special Effects (Roy Seawright and Elmer Raguse)

That Uncertain Feeling—Scoring of a Dramatic Picture (Werner Heymann)

1942 *Take a Letter, Darling*—Cinematography (John Mescall), Interior Decoration (Hans Dreier, Roland Anderson, and Sam Comer), Scoring of a Dramatic or Comedy Picture (Werner Heymann)

1943 *The More the Merrier*—Picture, Actress (Jean Arthur), Director (George Stevens), Original Story (Frank Ross and Robert Russell), Screenplay (Richard Flournoy, Lewis R. Foster, Frank Ross, and Robert Russell)

1944 *Hail the Conquering Hero*—Original Screenplay (Preston Sturges)

The Miracle of Morgan's Creek—Original Screenplay (Preston Sturges)

Up In Mabel's Room—Scoring of a Dramatic or Comedy Picture (Edward Paul)

Selected Bibliography

ALBRECHT, Donald. *Designing Dreams*. New York: Harper and Row, 1986.

BAILEY, Margaret J. *Those Glorious Glamour Years*. Secaucus, N. J.: Citadel Press, 1982.

BEHLMER, Rudy. *Inside Warner Bros.* New York: Simon and Schuster, 1985.

BERGMAN, Andrew. *We're in the Money: Depression America and Its Films*. New York: New York University Press, 1971.

BORDWELL, David, Janet STAIGER, and Kristin THOMPSON. *The Classical Hollywood Cinema*. New York: Columbia University Press, 1985.

CAMPBELL, Marilyn. "*His Girl Friday:* Production for Use." *Wide Angle,* vol. 1, no. 2, Summer 1976, pp. 22–27.

CARNEY, Raymond. *American Vision: The Films of Frank Capra*. New York: Cambridge University Press, 1986.

CARTER, Hugh, and Paul C. GLICK. *Marriage and Divorce: A Social and Economic Study*. Cambridge, Mass.: Harvard University Press, 1976.

CAVELL, Stanley, *Pursuits of Happiness*. Cambridge, Mass.: Harvard University Press, 1981.

CHAPMAN, Robert, ed. *The New Dictionary of American Slang*. New York: Harper and Row, 1986.

CHERICHIETTI, David. *Hollywood Director: The Career of Mitchell Leisen*. New York: Curtis Books, 1973.

————. *Hollywood Costume Design*. New York: Harmony Books, 1976.

CURTIS, James. *Between Flops*. New York: Limelight Editions, 1984.

DICKOS, Andrew. *Intrepid Laughter: Preston Sturges and the Movies*. Metuchen, N. J.: Scarecrow Press, 1985.

DILIBERTO, Gioia. *Debutante: The Story of Brenda Frazier*. New York: Alfred A. Knopf, 1987.

EMERY, Edwin, and Michael EMERY. *The Press and America: an Interpretive History of the Mass Media*. Englewood Cliffs, N. J.: Prentice-Hall, 1984.

EVERSON, William K. "Screwball Comedy: A Reappraisal," *Films in Review,* vol. 34, December 1983, pp. 578–584.

FACEY, Paul W. *The Legion of Decency*. New York: Arno Press, 1974.

FISHER, Anne B. *Brides Are Like New Shoes*. New York: Dodd, Mead and Co., 1938.

————. *Live with a Man and Love It!* New York: Dodd, Mead and Co., 1937.

GALBRAITH, John Kenneth. *The Great Crash 1929*. Boston: Houghton Mifflin, 1979.

GOMERY, Douglas. *The Hollywood Studio System*. New York: St. Martin's Press, 1986.

GRANT, Barry Keith. *Film Genre Reader*. Austin: University of Texas Press, 1986.

HARVEY, James. *Romantic Comedy*. New York: Alfred A. Knopf, 1987.

HAVER, Ronald. *David O. Selznick's Hollywood*. New York: Alfred A. Knopf, 1980.

HECHT, Ben. *Charlie: The Improbable Life and Times of Charles MacArthur*. New York: Harper and Brothers, 1957.

————. *A Child of the Century*. New York: Simon and Schuster, 1954.

JEWELL, Richard B., with Vernon Harbin. *The RKO Story*. New York: Arlington House, 1982.

————. "How Howard Hawks Brought Baby Up: An Apologia for the Studio System." *Journal of Popular Film and Television,* vol. 11, no. 4, Winter 1984, pp. 158–165.

JOHNSON, Diane. *Dashiell Hammett: A Life*. New York: Fawcett Columbine, 1985.

KAEL, Pauline. *The Citizen Kane Book*. New York: Limelight Editions, 1984.

————. *Reeling*. New York: Warner Books, 1976.

KATZ, Ephraim. *The Film Encyclopedia*. New York: Perigee Books, 1979.

KEPLEY, Vance, Jr. "Spatial Articulation in the Classical Cinema: A Scene from *His Girl Friday*." *Wide Angle,* vol. 5, no. 3, 1983, pp. 50–58.

LA VINE, W. Robert. *In a Glamorous Fashion*. New York: Charles Scribner's Sons, 1980.

LEISEN, Mitchell. *The Reminiscences of Mitchell Leisen*. American Film Institute Oral History Collection. Glen Rock, N. J.: Microfilming Corporation of America, 1977.

MARTIN, Jeffrey Brown. *Ben Hecht: Hollywood Screenwriter*. Ann Arbor, Mich.: UMI Research Press, 1985.

MAST, Gerald. *The Comic Mind*. Chicago: University of Chicago Press, 1979.

MCBRIDE, Joseph. *Hawks on Hawks*. Berkeley: University of California Press, 1982.

MOORE, William T. *Dateline Chicago: A Veteran Newsman Recalls Its Heyday*. New York: Taplinger Publishing Co., 1973.

PAUL, William. *Ernst Lubitsch's American Comedy*. New York: Columbia University Press, 1983.

POWERS, Tom. "*His Girl Friday:* Screwball Liberation." *Jump Cut,* no. 17, April 1978.

PRINGLE, Henry F. "Screwball Bill." *Collier's,* February 26, 1938.

QUIGLEY, Martin Peter. *The Crooked Pitch: the Curveball in American Baseball History*. Chapel Hill, N. C.: Algonquin Books, 1984.

QUIRK, Leonard. *Claudette Colbert: An Illustrated Biography*. New York: Crown, 1985.

RUSSO, Vito. *The Celluloid Closet*. New York: Harper and Row, 1987.

SALGADO, Gamini, ed. *Three Restoration Comedies*. New York: Penguin Books, 1986.

SANN, Paul. *American Panorama*. New York: Crown, 1980.

SARRIS, Andrew. "The Sex Comedy Without Sex." *American Film,* March 1978, pp. 8–15.

SCHULTHEISS, John. "Director Mitchell Leisen: An Annotated Filmography." *Journal of Popular Film and Television,* vol. 8, no. 3, Fall 1980.

SENNETT, Ted. *Lunatics and Lovers*. New York: Limelight Books, 1985.

SKLAR, Robert. *Movie-Made America*. New York: Vintage Books, 1975.

SPIEGEL, Ellen. "Fred and Ginger Meet Van Nest Polglase." *The Velvet Light Trap,* no. 10, Fall 1973.

SULLIVAN, George. *Pitchers and Pitching*. New York: Dodd, Mead and Co., 1972.

THOMPSON, Frank T. *William A. Wellman*. Metuchen, N. J.: Scarecrow Press, 1983.

Webster's Sports Dictionary. Springfield, Mass.: Merriam-Webster, 1976.

WEINER, Bob. "Is Bruce Millholland the World's Greatest Freeloader?" *New York,* March 20, 1978.

WILEY, Mason, and Damien BONA. *Inside Oscar: The Unofficial History of the Academy Awards*. New York: Ballantine Books, 1986.

WOOD, Robin. *Howard Hawks*. London: British Film Institute, 1981.

WOOD-COMSTOCK, Belle. *Is Love Enough?* Mountain View, Calif.: Pacific Press, 1940.

Acknowledgments

True to the spirit of screwball, I would like to express my love and gratitude to everyone who helped me write this book by punching and insulting them as viciously as possible. In the meantime, I'd like to thank them. William K. Everson, Eric Spilker, Barry Gillam, Bobby Rivers, and Ron Magliozzi graciously took the trouble to locate the movies I thought I'd never get the chance to see. Ron Haver, Jeffrey Wise, John Belton, and Vito Russo shared their extraordinary knowledge without ever asking for anything in return. And Bill Paul and Chris Bram had the patience to read early versions of the book without complaining; they corrected my mistakes and offered desperately needed advice.

My swell editors, Gail Kinn and David Groff, must be the best hand holders in the business; if my anxieties rattled them, they never showed it. We jointly decided not to use footnotes in the text, so I'd like to take this opportunity to thank all of the writers, scholars, and critics listed in the bibliography. Their research and insights made this book possible, and I'm very grateful to them. In particular, I'd like to thank Andrew Sarris for teaching me how to look at movies and Mason Wiley and Damien Bona for showing me how to have fun with them. Ted Sennett and James Harvey steered me through hundreds of comedies; Andy Dickos's book on Preston Sturges and David Cherichietti's books on Mitchell Leisen and Hollywood costume design were invaluable.

Howard Mandelbaum, Ron Mandelbaum, and Ed McGuire at Photofest made photo research a lot more fun than I thought it would be; their input was tremendous. Also helpful were the staff of the Academy of Motion Picture Arts and Sciences, the Museum of Modern Art, and the New York Public Library. Special thanks to Kathryn Leigh Scott and Michael Hawks for their generous contribution of lobby cards.

Special thanks to all the sung and unsung people at Crown who made this book happen. Particular thanks must go to Fred Goss, my production editor, for his beyond-the-call-of-duty efforts, and to Ken Sansone, design director extraordinaire. I'd also like to express my gratitude to Laurie Stark, Amy Boorstein, Kay Riley, Joan Denman, and J. Wilson Henley.

Draper Shreeve designed this book and made it as beautiful as it is; I couldn't be more thrilled.

Finally, I'd like to thank everyone who put up with me, both personally and professionally: Howard Karren, Ira Robbins, Michael Kaniecki, Charles Silver, Howard Feinstein, Barbara Zitwer, Matthew Mirapaul, Rosalind Lichter, Troy Alexander, Nick Poser, Joe Smith, Tom Rhoads, Bill Condon, Frank Roma, Irving and Betty Sikov, Barry Adkins, and of course my suave agent, Eric Ashworth.

Photo Credits

Grateful acknowledgment is made to the following archives and collectors who have given permission to reprint still photographs.

Photofest: pp. 20, 21 (left), 22, 25 (top), 25 (bottom), 26, 27, 29, 35 (left), 35 (right), 40, 40 (inset), 41, 43, 47, 49, 55, 57 (top), 63, 65, 67, 70, 73, 75, 75 (inset), 76, 86 (left), 87, 91, 93, 94, 96, 98, 99, 100, 110, 111, 112 (right), 113, 114–115, 117 (top, bottom), 119 (top), 119 (inset), 123, 129, 130, 131, 136, 137 (top, bottom), 138, 139 (left, right), 144, 150–151, 151 (inset), 152 (bottom left, top left), 154, 160, 163, 164 (top, bottom), 166 (all), 172–173, 174, 176, 181, 185, 189, 190, 192, 194, 198 (top, bottom), 199, 205 (left, right), 206 (inset left, inset right), 207, 208, 210, 215, 216, 218 (Irene Dunne).

Fred Goss Collection: p. 152.

New York Public Library: pp. 127, 149.

With permission from the Michael Hawks Collection; from *Lobby Cards: The Classic Comedies* (1988): pp. 34 (left), 53, 154, 142, 169 (top), 209.

Courtesy of the Academy of Motion Picture Arts and Sciences: pp. 21 (right), 33, 42, 44–45, 46, 68–69, 74, 79, 81, 85, 101, 102, 103, 106, (top, bottom), 107, 109, 114, 124, 133, 140, 141, 145, 147, 150 (inset), 150 (left), 213 (top, bottom).

Museum of Modern Art Film Stills Archive: pp. 2–3, 7, 11, 14, 18, 24, 29, 34 (right), 37, 51, 56, 60, 61, 62, 72, 78, 81 (inset), 82, 86 (right), 89, 103 (bottom left, bottom right), 104, 104–105, 105, 120, 121, 126 (top, bottom), 128 (bottom), 130, 131 (left), 143, 146, 153, 157, 161, 169 (bottom), 170–171, 178–179, 180–181, 186 (top, bottom), 187, 191, 195, 197, 202 (top), 203, 206.

Index

Page numbers in *italics* refer to captions.